READ YOUR MIND

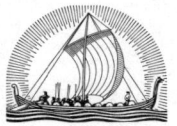

READ YOUR MIND

Proven Habits for
Success from the World's
Greatest Mentalist

OZ PEARLMAN

VIKING

VIKING
An imprint of Penguin Random House LLC
1745 Broadway, New York, NY 10019
penguinrandomhouse.com

Set in Garamond MT Pro

LIBRARY OF CONGRESS CATALOGING-IN-PUBLICATION DATA
Names: Pearlman, Oz author
Title: Read your mind: proven habits for success from the
world's greatest mentalist / Oz Pearlman.
Description: New York, NY: Viking, [2025] |
Includes bibliographical references and index.
Identifiers: LCCN 2025028410 (print) | LCCN 2025028411 (ebook) |
ISBN 9798217059041 hardcover | ISBN 9798217059058 ebook
Subjects: LCSH: Self-actualization (Psychology) | Success
Classification: LCC BF637.S4 P424 2025 (print) | LCC BF637.S4 (ebook)
LC record available at https://lccn.loc.gov/2025028410
LC ebook record available at https://lccn.loc.gov/2025028411

Printed in the United States of America
3rd Printing

The authorized representative in the EU for product safety and compliance
is Penguin Random House Ireland, Morrison Chambers, 32 Nassau Street,
Dublin D02 YH68, Ireland, https://eu-contact.penguin.ie.

TO MY CHILDREN:
YOU'VE GIVEN ME JOY BEYOND
ALL MEASURE.

TO MY WIFE:
YOU'VE GIVEN ME EVERYTHING
AND ARE MY EVERYTHING.

CONTENTS

READ YOUR MIND

ONE

Channel Your Inner Mentalist

Picture this.

I'm a guest on a private island in the British Virgin Islands. A band plays steel drums as the clear waters of the Caribbean Sea gently lap the pristine shoreline. Chefs tend to jerk chicken sizzling on an elaborate barbecue while a team of uniformed servers weaves in and out of the crowd. The breeze smells like spices, hibiscus, and money. It's magic hour, the last golden light of day washing over us. All the beautiful people are enjoying bespoke cocktails. The other guests and I can't help stealing glances skyward; our host on Necker Island has just returned from the edge of space on his Virgin Galactic rocket.

Sir Richard Branson's people could have hired anyone to celebrate the occasion. I mean, this is a man who has Mick Jagger on speed dial, right between Paul McCartney and the King. To my surprise and delight, his team chose me. I'm working the crowd, going from group to group, building up excitement and momentum as we all wait for the guest of honor. Suddenly, his friends and family part like the Red Sea. The barefoot billionaire appears, sporting a deep tan that contrasts with his iconic white-blond hair and open linen shirt, flashing that un-forgettable smile. Everything about the scene feels surreal.

A moment such as this demands nothing less than the best, and I'm ready with one of my strongest reputation-making tricks. I lock eyes with the man, the myth, the legend, and it is go time.

"Imagine someone's face, anyone at all, and see them in your mind's eye," I say. Then, using a small pair of scissors, I start slicing and dicing one of my business cards, like a child carving out a meticulous snow-flake. Everyone around me whispers as they start to anticipate where this might be going.

When I ask him who he is thinking of, he casually says, "Barack." Then he adds, "Obama," in case I wasn't sure which Barack he has in mind.

I unfold the paper and hold it up against my dark gray suit, revealing the freshly cut silhouette of the former president. The audience gasps in astonishment, but Branson, who does billion-dollar deals before break-fast, isn't so outwardly effusive. Instead, he gives me a sly little smile. The best way I can describe his reaction is that it's like having the God-father reach over and pinch you on the cheek as an understated sign of respect and affection.

Sir Richard tucks the piece of paper into his breast pocket. He looks over his shoulder to make sure no one else hears him, leans in close, and whispers, "I'll give this to him tomorrow when he arrives."

What If You Could Read Minds?

Who hasn't wished they could read someone else's mind? How much easier would everything be if we could just figure out what other people were thinking, right? I mean, you'd probably never fight with your spouse again because you'd understand that should he or she say, "It's nothing," it would *definitely* be something, and you could act preemptively.

What if reading minds gave you practical skills, enabling you to predict the right time to ask your boss for a raise, to cease self-sabotage, or to stop procrastinating and start doing? You'd be more confidently persuasive, able to influence those around you in an effortless manner. How great would that be?

Of course, mind reading would be nice to have if you found yourself in a position of weakness, because you'd have the formula to flip that power dynamic to your benefit. By knowing what's in another person's head, you could get a gatekeeper to give you what you want, whether it's an extension on an assignment or a waiver from your homeowners' association. Reading minds would make you better at understanding human nature, which makes it the ultimate cheat code in life.

What would be even *more* useful than reading other people's minds? The ability to read your own. Picture the results of tapping into your motivations and learning how to change your outcomes; of pushing past what's kept you stuck. What if you could set yourself up for success in the long term?

You can do all of this using the skills of a mentalist.

I've spent almost thirty years learning how to reverse engineer the human mind. Knowing *how* you think reveals to me *what* you think. From Tom Brady to Serena Williams, Howard Stern to Shaq, I've convinced some of the most notable people on the planet that I can access their innermost thoughts. But guess what? My entire career is built on a lie.

Ready for a bombshell?

I can't actually read minds.

What I can do is read *people* . . . and so can you! You already do it hundreds of times a day, every time you interact with another human being at home, at work, on the street, and everywhere in between, and I can help you be even better at it. Few skills will take you further in life than learning how to channel your inner mentalist. Reading people is a critical step to achieving what you want in this world. From getting ahead to getting what you want, the tactics I employ as a mentalist can be repurposed from entertainment to success in everyday life.

All of us have an internal BS detector that we developed from being around people, from getting social stimulus. What you may not realize is you were born being able to read minds. You can tell when someone's not paying attention to you. You can tell when someone's lying to you. (If you're a parent, you're *really* good at this.) You can tell when someone's interested in you or when they're faking it. We all have this sense. Well over two-thirds of communication is nonverbal[1], so it's not a matter of *what* people say but *how* they say it, and even what they leave unsaid.

Mentalism is magic of the mind. Rather than using fast hands to fool your eyes, I watch the way people move. I listen to the words they choose. I study their patterns and behaviors, often without them realizing I'm doing so. Mentalism is all about psychology, observation, memory, and communication. These small signals tell a much bigger story—and once you know what to look for, you can "read" people almost instantly. When I say to channel your inner mentalist, what I mean is this skill is instinctual. When you were a baby, long before you understood spoken language, you were able to interpret your parents' thoughts by studying their faces. The furrow of a brow, the flicker of an eyelid, the pull of the upper lip; all of it infused with meaning. The first time we smiled at our parents and they smiled back, we said to ourselves, *Oh God, when I do the thing with my mouth, that makes people pay attention to me!* And it's that first bit of dopamine that gets us going. The ability to interpret other people is innate in all of us because we're social creatures; it's why our species has survived.

The question isn't *Do you have the skills?* because the answer is *You do.* The question is *How do you take your skills to the next level?* How do you improve on your instincts and learn to trust them more?

This isn't about tricks. It's about transformation. I'm going to teach you the very techniques I've used to perform for millions of people around the world—but more important, I'm going to show you how to apply them in your own life to create real, lasting change. You don't have to be a mentalist to think like one. You just need a shift in mindset—and a few powerful tools.

So, I'll walk you through how I became a mentalist and start you on the path to honing your skills so you can learn to read people and apply the principles of mentalism to your everyday life. And, crucially, to develop the ability to look into the mirror and start to read *that* person's mind, which seems daunting, but it's not. In fact, it's easier than you think!

Like Magic

When I was thirteen, my parents took me on a cruise where I saw a magician perform for the very first time. I was captivated as I watched miracle after miracle. And then the most incredible thing happened: He picked me to join him onstage. The magician performed a classic known as "the sponge balls," where the balls appeared, disappeared, and changed in number and size in my hands. An obsession was born and, from that moment on, I spent my time stalking him because I just had to see more. (FYI, there are surprisingly few places on a ship a grown man can hide, especially from a determined kid with nothing better to do.)

When I got home, I checked out every single book on magic at the library and read them from cover to cover . . . twice. You could not find me at any point of the day without a deck of cards in hand, literally: I found waterproof cards to practice with in the shower. By the time I'd turned fourteen, it was apparent that magic was more than a passing fad for me. But I didn't need to be a mentalist to understand that my mother was tired of driving me to Wunderground, the local magic store in metro Detroit where I grew up, and paying for the tricks to satisfy my obsession. Ever pragmatic, my mom told me if I was serious about pursuing magic, I needed to get a job and start supporting my own hobby. My folks were on the cusp of divorce back then, so it's possible that my bending of spoons at the breakfast table didn't exactly ease collective stress.

Anyway, instead of taking a paper route, babysitting, or shoveling driveways, I did what seemed the most logical thing for a kid in my position—I decided to try and get a job as a strolling magician, who does close-up magic while mingling with the crowd. I imagined all the tricks I could buy and how I could take my magic to the next level. At no point did it occur to me that my idea was (a) half-baked or (b) almost certainly destined to fail, because otherwise I'd never have tried in the first place. Ignorance can be bliss. If I'd asked someone else how to land that job, they'd have told me, "First you have to do this, then you have to do that," and I would have psyched myself out of even trying.

Zia's, a family-style Italian restaurant in a strip mall a half mile from home, seemed the most logical place to give my magic gig a shot because its location was cursed. Every restaurant that opened there failed after a couple years. So I figured they could use my magical touch, pun intended.

I decided to go in one day after school with my mom, which happened to be perfect timing because at 4:00 p.m. the place was mostly empty between shifts. We sat at the bar alone, ordered some beverages and appetizers, and I started performing for my mom. This caught the bartender's eye, so I asked him if he wanted to see some magic, too—which was exactly my plan. Had I gone in during the lunch rush or at dinner, he probably would've ignored me. But because he and the rest of the staff weren't busy, he said, "Let's get a bigger crowd going." He called over several servers and, the next thing I knew, the general manager was coming by to see what was going on.

My mom, always my number one fan and a slightly pushy Israeli, gave me the eyebrow raise that indicated this was my moment. It was time to start selling. My mother and I tag-teamed, asking when their slowest night was and if they ever had entertainment. Like any good attorney, we asked our questions already knowing what answers we wanted them to give, leading them to the conclusion that I was what their restaurant was missing.

Why were they so willing to give me that shot? Maybe they were grasping for straws and thought, *We need whatever hook we can get to have this restaurant take off.* Lo and behold, I landed one night per week of strolling magic, going table to table. I was too young to drive so I walked there carrying my small bag of tricks, freshly printed business cards, and a dream.

The one thing I already understood was the concept of "Fake it till you make it." My superpower was acting like I knew what I was doing even when I didn't. I had my pitch perfected because I'd gone over it in my head a hundred times. That's why when I got in front of Zia's owners, with a proud Jewish mother behind me, I projected an aura of confidence and pulled out my best tricks. They bought it; I was *in*.

Pick Your Moment

Performing close-up magic at Zia's was probably the best education I could ever receive about learning to read people. I was able to iterate how to approach strangers and how to get a sense of what they thought of me even before I began performing. My mind would race trying to answer the questions: *What do they think of my act? How do I win their favor? How can I get them to want more?*

Through trial, error, and all kinds of rejection, I learned that my tricks were only a small part of the show as a whole. Everything counted, from my personality and my energy to the statements I'd make upon greeting them.

When I'd walk up to the table, every factor made an impression, even my smile and my body position. I learned fast that timing is everything. If people had just sat down and hadn't yet ordered, they could be flustered or get angered by my presence. They hadn't unpacked their day yet. They needed a minute with their drinks and a few calories from the bread basket to ease their tension. I used all these little bits of info when deciding the right moment to visit a table.

The sweet spot was just after they'd ordered, when the excitement of making their choices was over and there was a lull in the conversation as they anticipated their meals. Diners were the most relaxed and their guards were down. That's when I could go up to them and say, "How's everybody doing tonight?" I knew that when they saw me come over— obviously not their server or the manager—their minds would race with questions, so I would address their objections before they were even consciously aware of them. While I'd yet to study any psychology in junior high, Zia's taught me about heuristics, meaning the mental shortcuts people take to make quick decisions. My customers' default setting was assuming I shouldn't be there, so I'd immediately counter that. I'd tell them, "The owners have a treat for you tonight!" indicating that not only was I welcome, but I was a value-add and management wanted me to be there.

You've likely been in very similar situations when wanting to get something from someone and trying to find the best moment to do so. Let's say you want to ask your boss for a raise. It's important to you, so you have it on your calendar to talk to him or her first thing on Monday morning, when they're back from their annual vacation cruise. It's a big deal, so you want to get it out of the way right now. But if you do it then, even though you've worked your butt off and may well deserve that raise, you may be shooting yourself in the foot. Because your raise is not necessarily as important and immediate a concern to your boss.

Put yourself in their shoes—does your boss have a million other things on their plate? Are they normally in the best mood first thing in the morning, especially after an extended break? You know this person. You've worked with them for years. You've seen when they're at their kindest, their most receptive, their most generous, and it's rarely at 8:30 a.m. on Monday when their phone is ringing off the hook, their inbox is full, and they haven't even touched their coffee yet.

When I was working the restaurant, was I technically employed if they paid me fifty dollars under the table and sent me home with some spaghetti? I quickly learned ways to hype up a table before I'd perform. I'd ask, "Did you hear what's going on?" They'd say no, but with that one question, I shifted their hesitation to anticipation, and instead of being bothered, they were now intrigued. I'd continue, "Then you're in luck!" further piquing their curiosity. Who doesn't want to be lucky? Who doesn't want to feel in the know? Every word and phrase was designed to grab their attention and not let them go. I was setting a path in motion and that is key to tapping into the minds of others. This is Human Behavior 101: learning to anticipate the thoughts of others before they even think them.

When I'm performing, I don't use this anticipation to amaze you. I use these little sweeteners to get you to like me, to get you interested in what I'm presenting, and to win you over so the experience is all the more memorable. And you can do the same. Like in the example above, when asking for a raise: You know your boss. You know when she or he is at their best, their happiest, their most generous. Learn their patterns, make an effort to actively pay attention to their moods, and use this knowledge to strike when the time is right!

Shift Out of Autopilot

Zia's taught me the value of being an active participant, one who remains present in every moment and pays attention to every little detail. More important, I learned that I needed to make an opportunity happen, rather than wait for others to take the initiative. This is something all of us can improve in our lives and occurs only when you take charge and assume responsibility. For example, think about your day-to-day life with your spouse. How often are you truly present? And how often are you just going through the motions? We are bombarded with so much information that, with our eyes alone, we're processing one megabyte of data every second.[2] To handle the thousands of tiny decisions we make every day—from seasoning our food to picking out a tie—our brains create habits to help us process this info. These habits we develop help us to not be overwhelmed by information, yet they also make us default to autopilot. We counter this by leaning into active participation.

In lieu of going through the motions, try to view things from your spouse's perspective. Consider what might be on their mind. Are they anxious about work? Are they worried about the kids? Are they stressed about everything on their to-do list? The simple act of being able to read the room can be a relationship saver. (Again, this is tied closely to timing.)

If I performed my show on autopilot, I would mess up all the time—even though I know every formal beat of my performance by heart. I must be hyperfocused when I'm with an audience. I have to study everything they're doing, like their traits, their mannerisms, their eyes, their body language, and even their pauses. The smallest "um" uttered by a spectator at the wrong moment might seem harmless at first glance and would likely go unnoticed by the audience. But for me, even a small moment of disconnection can spell doom if not immediately addressed. That "um" may indicate that something was missed or that my participant may be mildly confused. This is a big red flag that I simply can't ignore. For example, this tells me their brain thought of one thing and then shifted to another. That one little pause could be the difference between succeeding and failing on a trick in front of thousands of people.

Failure was my teacher and my motivator in the restaurant days. When I first started working the gig, I'd walk up to a table and say, "Oh, are you ready? Let me do some magic." Then many of the diners would just laugh and go, "No thanks, kid." You're walking up to someone, ready to give them your all and they reject you? What a gut punch. (We'll delve deeper into dealing with rejection in a later chapter.) It's hard to move past that.

I could have left the rude table and thought to myself, *What a bunch of jerks.* The easiest thing is to shift the blame onto them rather than learn from this situation. Then I'd be annoyed, that tension would impact me, and I'd bring that kind of negative energy to the next group. When you're going up to fifty or more tables in a shift and three in a row treat you poorly, it can ruin your whole attitude.

My tricks weren't paying for themselves, though, so I had develop thicker skin. Instead of quitting, I tried to figure out what I could do that might yield different results, and I learned that every "no thanks" was giving me the data I needed to turn my next interaction into a "yes, please."

I discovered that instead of being mad at them, I'd be more effective in the long run if I tried to understand them. I couldn't let myself wallow in that rejection. Our brains are hardwired to register and dwell on negative events. This is called "negativity bias" and it means we feel the pain of rejection far more deeply than the balm of praise.[3]

I didn't know anything about neural processing back then. I had no idea that a negative stimulus resonated more strongly in my cerebral cortex. All I knew was that I'd feel better if I tried to put a positive spin on the situation—I'd be more focused on the task at hand instead of distracted and diminished by the recent past. So I'd say to myself, *What if their kid is sick at home? What if they had a huge fight right before they came? I feel really bad for them. They must be having a rough night. I can't wait to bring joy to the next person.*

I also started conducting after-action reviews to see where I may have veered off the rails. Maybe I'd realize that they'd been talking and I had interrupted. How would I feel if someone interrupted me? I had already started on the wrong foot when I walked up to them, and so I'd had to climb up a hill just to get their attention to win them back over. That was *my* fault, not theirs. In so many instances we tend to blame the other person instead of examining our own behavior to see what we could have done better instead—as if in a failed interaction there is only one party to blame.

When you walk up to somebody and they don't know you, what's the first thing that often happens? They get tense. You can see it. I mean, imagine you're standing at the ATM and someone approaches you—that's anxiety-provoking for sure. Your body goes into fight-or-flight. This happened to me a couple months ago. Someone was panhandling and they came up to me as I was putting in my PIN. I said, "Listen, I'm getting money out. I'm willing to help you, but give me a minute and I'll meet you outside." A better way of handling this would be if he held the door for me on my way out and then said, "If you can spare any change, that'd be amazing." He would have created a totally different feeling in me. Ultimately, I still helped him, but this is something to keep in mind if you're ever trying to solicit signatures for a petition or donations for a nonprofit. It's so important for you to consider the other person's reaction, making sure you don't interrupt or impose. In a situation where you're, say, trying to collect signatures, you're going to find the most success if you acknowledge the other person by saying something like, "I can tell you're so busy, but I have to quickly share this with you." Speak with light urgency, empathize, and validate their reactions and don't be surprised when you're able to get what you need.

Find the Right Energy

A couple of years ago I was presenting and performing at the ESPY Awards, standing arm's length from LeBron James, arguably one of the most famous people in the world. We were elbow-to-elbow backstage, and he was getting ready to go up and give a speech. We said a brief hello and exchanged pleasantries. I knew that was the absolute worst moment to say, "Hey, LeBron, can I get a selfie?" The timing was just off. Plus, I want to be seen as an equal, and coming up to him as a fan was the surest way to not get what I wanted. For him to give something of value (in this case, the selfie), I would ideally provide him with something of value first. So backstage, pre-speech, just wasn't the right moment.

However, seconds later, I met Patrick Mahomes, and he was in less of a time crunch, having just wrapped up his stage portion. I ended up talking to him and getting a good vibe. Plus, he knew who I was because earlier I'd performed for his wife, making her the star of my act; I won him over right from the start as I'm sure he typically gets most of the attention. At the end of our conversation, I said, "Patrick, it's been a real pleasure hanging out tonight, let's get a picture to remember it!" Without hesitation, he wrapped his arm around me and said, "Oh my God, get in here!" and we took the photos.

I didn't really need to ask for permission, and I could assume the close, because the timing was right and I'd locked in what matters to him most: his wife's happiness. So, when I asked for something in return, he was more likely to accommodate wholeheartedly. If I'd tried the same move with LeBron, he probably wouldn't have acquiesced because he was concentrating on what he was about to say to a huge audience, plus there was nothing in it for him. Often, getting in touch with your inner mentalist is as easy as thinking about what's going through the other person's head.

A while back, I was at an incredibly high profile event. This room was filled with the heaviest of heavy hitters in the sports world, including most of the team owners along with the commissioners of the NFL, NHL, NBA, MLB, WNBA, the World Surf League, the IOC, etc. Rarely do you get the chance to be in a room with this many powerful people at the same time. There was an über-successful attendee named Michael. One of my major objectives was to impress and win him over because he throws arguably the most exclusive party in the country each summer.

Always scheming, I planned to punch my ticket to his party that night. I was with Roger Goodell and a couple other people, and I'd already performed three close-up tricks for them while working the crowd during cocktail hour. I always aim to leave people wanting more. One of the biggest rules of success is to never overstay your welcome. If you get to a moment where you see somebody looking down at their phone or starting to check the clock, then you've missed the boat. Think about it: Let's say you're the biggest Ryan Reynolds fan in the world. You're having coffee, and Deadpool himself walks in the shop. You're not going to get distracted and check your phone. You're not going to look at what time it is. The world has ceased to exist. You could forget to pick up your kids from school at that moment because you're so focused.

Michael moseyed over right as I was finishing my very best trick. My act is structured to end on the highest note. I'd basically hit a walk-off grand slam and was leaving them on cloud nine . . . and there's no such thing as cloud ten. But then someone from the group goes, "Michael, you've got to see this!" That wasn't good. I needed to peel off and plant Michael in a group that was starting from scratch if I wanted to leave him amazed, but I had lost control of the situation. At best, I could keep going and hold the vibe at a plateau. But plateauing wasn't an option. I had to do another trick for the group, and it had to kill. Michael wasn't at the same energy level as the rest of the people in this already engaged group, though. It would be like if you walked into the end of a Bon Jovi concert and everyone else has been on this epic journey the whole night. They're screaming the lyrics to "Livin' on a Prayer" at the end of his set, but you can't match their energy because you didn't have the chance to build yours up yet. Same thing happened here. I did the trick, and it was fine, but because of the energy mismatch, it didn't produce the results I'd hoped.

I wasn't invited to perform at his party. I wanted it, but this ended up being a missed opportunity because the situation was out of my control. It's frustrating, and I've played this scenario back in my head dozens of times since. The best I can do is to learn from it. But mark my words—I haven't given up. I *will* be at that party one summer soon, because I am relentless once I set a goal.

Here's what you need to remember: In your head, replace the word *no* with *not yet*. Let's rewire your brain against what you perceive as rejection. When you're frustrated by a no, you create a self-fulfilling prophecy because you believe that your dream is not going to happen and you stop taking strides toward it. Instead of thinking of "no" as a locked door, think of it as a jammed door. A locked door is final—you can't get through. But a jammed door isn't permanently closed; it just needs a bit more effort and finesse to open. It's not a "no," it's a "not yet." If you keep at it. you'll eventually get through.

Kill with Kindness

The first rule of working in the service industry—and all industries are, fundamentally, service industries—is that the client is always right. And even if they're not right and truly unpleasant, as long as you're not in physical danger, the best approach is to kill that person with kindness. When people would snap at me during my restaurant-working days, I'd say, "Oh, I completely understand. Have a wonderful dinner and if you need something, I'm happy to send the manager right over."

When you meet negative energy with negative energy, it's just going to fan the flames.

The smartest plan is always to de-escalate a situation. A vital rule of de-escalation is that you don't charge up on someone who's running hot, who's already in a fury and wants to fight. You're far better off approaching them with a calm you may or may not feel. You want to make yourself seem smaller to calm them down. You don't match their energy, because then it turns into a competition for who can be more alpha, and that will only heat things up.

I often run into similar issues onstage. Someone in the audience wants to be combative, wants to heckle. I have learned to look at the root of what's causing them to act this way: This person wants attention. They don't want to feel like I'm putting them down, but because I'm the one in the spotlight, the power dynamic has me in a superior position. I know how to do something they don't, and it makes them feel stupid—out of place, insecure, unengaged, or not on the same wavelength as everyone else in the room. That's when I need to downshift my energy. I need to alter our power dynamic in their mind.

In situations like this, I find a way to communicate that doesn't place us in opposition, but lets them understand that we're on the same team. If you and I were on the same team, why would I ever try to steal the ball from you? If we're both trying to score together, that would be silly. I want them to know that we're on a level playing field, that I'm not some mythical messiah figure or a psychic: What I do is learnable.

What you have to understand is that my career is built on secrecy. If you get to the core of it, the truth is just that I know how to do something you don't. I build rapport with the audience, and earn their trust, by dropping little breadcrumbs of how I do it along the way. I'll create an environment where I open up to them and let them in on the secret, showing them how one of the tricks is done behind the curtain. Suddenly, they'll say, "That's so cool!" And I'll say, "Isn't it amazing?" Then I'll raise the bar and use that knowledge against them by employing a different method, and I'll use the element of surprise to my advantage, leaving the audience even more astounded. Of course, they'll want to know how I did that, too, but I'll say, "I have to keep some secrets here. I've got to try to impress you now that you're a mentalist yourself."

Letting people get a win, giving them that win, or inviting them to feel like they're in on the trick tells them you're not trying to steal the attention away from them. It's a great way to shift the energy, to de-escalate. In many instances when I walk up to a group there's often a person who wants to be the dominant alpha. They want all eyes on them, which generally stems from a feeling of insecurity. So I give them their moment. I let them call the shots within the framework of the trick I'm doing. I have them make the choices. It's no different than how I parent my children when asking them, "Do you want one carrot or two broccolis?" because it gives my kids the feeling of having control . . . and either way they eat their veggies.

It's important to make people feel like they have agency, that they have choice within the set of parameters you give them. Then, they will choose within that set of constraints, especially if you deliver that choice with a genuine smile and a kind tone. Ultimately, your hecklers can become your biggest cheerleaders. The people you think are going to be the worst in your day-to-day life can end up as your greatest allies if you get inside their heads effectively and learn what makes them tick by trying to assess their true motivation. With hecklers, what drives them is the desire to feel smart, to feel validated. They don't like when they feel lesser than, and they probably don't encounter a lot that defies logic. So they won't just let themselves lean into the wonder of it all.

People want to be seen and heard. They want to feel special. If you can win them over, it flips the script. They want attention, so give them what they want. When I work with football players, I always look for the guy who has his arms crossed, who's not smiling, because if I can win him over, everyone else will be won over as well. Here's the thing: Someone in the crowd who's negative is still engaged. If you give them a win, you can exploit that.

When I was working the private party circuit, I knew that, almost universally, people also wanted to feel like they were getting a deal. Let's say my goal was to make $500 for a show. (Thankfully my rates have gone up since then!) To get there, I'd give clients an option of three pricing packages: the bronze, the gold, or the platinum.

Human instinct is that no one wants the bronze. They want one of the better options. People will naturally gravitate toward the one in the middle, so I'd ask for $400 for the bronze, $500 for the gold, and $750 for the platinum. People don't want the basic package because there's not enough stuff in it—they easily convince themselves it's missing one or two key pieces. But the extras I'd add on to the more prestige packages are things I would have wanted to incorporate anyway, like strolling around and meeting the audience in advance because that would actually help me when I went onstage. But the client doesn't know this is something I love doing.

Even now, I run my events this way. I still want to shake hands and perform close-up mentalism. What makes mentalists unique is that there are no other entertainers—comedians, singers, athletes, keynote speakers—who work close-up for groups of two to twenty people at a time. It's such a powerful experience to be immersed in the show from only a few feet away. When potential clients see that, if they get the gold package, I'll do the close-up work, they go, "That's amazing, thank you!" When you price yourself this way, you increase your revenue by providing something extra you'd have provided as a matter of course.

What's interesting in this example is that sometimes what feels natural or easy to you has its own worth. In my case, talking to people beforehand is fun for me, so putting a price on an element of my work that I love not only increases my revenue but also helps me clearly value my own work.

Bottom line, everyone wants to feel like a VIP, and that became evident in my restaurant work. There are simple ways to create that feeling that don't cost you more than you want to invest. This is why I would walk up to people at their tables and say, "I'm here compliments of the owner, and it's your lucky night!" When you approach with that energy, right away you've established a good feeling. If, instead, I walked up and said, "Do you want to see some magic?" I'd have given people a very easy path to saying no. Human nature positions us to respond positively to hearing that it's our lucky night, especially when it's free.

Sometimes despite my best efforts, diners were rude, but I'd never give that energy back to them. Rather I'd be polite and direct, saying, "I'll see if I can come back later. Several tables have requests for me. Have a wonderful night and enjoy your meal." Then I would walk away. I wouldn't be curt; I wouldn't be emotional about their response. If I had performed one trick and they were rude, disrespectful, or apathetic, I'd think, *Okay, you're cut off. I have something special to share. Other people want it, and I'll give it to them instead.* In that moment, when they realized I was taking my talent away, many would pull a 180 and try to get me to stay. Often, if it was just one person who had been rude, the whole group would turn against them. They'd realize they'd all collectively lost something of value.

The restaurant gigs taught me the importance of aligning myself with people. One person who is an ally can open so many doors. This is basic sales. Generally, about 5 percent of your clientele absolutely love you and they become your champions. They become your promoters.

They're your hype men or hype women. Recently, my good friends had their first child and asked me if I knew anyone who could help with life insurance. I responded, "Yeah, of course! I'll put you in touch with Frank, he's my guy, he's great!" And that's what you want to be: the *go-to* guy or gal for that niche, so much so that nobody else is even considered, it's a lock.

Your fans will talk about you, whether it's business or personal. When somebody gives you a glowing over-the-top review, that is worth its weight in gold. When you get people to be your champion, you're unstoppable. So many instances in my career have come down to a handful of people who supported me. In turn, I've nurtured those relationships. I've tried to make myself valuable to them, done favors for them, gone above and beyond for them, and shown appreciation for the ways they've gone above and beyond for me, because these relationships should always be a two-way street.

Play the Long Game

Some of the biggest TV appearances I've landed I can trace back nearly twenty years to my finding the name of an event planner in the yellow pages. (For my Gen Z audience—google that move for a blast from the past.) Back then I would call event planners, saying, "I would love to swing by and give your team a very unique treat and perform a gratis show during lunch, or whenever you have downtime," knowing that they were the gatekeepers responsible for booking acts like mine. Impress a prospective client and maybe you score a show or two, but impress the right event planner and it could mean dozens of gigs down the line. This was a force multiplier and a way to work smarter rather than just harder. With a planner shilling for me, I booked my first bar mitzvah through what had been a free performance. That bar mitzvah led to another bar mitzvah, which led to a holiday party and a birthday party, and on and on. We went many levels deep into Jewish geography. Eventually this led me to the bar mitzvah of the son of a very prominent NFL correspondent on ESPN named Adam Schefter. I kept in touch with him. I made sure that I never fell off his radar, that he always received my newsletter.

Now, this is one of my best pieces of advice: Always take notes. Whenever I met someone new, I'd be sure to jot down a few lines about what was happening in their life. If someone handed me their business card, the moment I was out of their sight I wrote down the date, where I was, and everything they had said to me in the smallest font you can imagine somewhere on that card. Adam and I continued to cross paths over the next few years on the bar mitzvah circuit, and whenever I'd see him at a party, I'd always know his kids' names and what the family had been up to. We were friendly. I wrote every detail down because we had a connection and I needed him to know that what was important to him was also important to me. You don't have to be a mind reader to know that people are flattered when you recall details from previous conversations.

A lot of the time, you'll find yourself moving in the same social circles. You get hired by one person, and then someone else in their group of friends or family hires you again in a year or two. This becomes another moment to shine in front of an already receptive audience. After well over a decade of knowing each other, Adam said, "I need you to meet my boss who runs ESPN's football content."

If I had met his boss twelve years earlier, I wouldn't have been ready. But by this point, I was a seasoned pro with plenty of TV experience under my belt and was ready for this opportunity. My confidence shined; I performed the right routines and highlighted how my act could be tailored to football, could connect with their audiences. I was in the right place with the right person at the right time . . . and it only took twelve years for me to get the chance. Ultimately, your biggest goals are going to be part of a long game, and every step along the way adds up. This is the same for nearly every profession. You show me an overnight success and I'll show you the ten plus years of grinding they did to land that big break. So if your long game as, say, a Realtor is to land a million-dollar listing, every lower-dollar condo and ranch home you sell along the way builds your record and your skills.

Flip the Power Dynamic

Now, you would think that, by channeling my inner mentalist, by paying attention to my timing and killing people with kindness and tapping into human nature, I'd make all the right moves and every decision I made would be the wisest one.

That's why I need to tell you about the time I almost blew it.

I met my wife, Elisa, when I was in my mid-twenties, living my big single life in New York City. We dated for a few months; it was great, but again, I was in my midtwenties. Sometimes you have the best thing in the world in front of you and you don't even know it. You could have a winning lottery ticket and not realize it. So . . . I tried to break up with her because I was immature, too scared to commit and focused on all the wrong things. But when I told her we were done, she rejected my move and just said, "No." I was completely confused, downright flummoxed. What did she mean, "No?" Can you even do that?

In the span of just a few days, I realized how right she was. Elisa explained to me pretty much exactly what was in my head because it seems she was a far better mentalist than I was at the time. She laid out how stupid I was being, how fickle, how the problems that I raised were minor and easy to overcome. She pointed out that rather than taking the hard road of doing the slightest bit of work, I was just going to throw our relationship away. As soon as I realized what a life with her would offer, suddenly I was the one who was begging for more. With our roles flipped and Elisa suddenly in control, I pleaded with her to move in, as I'd recently bought my first apartment. She just replied, "Slow down, buddy." The shift in our dynamic reminded me of my early magician days working restaurants, when I'd walk up to a group: They didn't know if they wanted me, and they held all the cards. A minute later when I would do the first amazing trick, they'd be blown away and they'd say, "Don't stop!" Suddenly, they wanted me more than I needed them.

Learning to rely on our inner mentalist can be a challenge at first, especially when we're so likely to default to autopilot. It requires us to take a pause, really assess each situation and person, and put ourselves in their shoes. But once you're used to taking that second to get your bearings, it becomes easier and easier to figure out your timing and not rush through things, as you're far more likely to get a negative response when you come from a place of impatience. By taking a breath to de-escalate a situation, and doubling down on kindness, you make space for everyone to have a positive outcome. And when you can prove to others that you've genuinely listened to them and what they've told you is important, you're far more likely to get what you need from them.

Remember, none of this is magic; it's mentalism.

TWO

Believe It to Achieve It

The old adage says, "If you fail to plan, then plan to fail."

That couldn't be truer in my case. I never go into a performance without a series of contingency plans, in case my initial parachute fails to open. To achieve the best outcome in whatever you do, from selling software to persuading a jury of your client's innocence, it's an absolute must to not only visualize your success but also your failure. Being able to anticipate what could go wrong—and create fallbacks—goes a long way toward ensuring a positive end result, so in this chapter we'll cover how planning for every eventuality is a counterintuitive key to "reading" the minds of others.

Theory of Mind

Much of my planning revolves around the concept of "Theory of Mind," both personally and professionally. Theory of Mind refers to our ability to attribute mental states to ourselves and others, and to understand that the mental states of others may be different from our own.[1]

Picture this: It's a rainy summer day during your childhood. You can hear the heavy drops pelting the windows as the wind howls. You're stuck inside while visiting your grandmother. You and your little sister are killing time until the weather breaks, so you've decided to play hide-and-seek. You've determined that the very best hiding spot is tucked inside Granny's closet behind her dresses. However, you also know that your sister is great at finding you. Maybe she even saw your eyes dart toward your grandmother's bedroom when you decided to play. So you choose a different area because you're pretty sure she'll look in the closet first, as she's also aware that it's the best hiding place.

Taking the effort to imagine what someone else is thinking lets you step into someone else's shoes and see the world from their point of view.

And *that* is a superpower.

When I was a kid working at the restaurant, I learned to take a beat to consider the diners' inner monologues. I knew they'd wonder, *Is he any good? Because there's nothing more awkward than having someone perform badly, like a lousy singer or an out-of-tune band, and we'll have to cringe-smile. How long is this going to be? Will he leave soon?* Using Theory of Mind, I realized there were at least ten questions people were asking themselves before they even blinked their eyes when I got to their table. My challenge became to answer all ten of those questions in ten seconds or less.

Your body language and eye contact play a huge role when approaching someone else. In fact, Albert Mehrabian, a body language researcher, found that when it comes to face-to-face communication, 55 percent of communication is nonverbal, 38 percent is vocal, and only 7 percent is words, so approach and eye contact have an outsize impact on the impression you make.[2] Think of it like looking at certain animals in the eyes. When you do this, they look down. Direct eye contact can be very awkward and threatening because it feels like you're crowding them. But if you walk up to an animal at an angle, where you're really only seeing them with one eye, they get the vibe that you're one step in, one step out. It feels safer. There's a similar way to approach people that puts you in a less tense situation. So I would always walk up to the restaurant's guests in a way that was almost like I was leaving, and that's when I'd instantly address what I knew they were thinking. This was another way I'd try to set myself up for success.

Let's say you're looking for a relationship. So you sign up for a singles event, and yet when you get there, no one's mingling. Everyone is standing around, looking at their cocktails and waiting for someone else to make the first move. Clearly, it's awkward, so you could break that tension and shift the energy by calling out how uncomfortable the situation is, saying something casually to your first date, such as, "I don't know about you, but I was a bit nervous to give this a shot," all with a grin on your face. The combination of vulnerability and confidence is refreshing to others, even if you don't really feel confident and are employing a "Fake it till you make it" approach. Maybe you won't meet the person of your dreams at this event, but at the very least, you'll break the ice and make some new friends because you verbalized what they were feeling. And who knows what that could lead to?

Here's another scenario—in this one, you're a teacher. If you walk into class on the first day, how do you instantly build rapport with your students when they're on edge and they're also thinking, *Ugh, is this guy going to be dull? Is this lady going to give us a ton of homework?* There are all these expectations that are built in, so if you come in and look at the class from the students' point of view and answer the questions they might not even realize they have yet, you're going to establish that rapport far more quickly. If you immediately let them know that you're more interesting than other teachers, those kids are going to want to come to your class—they will look forward to it.

The same holds true if you're in sales. Every salesperson opens their laptop and says, "Now I'm going to work through my latest product catalog," and the potential customer's eyes are likely to glaze over, as they're so accustomed to this tactic. But if you come in and immediately address what they're thinking—especially if you guide them there by asking questions—you're going to have a more receptive audience.

The real power comes from leading with empathy. I like to present my inner monologue out loud when I perform for a big audience. When I get onstage, after the crowd has just watched a minute-and-a-half, high-octane video of supercuts of my most amazing tricks from past TV appearances, people are both intrigued and naturally skeptical. Many of them think this must be fake and like every magic show they've seen in the past, filled with sleight of hand tricks. So I'll say, "You saw my hype reel and you know what? I don't buy it. Gimme a break . . . mind reading? We all know that's impossible. Guess what, I'm the biggest skeptic in the room. If someone was up here telling me that they could read my mind, I wouldn't buy it either."

That's when I'll add, "Here's what I want you to know. I don't read minds; I read people. And each and every one of you can do the same thing, as this is a learnable skill. I just happen to have been practicing for nearly thirty years. Talk is cheap, let me prove it." Right there, I'm breaking down boundaries and promising them I'm not going to reveal what they'd prefer to keep hidden.

If I were that teacher in front of a new group of students, the first thing I would say is, "If I were you and I was sitting here thinking this class was just going to be dry lectures, I'd be bored out of my mind. So the question I have to ask myself is *How do I make this a class that you'll never forget?* One that will make you come in and you're waiting for the clock to start so we can learn about world history. I want to know from you guys how we can do that because I think this is the most fascinating topic ever, and if I do it right, you will, too."

I like putting words in people's heads. Feeding others the vocabulary I want them to use is a way of influencing them, but doing it openly, not secretly. The best speakers lead their audiences to a series of specific conclusions; keeping them engaged and entertained and unaware of the changes taking place in their minds, that is *real life mentalism*.

The first ten seconds you stand in front of someone are critical; you have to pay attention to everything the other person is giving you, from body language to facial expressions. You have to be aware of everything that might occur to someone when they look you over—how they might judge you. Their assessment of you is set in stone during those first ten seconds. I want you to ask yourself, "Have I ever been in a situation like this before?" If so, look for a pattern. What worked before? Scope out tension or resistance. It's also useful for you to be conscious of how quickly *you* judge others and understand that they're doing the same to you. What are you transmitting and what are they thinking of you? It's necessary you use that time to set the tone and take control. Verbalize what you believe they're thinking, expressing their inner voice aloud. Then, you either keep qualifying what they thought initially, such as, "I don't actually read minds," or you break down their barriers and burst the stereotypes they had of you from the start.

People always judge a book by its cover—publishers *literally* design them so you do—and that's why there's an adage telling you not to. But it's futile, because you can't avoid making a split-second decision about whether a book is for you. The beauty of mentalism is *you* get to decide what your own book cover looks like. You've got to become your own director, acquiring a real, objective perspective on yourself, which is very hard to do. We're so used to being ourselves that we can't even imagine listening through someone else's ears. We all have so much baggage that sometimes we can't see ourselves the way others do. But when you're able to step back and assess yourself, to take an unbiased, 360-degree view of how you're coming across both verbally and non-verbally, it suddenly becomes very easy for you to use that same skill to assess others.

The bottom line is that mentalists use Theory of Mind to predict and plan for what's going to happen next . . . and so do you! You probably don't realize you're already doing this. You use it every day because it helps you build relationships, solve problems, and understand the world around you by anticipating and being ready to react to what's going to happen next. It's a way of taking what people believe, what they perceive, and what they want, and then using that information to predict how they will behave.

By the way, Theory of Mind isn't just good at predicting how people will react in the future, but also helps if you're planning to try to change their reactions.[3] And it's a particularly helpful skill to hone when an unexpected event occurs . . . like when you appear on the *Today* show in front of millions of viewers watching at home and your trick goes wrong. (More on that later in this chapter.)

Game It Out

Mentalism isn't that different from cooking in a way, as both are designed to elicit primal reactions from your customers and make them feel good! Think of it like this: Chefs know the ingredients they have to work with, the sauces they can make, and have likely perfected their craft over many years of hard work, coupled with trial and error. This gives them a tremendous sense of what works . . . and what doesn't.

That foundation and knowledge allows them the option to throw this ingredient together with that ingredient and make a gourmet dish on the fly, if need be. There is a beauty to winging it and making it look easy, and that ease sometimes takes decades to achieve. I've been known to come up with my ideas for certain low-stakes TV appearances only a day, or even just a few hours, before they were set to take place. Never underestimate the power of a deadline to elicit creativity! But even on short notice, you still have to map out everything that could happen and plan effectively, not just for success but, even more important, for failure.

When it's a higher-stakes performance, you can bet that I have gamed out near infinite possibilities. I look at every step of the trick and make a contingency plan for how I'll right the ship if we veer off course. I will plan for every eventuality, storyboard each trick in my mind and on paper, and analyze the most minute details to see where I could make a mistake (or where an audience member could), and what I would or could do in each scenario. This type of stress testing is so critical and can make a massive difference in your life.

During my shows, if something goes wrong, the first thing I tell myself is to relax. I mean that on both a mental and physical level, as an audience can "smell" tension and discomfort from a mile away. Sometimes your expressions betray you, whereas with the proper practice, you can maintain a poker face even through a disaster. In fact, there have been times where I've messed up royally, but my attitude was so nonchalant and my demeanor so serene that my audience assumed my performance was going great. As Miles Davis put it, it's the *next* note that makes the note wrong.

Imperfection demonstrates that what we're doing is difficult. For example, let's say you're about to watch someone walk a tightrope strung between two skyscrapers. Nerve-racking, right? Now, if that person just flies across the rope, as effortless and sure-footed as a mountain goat, it sort of feels like something anyone could do. They made it look too easy. But if you were to watch that same person shaking on the rope, the sweat on their brow, the veins popping on their arms as they grip the wobbling balance stick, you get a visceral response right there in the pit of your stomach, your palms suddenly sweaty, because you're literally *feeling* the danger.

But it's not as dangerous as everyone thinks, because they've already gamed it out.

Visualize This

Visualization is something all top-tier athletes include as part of their training; they know the mental component is as important as the physical. Let's say the athlete is a runner: Before that starting pistol sounds, they'll have run that race in their head dozens of times, from the start all the way to breaking the tape at the finish. They'll figure out, *Here's what I'd do if my biggest competitor makes a move. Here's what I'd do if my energy flags on the last lap. Here's how I'd handle the curve in the track if it's raining. Here's how I'd proceed if my shoe rips.* And so on. They'll also envision themselves winning, again and again.

Bob Bowman, Michael Phelps's swimming coach, has had Phelps use visualization for years, and both swear by its use. Bowman says the key to visualization is starting with relaxation techniques, as relaxation helps your brain focus more on what you're trying to imagine. In fact, when Phelps was younger, Bowman gave Phelps's mother a book on progressive relaxation that she would guide him through at night, and often he'd become so relaxed after a few exercises, he'd immediately fall asleep.[4]

Whether it's Phelps picturing his pending heat, or you dreaming of winning your country club's mixed doubles tennis tournament, it's important to bring as much detail as possible to visualizing. What's the weather like at the club in your visualization? Is it bright and sunny? Or is it overcast and breezy—and how would your play differ, given those conditions? What kind of day is your opponent having? Do they play more aggressively—or less carefully—if they're tired or angry or pumped up on energy drinks? Is there a crowd gathered to watch you? Are there other matches happening close to you? How does the weight of the racket feel in your hand? How does it sound when you swoosh it through the air? Can you hear the clink of silverware coming from people dining on the club's terrace, or the rattle of ice in glasses? The more you put yourself in the scene of what you're likely to encounter, the more you'll be able to tune it all out and focus on your performance when it's the real thing.

Phelps would play out every scenario—what he wanted to happen, what he didn't want to happen, what might happen. While he went through the paces, I'm sure he could hear the din of the audience on the bleachers in the natatorium, could feel the grit under his feet on the starting block and the pinch of his goggles on his face, could taste the chlorine he'd have to expel from his mouth as he sliced through the churning water. Per Bowman, when we use vivid visualization and we've rehearsed many times, our brains can't distinguish between what is real and what's been imagined, and our bodies go into autopilot. That way, if anything goes wrong, your body is ready for it.

The more you play the mental movie in your head where you complete the task successfully, whether it's nailing your speech in front of the Rotary club, convincing your boss to give you a raise, or blowing away the *Today* show hosts, the more likely you are to succeed. That's why visualization is one of the most powerful tools you can use in your planning. Hand in hand with practice, visualization will build your confidence, help you manage pressure, maintain your focus, reduce your anxiety, and create muscle memory. I create that muscle memory by constant rehearsal, which is why my seatmate on the airplane on the way to my TED Talk likely thought I was insane, watching me panto-mime with full hand motions and body language and giving my speech over forty times during that flight. While it's incredibly helpful to visu-alize yourself asking your boss for a raise, sometimes you need to say it out loud to yourself so you can actually hear how it's going to sound.

When I think about the value of visualization, I call to mind a classic anecdote about Neil Armstrong's moon landing. Armstrong is en route and knows he has a very limited amount of fuel, so he must execute his tasks as perfectly as possible. Due to the angle and the lunar module's position,[5] it's hard for Armstrong to identify the best landing spot. He's at the point in the journey where he's had to switch from automatic to manual control of the landing module—the computer wouldn't be able to dodge the boulder fields that scattered across the surface of the Moon. There are alarms going off throughout the capsule, which Mis-sion Control quickly determined were harmless, but they intensified an already high-octane situation. Despite having run this—and every other scenario—over and over in their minds. Until those last few seconds, Armstrong's heart is pumping at 75 beats per minute, only slightly lower than the 110 BPM he'd experienced upon launch. While his heart rate spikes to 150 BPM in the final seconds, he still manages to put Apollo 11 on the ground perfectly, and then calmly announces, "The *Eagle* has landed."[6] (Interestingly enough, fellow astronaut Buzz Aldrin's average rate was 88 BPM, possibly because he had trained to be a fighter pilot and had shot down MiGs in combat, so he was likely better versed in visualizing everything that could go off the rails. Compare this with your own heart rate the next time you experience some nasty turbulence.)

With the Al Roker example I'll share shortly, I could not afford to panic on live national TV. But I used my time leading up to that appearance on the *Today* show to my advantage by rehearsing the entire sequence countless times assuming different outcomes, because I understood the value of having a contingency plan, and you should, too.

Account for Every Contingency

Around 2004, my sister surprised me with an announcement that she was going to run the New York City Marathon. Honestly, I thought the idea was ridiculous, especially as this was before celebrities decided to run marathons, before it became quite mainstream. In the past decade, everyone's started running marathons, from Kevin Hart to Karlie Kloss to Diplo. Back then, the notion of running 26.2 miles was absurd to me. But the only thing that was more absurd was knowing my older sister was going to suddenly be better than me at something, and sibling rivalry quite simply would not allow for that.

I couldn't get into the NYC race, so instead I signed up for the Philadelphia Marathon. Lo and behold, after a few months of mediocre training, I lined up at the start and went for it. Mind you, it didn't go well; I was crying (not afraid to admit it, full-on tears . . . and not of joy!) at mile 23, but I sucked it up and got it done. It wasn't pretty, it wasn't what I would describe as "fun," but I finished! And found myself suddenly hooked . . . with a desire to see if I could run the next one faster.

Over the next few years, I went from running marathons to the greater challenge of ultramarathons, which refers to any distance longer than 26.2 miles. Something I learned pretty quickly when I started to run these long-distance races is that at a certain mile marker, your mind will try to convince your body that you can't do it. Your mind will lie to your body. The worst thing in the world while you're running an ultramarathon is when your mind tricks you into giving up and starts to write your DNF (did not finish) speech.

A while back, I ran a race called the Keys 100. This is a one-hundred-mile run from Key Largo to Key West. It's really beautiful in certain spots, especially on the Seven Mile Bridge. The water all around is crystal clear and brimming with wildlife. The downside is it's hot as hell in mid-May. I've done this race twice, and each time, I've had a very rough go. The first year, I got full-blown heatstroke, which is different from heat exhaustion. Heatstroke is extremely dangerous. Your body overheats. In the span of half a mile, I went from running to walking to not being able to stand up. I was slurring my words and I couldn't tell you what day it was or even my name. Because ultramarathons are so grueling, runners typically have a race crew to help along the way. My buddies and fellow ultramarathoners, Ryan Dexter and Michael Halovatch, took time out of their busy lives to get me through this challenge. They were dumping ice under my armpits, down my back, on my crotch, and yet I had zero physical response. My body was overheating, and no matter what they did, my core temperature wouldn't seem to go down. My team attacked the problem piece by piece, never getting ahead of themselves. First things first—they had to force me to consume fluids and food. They knew they had to stabilize all my systems and try to get me back to neutral at the very least. Once I was back to talking, they saw if I was up to standing. Once I was standing, the goal was to start walking. Which I did for hours. And ready for the craziest part? I somehow got back to running and went so fast the last fifteen miles that my crew couldn't keep up with me . . . and they were in a car! I managed to finish in third place, and you bet your ass I remembered my name by that point in time.

The next year, I did the same race again, and by mile 27, I was throwing up. By mile 36, I was climbing into my stopped crew car to soak up a minute of air-conditioning. In my head, I was already rehearsing my DNF speech and preparing to tell Dexter to take me back to the hotel. You know the flowery social media posts: "It wasn't my day, but I will grow and learn from this experience, blah blah blah." But I had a contingency plan in place, by way of my crew. I knew my mind would lie to me, so I needed backup. Michael Halovatch, one of my team members who had crewed me the year before, gave me the pep talk of a lifetime over the phone. He wasn't even there with me this time, but back in New York. He said, "We're going to throw the kitchen sink at this. We're going to pull out all the stops. If you're taking ibuprofen, you're going to take more. You're taking caffeine, so we're going to double that, too. We're going to put calories in you. You've got music: Put it on, turn it up, and get your ass moving. Once you're walking, you start running. Don't give me any speeches. I'll talk to you again in five minutes."

And that was exactly what I needed. Physically, I could continue. But I needed someone to convince my mind that I wasn't done. What was so useful is that he made me stop thinking about the future and got me concentrating on the present moment, pulling every ace out of my sleeve that I'd been planning to save for later. Forget about later; all that matters is *now*. My crew member gave me exactly what was called for. I needed someone shoving me out of that car, pumping me full of everything, and bringing me back to life. The Oz Pearlman that never gives up was still in there, trapped somewhere in my mind, like a caged animal that needed to be released. When you find yourself in a situation where it would be so much easier to quit or to fail, have some tricks up your sleeve so you don't give in to what's easiest.

You might not even know what those tricks are until you're experiencing a low. Let's say you've decided to start your own business, as that's always been your dream. You don't want to work for The Man; you want to control your own destiny. Congratulations! But . . . you're not selling anything yet, and you've been at it for a while. You're not getting potential customers to call you back. You're thinking of giving up, even though you have enough of a financial cushion to tough it out.

What do you do?

At this point, you have to ask yourself, *What can I still put into this? What do I still have? Does anyone else do what I do? Is there some sort of information that I'm missing? Can I call in reinforcements?* When you get into a situation like this, set yourself up with guardrails and force yourself to utilize them, like having someone who can talk you off the ledge, buy you a beer, and tell you about the business that Bill Gates failed at before he started Microsoft. (It was called Traf-O-Data and it was a big goose egg.)

When I was in Florida running my race and it looked like the end, my buddy Ryan Dexter (aka "the Iceman") is the one who thought to call our other former crew member Michael Halovatch back in New York City. He gave the play-by-play: "He's been throwing up for nine miles. He's walking, he's a wreck. It's so early in the race." Usually in races like this, the breakdown comes 60, 70, or 80 miles in. Mine happened 27 miles into 100. The thought of walking 73 miles at a snail's pace while puking, otherwise known as a "death march," can break your spirit and overwhelm your determination. I thought to myself, *Oh my God, I'm going to have to walk the next twenty-four hours straight while feeling like this.* I would have done it but, man oh man, I didn't want to. Michael said, "We need to get you going because what you do well is run. You don't walk well, you run well. You need to get those miles in the bank. So if you can front-load those miles, you can use that to your advantage."

That's what you have to do—have plans in place that you can use to your advantage. I was in a crack-glass-in-case-of-emergency situation, and I needed someone to remind me that this was the time to crack that glass.

I was my own worst enemy in this situation. I was willing to quit instead of trying all the things my crew suggested. I was scared to take his advice because the easy way out was quitting. And in the moment, it feels good to say, "Oh, I just want to get rid of this pain and suffering and be done." But then I would have had to live with that decision for the next month, the next year, and on and on. Every time I looked in the mirror, I would know the truth, which is that I *chose* to quit. It's easy to give excuses to others, but it is very hard to lie to yourself. Quitting would have eaten me alive. I would not have dodged the pain and suffering; I would have transformed it from a short-lived experience to a long-term haunting. Knowing that your potential has not been achieved—knowing that you won't know the answer to *What if I had just done X, Y, or Z?*—will tear you apart. Do not let failure sneak up on you, but instead plan for that moment, prepare for that moment. Look failure right in the eyes and say, "Not today, I know what to do and I'm not giving up that easy."

You're not only going to succeed; you're going to improve your own brain chemistry.

The scientific effect of making plans, of having considered various backup plans, actually benefits your brain. Having something in reserve on your mental back burner will enhance your cognitive function for a couple of reasons. First, it's going to help improve your memory, because you're actively encoding that information. Planning will reinforce those neural pathways and make it easier to recall details, even under pressure; that will dovetail with improving your problem-solving skills, which will make it easier for you to decide on the fly. It's going to spark your creative thinking. In scientific terms, planning creates an interplay between our brain's prefrontal cortex and hippocampus, and that gives us the latitude to better guide our decisions and imagine our outcomes.[7] In plain English, let me break this down. The prefrontal cortex is like your brain's chief operating officer, in that it helps you with your decisions, with your goal-setting, and with thinking ahead. The hippocampus is more like the librarian who lives in your head and helps you retrieve your memories while also imagining future scenarios. When these two areas work together, you're engaging both your memory and your judgment to picture what may happen. This is key because it helps you decide what *should* happen. This interplay gives you more control over your choices and it allows you to envision different outcomes before they happen. Essentially, when these two are on the same team, they enable you to run mental simulations of the future. Imagine how useful that would that be. Plus, there's the added benefits of increasing our motivation and focus and reducing our stress when you know how it could turn out.

Planning, and including all variables, is simply a win-win.

Control the Variables

One of the best ways you can set yourself up for success is finding the means to control the variables. In a laboratory, variables are easy to control. You can isolate the experiment or the study, you can standardize the process, you can maintain a steady environment. But in life, it's not nearly so simple. Life is not a closed system. Social situations prove far more complex than a sterile lab.

The key here is figuring out what the variables are for your unique situation and how you may have a hand in guiding them. If you're a salesperson, you can't control how the potential clients react. However, you *can* schedule your pitch when you know people are most apt to pay attention or be receptive. If you've been in the business for a while, you've likely noticed patterns of when people are most alert, and you're well aware that right after lunch is the kiss of death, so you plan accordingly. If you're a teacher, your students are likely far more receptive at the top of the hour, rather than in the five minutes before class ends, so you hit them with the important concepts early. If you're wrangling your toddler, you're going to learn the hard way not to go anywhere with them right around naptime.

When I'm performing, sometimes the variable is as simple as getting a proper introduction to the audience. I never realized how important this was until I was slated to open for comedian Jim Gaffigan shortly after I was on *America's Got Talent.*

Right after *AGT,* I was hot. In showbiz, you get these moments where there's momentum and everyone's seeing you and recognizing you and it almost gives you a pass to not be as good. Stand-up comedy is my favorite form of entertainment and there is no better place in the world to see the best comics than the Comedy Cellar in New York City. The most famous comedians in the world will "drop in" unannounced, and for the first five minutes, they can just rest on their laurels. Everyone in the audience is just so blown away they are getting to see Chris Rock or Dave Chappelle from ten feet away, having paid only fifteen bucks! But if, five to ten minutes later, he's not funny, you're not going to be laughing anymore and his fame evaporates, at least in your view. With this in mind, I threw myself into improving my act because I promised myself that *AGT* was just the beginning for me, not my peak.

I was booked in early 2015 by a group of Modern Orthodox Jews that owns a very successful commercial mortgage business to perform at their client dinner later that year. This event was scheduled to take place two weeks after the finale of *AGT.* The fact that I was a fellow Jew gave me a major home field advantage. My humor was naturally going to hit better because I knew their terms, their inside jokes, I had the right "chutzpah." I knew *them.* We were just very simpatico.

It is important to note that they hired me before I'd even auditioned for *AGT*, much less made it through round after round and eventually into the finals. Their entire company watched every episode and rooted for me along the way, becoming emotionally attached as if I were their favorite sports team. And they got me for about 10 percent of the price I would have charged the day after getting third place on *AGT*. It was like buying a biotech stock whose blockbuster drug later gets approved by the FDA. They also hired superstar Jim Gaffigan, for a huge sum of money, to headline the event, and I was so excited to open for him.

The event was in Puerto Rico. It was an outdoor show by the beach, which is a kiss of death for live entertainment because there's lots of noise from the ocean and from animals, and the laughter and applause doesn't reverberate effectively with no walls to bounce off. The show is already going to be only 50 percent as strong as it could be. Then they told me to do forty-five to fifty minutes, the same as Jim. That was strange. Openers don't normally do the same amount of time as headliners. An opener should be more like the appetizer before the meal, especially because people only have so much energy to commit to entertainment on a given night.

I did forty-five minutes and I got two standing ovations. I absolutely killed it with this crowd because they got me; I was one of them. However, when I was done, they had *me* introduce Jim Gaffigan instead of an emcee. This was not the initial plan and took Jim by surprise, so he wasn't yet ready to come onstage. I read his intro and looked around, but he was nowhere to be found. About a minute or so later (but what felt like an eternity to the crowd), he made his way, flustered, to the stage. So, already, he had to contend with a bad introduction. After that, even though he's one of the biggest comedians ever, he just bombed. It was horrible, like, gut-wrenchingly bombed. It just wasn't the right crowd, and I'd inadvertently been at fault with the entrance.

And they had already been blown away by me—my show had both major moments of amazement and big laughs given our common sense of humor. (Full disclosure: My wife says that no one finds Oz Pearlman funnier than Oz Pearlman. She's right, as I just laughed out loud reading this, even though I wrote it!)

Afterward, I apologized profusely to Jim backstage about the intro because I felt terrible. I said, "You're one of the most legendary comics in the world. What went wrong?" Jim was really Zen about it, saying that bombing happens and you have to learn from a bad show and let it motivate you to do better next time. This was on a Monday night, and four nights later, he was back in New York, selling out Madison Square Garden, so I suspect he got over it. He wouldn't be where he is today without having cultivated some resilience. I learned an important show-biz lesson that night, which is: Everyone eats shit sometimes. Never forget it.

There are variables in life you can't control. There will be moments that, no matter how hard you try, you'll still fail. It's not about *if* that happens, but rather *when*: What will you do in those pivotal moments? That is what will define you. Determine what went wrong, learn from it, accept your feelings as valid, and keep moving forward. And that's exactly what I did when I didn't win *AGT*. (More on that in a later chapter.)

But failure wasn't going to be an issue on *Today*, because I was way too prepared.

The Big Reveal

When I perform on live TV, there is no safety net. There's no editing, no second take. If something goes wrong, my clock doesn't start over.

For me to extricate myself from the situation almost always involves more time. I need more time. Often, I don't have that time, as we are going to commercial or another segment, and so it's incredibly high pressure because the backup measures require me to dig myself out of a hole. And digging takes time! Now, if I'm at a live performance on-stage, that's rarely a problem. It doesn't go right? It's fine because I had a plan and plenty of time to fix it. You might not even know it went wrong because it's so effortless as I swoop in with something that you didn't know I was going to do.

Live TV is more of a pick-your-own-adventure in terms of planning. On one of my *Today* show appearances, when we had about forty-five seconds left, on a whim I asked Al Roker to name any celebrity he thought could be elected the next president of the United States. When I gamed out this trick, the Theory of Mind led me to believe he'd choose Taylor Swift. I set up the trick around that specific predicted outcome. Everything I did should have led him to that choice. Unbeknownst to him, I was even wearing a Taylor Swift T-shirt under my suit for my big reveal.

Confident in Roker's answer, I said to him, "Al, who's running? Shock us."

With great confidence, Roker replied, "George Clooney," which *was* a shock, as he wasn't who I'd envisioned him picking! He had no idea that, at that moment, my blood pressure was spiking and there was the potential for millions to see me implode on national television.

And yet, in the month that I'd planned for this trick, I knew that him picking Taylor wasn't a given, although she was the most likely choice. I had visualized this scenario in my mind hundreds of times, figuring out how I could quickly get him to choose the answer I'd anticipated if he didn't pick it on the first try.

Al Roker had no idea how wrong this had just gone, and I did not allow my body language to betray my true feelings. He'd given me a catastrophically wrong answer, but he didn't know there was a *right* guess I'd anticipated. When you find yourself in a moment like this, even if the stakes aren't quite so high, the way you handle the situation determines your outcome. You keep cool, you keep calm, you shift gears. Control your emotions and take charge.

At this point on *Today*, we had maybe half a minute left of airtime. Not a lot of time to pull out the win and prompt Roker to re-guess Taylor Swift. In Taylor's own words, I was "Down Bad," and maybe even ready to cry at the gym. The clock was ticking and I had the wink of an eye to make it seem like this had been my plan all along, as the unexpected correction with seconds to spare would make the trick seem even more powerful and deliberate.

There are certain moments where you go, "Oh, he's getting it wrong but he's going to come back." But in front of millions of viewers drinking coffee in front of their televisions as they get ready for work? That's not a get-it-wrong-to-come-back moment from my perspective. I knew I couldn't lose my cool. Animals sense danger on an instinctive level. They can see it. They can smell fear. If you run from a bear, it considers you prey and it will hunt and kill you even if it doesn't want to eat you. The same thing applies when you're trying to influence people. They can sense fear, and sensing fear is almost like a smell. Your body tenses. In that moment, I had to turn into a quarterback with five seconds left on the clock. When time's running down, a good quarterback knows they have to throw a perfect pass.

I knew if I panicked, Roker would panic, and then I would not be able to impose my will on him. I wouldn't be able to get out of the situation. If you happen to watch the clip on YouTube, you'll see that I'm calm as can be.[8] Roker didn't even know that the trick wasn't on plan.

In situations like this, you must maintain your calm and composure or it actually will not work. It's sort of a catch-22; if something goes wrong, you inherently want to panic and tense up, and often that will make it even worse. In flight training programs, they do heart rate analysis on fighter pilots and astronauts. In situations of extreme tension and stress, the people who make it through are the ones who are able to maintain a low heart rate to keep their disposition, even in a situation that's life-or-death.

The stakes were high. If I failed, I would die of old age before the video clip died on social media. I can tell you about past instances when I've panicked onstage—the audience senses it and things spiral. Having visualized and having planned will help you maintain composure. It's physical. Your mental controls your physical. I've reviewed plenty of my old tapes and there are times I could see in my body if things were going wrong. I've had flop-sweat moments when suddenly my brain turns off and I go offstage and ask myself, *What just happened? I don't even remember; I was so stressed.*

I said to Roker, "Listen, the world is changing. What if it wasn't a guy who was elected? What if I was anybody else? Any women?" Instead of thinking that my setup was unsuccessful, Theory of Mind indicated that Al Roker suddenly took pause to worry that he'd inadvertently been sexist to not consider a woman.

Roker screwed up his face for a couple of seconds (that felt like an hour) and thought hard before he said, "Um . . . Taylor Swift."

I shrugged nonchalantly and repeated it slowly back, "Taylor, Swift," as if to emphasize how impossible it was that he had changed his mind, seemingly of his own volition, and with only seconds remaining before the commercial break. As he pondered, I removed my blazer and button-down to reveal my T-SWIFT FOR PREZ T-shirt. And then I asked his cohost what the word was that she'd associate with the campaign, and she spontaneously said, "Independence." Then I turned around ard showed them the back of the shirt, which read #INDEPENDENCE . . . snatching victory from the jaws of defeat as Roker exclaimed, "Mind blown, again!" They were so shocked by what just took place that they bumped the next guest and kept me on for another segment. This was a near unprecedented occurrence on a show that is so tightly scheduled.

All thanks to planning for the unexpected!

(Whew!)

THREE

Make Your Fear of Rejection Magically Disappear

All too often, people shy away from accomplishing big goals because they fear rejection. What they don't realize is that by eliminating the chance of failure, there's also no chance of success. But anyone who says rejection doesn't hurt is either a liar or a masochist. It's always painful, and no one figured that out faster than me as a sensitive teenager.

Listen, I can't make the sting of rejection vanish completely, but in this chapter, I can help you shift it elsewhere. I'll show you how to separate and disassociate yourself from the skill or task at hand, to not internalize the guilt or rejection, and to prevent those bad feelings from bleeding into other aspects of your life. It's a technique I call "magic mode."

And barring that, I'll show how to let the haters fuel you, something I experienced myself after a Super Bowl trick didn't go as planned. Is it as easy as flipping a switch?

Yes, it is, and I'll show you how.

Weird Science

Rejection doesn't just hit us in our feelings. What you may not know is that social rejection causes a process in our brains that's akin to physical pain. According to the American Psychological Association, rejection can impact our emotions, our cognition, and even our physical health.[1] This stems from evolution and our biological need to be included, because being ostracized from the group and cast out of cooperative society thousands of years ago meant certain death.

Social psychologist Naomi Eisenberger of UCLA conducted a study to investigate the brain's response to rejection. Volunteers were placed into a functional magnetic resonance imaging machine, which is a type of MRI that can read brain activity, and given virtual reality goggles with which they would throw a virtual ball to other players. The subjects were told they were interacting with other volunteers, but the ball's progress was really controlled by the research team. Researchers wanted to determine what happens in the brain when we are excluded.

For those singled-out players, researchers noted that the anterior cingulate cortex, which is what responds to pain, would light up in accordance to exactly how strongly the participants felt excluded and rejected.[2] The emotional pain manifested itself into a physical response. So if you're still having flashbacks about what happened during a game of dodgeball when you were in junior high, this is why.

Rejection triggers our fight-or-flight response, meaning our heart rate increases, our blood pressure spikes, and our stress hormones are activated.[3] And that's not to mention how it hurts our self-esteem, especially if it sends us down the rabbit hole of negative self-talk and feelings of worthlessness and inadequacy.[4] Plus, being rejected can cause a drop in dopamine and that opens a whole Pandora's box of sadness, grief, and the loss of motivation.

That's a lot of baggage to lay on a kid who just wants you to pick a card before your linguini arrives, know what I'm saying?

I had no clue why being turned away made me feel bad; I just knew I wanted to *stop* feeling bad. When I was at the restaurant, my mind was constantly racing. I was always trying to find a way to be better received. In some respects, it was like I was working out a recipe; I'd see what happened if I changed an ingredient here or there and then taste-test to see what worked.

My solution then to deal with the rejection was to disassociate myself from my fear of being hurt and embarrassed. In terms of personal phobias, the fear of being embarrassed is one of the most common. It's like that Jerry Seinfeld joke where he says that more people are afraid of public speaking than they are of dying. Which means that at a funeral, more people would rather be in the coffin than giving the eulogy.

Through my trial and error, I stumbled into something that researchers describe as the ability to go from being the "actor" in the situation to being the "observer."[5] (Now I call this "slipping into magic mode" and we'll go into further detail on how to do that later in this chapter.)

What I mean by being the observer is that when I was about to perform—way back when I put on my bar mitzvah suit and walked into Zia's—I'd tell myself that I wasn't Oz Pearlman. Instead, I was Oz the Entertainer, the precursor to Oz the Mentalist. And if people rejected or didn't like Oz the Entertainer, that wasn't Oz Pearlman's problem. I turned myself into a character, meaning I separated myself and my psyche from the task at hand. I was no longer the actor; I was the observer. I made a conscious decision to not internalize how people would react to me because they weren't reacting to the *real* me.

Essentially, I would silo myself. I like to explain this with the analogy of having a bucket of fresh drinking water. If you add salt to that bucket, the whole thing is ruined; you can't drink it. But, if you were to put a divider in that bucket, you could dump salt into a little section and the rest of the water would be free and clear. I realized that if one element could ruin everything, then I had to figure out how to create silos so the salt—meaning the rejection—would only impact a small portion. That way, I wouldn't shuffle home thinking *Ugh, I'm terrible at everything*, and I wasn't derailed from my goal of scoring party gigs, which would allow me to buy more tricks. I quickly began compartmentalizing my feelings, so those negative thoughts didn't paralyze me. I'd rationalize that those patrons didn't know Oz Pearlman, and they weren't rejecting *him*; instead, they weren't into Oz the Entertainer's tricks. And that was their loss.

Ironically, while you may imagine that the pain of rejection goes away as you grow up, research shows it's just the opposite—studies show that older adults feel the sting of hurt feelings more than younger adults.[6]

So I want you to consider how disassociating could apply to the rejection you may face. Where would it be useful for you to step outside yourself and observe? If you could detach, would you feel more free to share your ideas in team meetings? Would you take the chance to talk to that attractive guy or girl you keep seeing in your apartment lobby? Would you be able to make the case to your boss for hiring an intern to help lessen everyone's workload? Could you take a bigger swing if you weren't so tied up feeling like everything was at stake?

Instead of thinking about all the ways your asks could go wrong, take a minute and envision all the ways in which they could go *right*. This is one of those "What could you try if you knew you couldn't fail" situations, so put this advice to use and prepare to amaze yourself. And if you ask and it's a no, remember, they're never rejecting you—they're rejecting one tiny piece that's separated from the rest and won't bring you down.

Failing Up

I've actually seen magicians quit performing because they couldn't deal with the rejection; they never learned to silo themselves. This is a lot like an athlete that never recovers mentally from an injury; long after they are physically healed, the fear of more pain ends their career.

This same fear can handicap you and keep you from chasing your big goals because you're not ready to risk rejection and failure.

Here's the quiet part that no one says out loud: If there's no chance of losing, there's also no chance of winning. Like in the above examples, while you may strike out, what happens when your shared ideas are implemented? When you find out the attraction to your neighbor is actually mutual? When your intern helps you shine because you're no longer bogged down with administrative work?

If you want to become stronger, whether it's mentally or physically, you must experience failure. Failure is the foundation for growth. Failing, especially multiple times, gives you the kind of resilience you just don't get from smooth sailing. Failure is the cornerstone of innovation.

Let's talk about some famous failures, like . . . one of our greatest living authors, Stephen King. King had started to write *Carrie* and became so frustrated that he ended up throwing out the entire manuscript. His wife, Tabitha, who couldn't help but be curious about his work, fished it out of the trash.[7] The manuscript was rejected 30 times before being picked up by Doubleday. It went on to sell over a million copies its first year in paperback and become a successful film.[8] Since then King has published over 60 novels, 200 short stories and won numerous awards for his contributions to literature."[9] (Imagine being the editor who told Stephen King he didn't have what it takes.)

Or how about we look at that big loser, Walt Disney? He got canned from his newspaper job because they said he "lacked imagination." (Seriously!) The Grand Ole Opry suggested that Elvis Presley return to his job driving trucks when they gave him the boot. The King of Rock and Roll! And do you clean your floors with a Dyson vacuum? Well, that's only because Sir James Dyson had the fortitude to fail 5,126 times before he created the working prototype.[10] No one sees failures in these instances; instead, they see dynamic individuals who didn't allow a bump in the road to knock them off their trajectories.

Let that be you.

Failure allows for growth. But so many have the tendency to not own up to the fact that it's easier to keep the status quo than it is to potentially suffer more along the road to greatness. Any athlete knows that if they want to get stronger, they have to break down that muscle. So it follows that, if you want to get stronger mentally, you can't protect yourself from the failure and rejection that can come from having tried.

At Zia's, one of the many things I learned (which is I why I keep bringing it up) is that landing outside gigs for my tableside magic was a numbers game. For every three tables that loved me, one would say, "Keep it moving, buddy," and for every fifty business cards I would hand out each night, maybe two would turn into a show over the next year. This required me to be patient, to plant the seeds and wait for the fruit to grow. What helped me reframe these rejections was knowing that X number of rejections would ultimately result in Y number of paying gigs. So the more rejections I collected, the quicker I could achieve my goal of working consistently as a party magician. Suddenly, rejection wasn't a failure; it was a necessary metric.

There was a popular challenge on social media called "rejection therapy," which is really just an updated term for exposure therapy. In it, people film themselves going places and asking for things, knowing full well they'll be rejected. Some of the most common challenges are asking a stranger to buy you a Slurpee at 7-Eleven or requesting a random person on the street give you a hug. The theory is that the more you accustom yourself to rejection, the better insulated you'll be. While this is not an evidence-based therapy, I have no doubt that this can help some people develop thicker skin, which in turn can help build character.

I feel lucky to have learned as a kid that getting knocked down wasn't pleasant, yet I was stronger every time I picked myself back up. It doesn't matter if you're fourteen or forty, every rejection moves you a step closer to where you want to land.

Expect the Unexpected

After *America's Got Talent*, my popularity grew exponentially, and I thought I could put worrying about rejection and failure in my rearview mirror. I assumed the road ahead would be smooth and easy from then on out . . . until the pandemic hit.

For people who held office jobs, the pivot to working from home was fairly easy. In fact, many people preferred not having to deal with commutes, dry cleaning, office politics, etc. Heck, even broadcasters were able to work from home. But when your job is to appear in a room in front of thousands of people, lockdown presented a real dilemma.

My peers began performing on and promoting themselves through social media, but I'll be honest, this scared me. Despite my best efforts,

I'm not immune to the fear of rejection, especially because social media allows for immediate responses that are easily measured. Plus there's the tendency for others to pile on when they sense sentiment has turned against the person posting. This was an entirely new medium for me. In some ways, it felt like I was starting over, though at least I was wearing better suits than my Zia's days.

Say what you will about social media; love it or hate it, the fact of the matter is it's here to stay. It seems like everyone's addicted. If you think social media doesn't impact your brain chemistry, think again. Researchers have found that the dopamine hit we get from positive interactions is similar to what's produced from using cocaine.[11] It can also diminish your ability to pay attention and to retain information, plus there's the possibility that it can negatively impact your mental health, so I'm saying all this with the caveat that it should be used responsibly. But in a time when the world was feeling so disconnected, social media was a bridge that helped us feel like we were all in it together, so I had to figure it out.

I knew that, to be successful in any endeavor, I needed to be able to scale, and social media allowed this to happen. Social media has changed our access to people, and it's the currency of our time. Think about it—you can reach out, and people can reach right back. I had no idea how mentalism would translate to a handheld screen, but I made myself try. My strategy wasn't to monetize, but to connect.

I began performing online when so many of us were still trying to figure out how to work Zoom, and I have to tell you, it felt like my early restaurant days when I was a research scientist, tweaking my experiments until they produced the desired results. At first, I was sure I was ruined and told my wife we should sell our home and move while we still could, that I'd never work again. Yes, I may be prone to catastrophizing. Yet I kept at it and within a few weeks of free shows offered to friends, family, and past clients, I came up with a successful formula of how to perform on Zoom.

Rejection is never going to go away. The possibility of failure is never off the table, no matter who you are. But the more you're willing to put yourself out there and try new things, the more success you'll experience. The ultimate failure is never getting to the starting line. When I began my career, I thought opportunities would fall into my lap, but that was never going to happen. For example, I was never going to get on television if I didn't force myself to try, so, as a bulwark against failure, I had to ask myself hard questions about what I wasn't doing.

Fortunately, during those strange pandemic times, I was able to slip into magic mode. Here's how you can do the same.

Flip the Script

I didn't have strong social skills when I was fourteen—but what kid does? If Clark Kent can rip off his shirt, throw on a cape, and become Superman, then why couldn't I do the same? In this case, my superpower was to go from Oz the nerdy, insecure teenager to Oz the Great and Powerful (as far as my audiences were concerned). Seeing people light up when I performed was a rush and I fed off it. I flipped that switch, went into magic mode, and suddenly shed the fears that otherwise held me back; I'd started on the journey to becoming Oz the Mentalist.

It's always scary to try new things. There's a possibility of failure and rejection. We worry that we're going to look stupid and feel ashamed. Neophobia is *real* and it can manifest itself in any area of your life, no matter how large or small, whether you're anxious about getting a new haircut or you're worried about making a cross-country move for that dream job. So often, our defense mechanism is to just give up instead of trying. It's easier to stay stuck, to not venture outside of that comfort zone. Keep your hair the same, stay in that dead-end job.

We've already established that visualization tricks our brain into thinking what we're seeing is real and puts our bodies into autopilot. But when you see yourself as the observer, your brain flips the script and gives you license to be a bolder version of who you are.

If you're ever going to try something new, you must be able to imagine that it's possible. For example, when I started training for my first marathon, I never allowed myself to believe that I would fail. I told myself that if I built up my endurance, if I cross-trained and fueled and hydrated properly, if I got enough rest, and if I held myself accountable to a series of small goals, there was no way I couldn't do it. I'd have built such a strong foundation that I'd be rock-solid on race day . . . and I was.

Having some healthy irrationality can be a motivating force, even though, in the back of my head, I wondered if running 26.2 miles was bananas. In marathons—and in life—the mental is just as important as the physical. You have to tell yourself you've got this, while concurrently putting in the work to make sure you've got it. Remember, *you* control that little voice inside your head. Flip that switch, and don't let it be a negative influence. Instead, become your own biggest cheerleader. Celebrate those little wins along the way, as they will add up to more than you expect over time. Repeat that positive self-talk until you believe it.

Rejection sensitive dysphoria is the name for the heightened emotional responses people can feel stemming from rejection, critique, failure, or even teasing. (This phenomenon is most common in adults with

ADHD.) One of the best ways to combat it—beyond therapy and medication if it's severe—is through focusing on the positive and your own personal strengths and abilities.

Part of magic mode is understanding the difference between rejection, critique, and feedback. Rejection is when your idea or effort doesn't work for the audience, which can be less about you and more about their individual needs. For example, you may be the best painter in the world, but if the end user wants a poem, your creation isn't going to work. Critique is more problem-focused, like when you're telling a joke and the punchline doesn't land. Feedback is solution-oriented, and it can include both strengths and weaknesses. Of course, you can certainly learn from and implement changes in each instance. The most important point is to concentrate on what is within your control. Using the Jim Gaffigan example from the last chapter: Although he couldn't control the outdoor venue's noise, he could take steps to better his outcome, such as insisting that his opener have a shorter set and getting a clear a signal before being introduced.

Magic mode is the difference between beating yourself up, and saying, "This was great, but next time will be even better," because it will help you enjoy every moment. For example, a few years ago, I ran my fastest time ever at the Philadelphia Marathon. I finished in 2:23:52, which, given my age, is likely to be the fastest time I'll ever run in my life. I was a lean, mean, running machine! Rather than savor that achievement, as I should have, I instead focused only on the negative, which was having not achieved my goal of breaking 2:20. I was hyper-fixated on that number to my detriment, and that caused me to lose sight of my incredible accomplishment during that race, which I will always regret.

When I look back at that day, I realize I robbed myself of what was an epic achievement because of my mindset. I should have taken a step back, been the observer, and said to myself, *You might never run this fast again, don't take your fitness, your focus, your unwavering dedication and commitment for granted. Enjoy this day!*

I didn't and I regret it. Not only was I miserable, but I let my bad feelings spill over, which impacted my family and my next performance. That wasn't fair to anyone. I should have celebrated clocking the best time of my life. I should have been grateful for having the capability to run any distance at all. I should have reveled in the beauty of speeding through a historic city on a beautiful day, through crowds of supportive spectators. There was so much to love in the moment and I didn't recognize any of it: I was too fixated on four stupid minutes.

To remind myself to not let this happen again, I like to look at a picture of myself finishing the Hartford Marathon a year earlier. I was nearly two minutes slower in that race, but I didn't expect to run as fast as I did. The look on my face when I crossed that finish was one of pure bliss, unbridled joy, distilled and injected into every cell of my being. It was so striking that the next year the race organizers used it for the posters to promote the race! And what was the difference? My expectations. Letting that negative self-talk creep in and not learning my own lesson of flipping into magic mode meant that I wasn't able to shake the negative and embrace the positive.

But we're all works in progress, so remember that.

The Future Is Now

When something does go wrong, there's a technique I like to use. I tell myself that no matter how awful this feels now, it will eventually get better. The pain, the unpleasantness, the discomfort will subside and you need to visualize the sunrise just over the horizon and be patient as it comes.

Having an awareness that this pain and shame and unhappiness is temporary will help save your psyche, especially the more time passes. Will you even remember said slight or mistake three years from now? I suggest you fast-track that set of emotions, which is what I ultimately learned to do at Zia's; it's a skill I've carried with me ever since.

When I'd walk up to an unreceptive table, I'd worry about how I'd feel in the moment that they shooed me away. If they were like, "Please get out of here," that was rough. The dejection right in the moment is huge. But an hour later, a day later, the pain is virtually gone. What I suggest you do is trick yourself into speeding up that cycle. In your mind, tell yourself it's a day later instead of a minute later.

Imagine you have a remote control you can use to fast-forward your life. Right now, I want you to workshop something in your head that you're dreading and you've been putting off. Let's say you have a call with somebody that you know is going to tell you no or be mad or disappointed. You do not want to do this call. It's awful and the anticipation makes it even worse. Or let's say you're dealing with somebody that you hate, or any other situation that has you tied in knots. The mere thought of dealing with it sends waves of dread pulsing through your core, hence you keep delaying the work. Unfortunately, avoidance is only a tactic, never a solution.

I want you to catalog how you feel one minute after doing the task— just write it down. You don't even have to make the call, just record how you imagine you'll feel once you do. Then set yourself a reminder in your calendar for twenty-four hours later. How do you feel now that it's a day later? See what the difference is.

For almost everything I can think of, barring life-or-death decisions, the negative swirl of emotions subsides within twenty-four to forty-eight hours of the work being addressed. Researchers have found that, without reinforcement, memories are actively suppressed and degraded.[12] You literally will get over it. The difference is, one minute later, you probably feel an eight out of ten on a scale of terrible. But a day later, you feel maybe two out of ten, right? So let's trick our brain. Remember, the more vividly you visualize it, the more your brain accepts it to be real, and the more your body responds appropriately.

Let's repurpose the very same mentalist tricks I use in my act to get in people's heads and manipulate the way they think, but instead do it to you. In this case, speed up the clock and take what you know you'll feel one day from now and trick yourself into feeling that one second from now instead. Picture yourself hitting fast-forward on a remote control. That's how I would do it at the restaurant. So when a table would say, "Kid, get out of here," I'd trick my brain into fast-forwarding to how I'd feel a day later. Couple that with magic mode—they had an issue with Oz the Entertainer, not me—and it was easy for me to go to the next table, pass out the cards, and get the gigs.

Mission accomplished.

(Not So) Super Bowl

All of this is to say that when I finally had my chance to perform on live national TV before the Super Bowl kickoff in 2023, I was as well-insulated as I could have been for when my trick failed. The trick hinged on NFL coach Rex Ryan using a stopwatch to time Matt Hasselbeck throwing a bunch of footballs to Randy Moss, and an impossible reveal at the end that I'd predicted how long this would take. To be safe, I had the coach practice using the stopwatch with me before we went on air, even though I was worried that he'd feel patronized. I mean, showing a coach how to use a stopwatch? Why not instruct Michael Jordan on how to put that bouncy orange ball in the net? And yet somehow Rex fat-fingered the stopwatch, pressing Start and Stop simultaneously, so that the recording of the seconds—the crux of the trick—never happened.

That's right, my trick went off the rails in front of a live audience that numbered in the tens of millions. I guess if you're going to fail, fail big?

The issue was I was still sort of new to massive broadcasts like this and I didn't have proper control of the situation. My tricks have layers and can sometimes be complex, so I need total and complete buy-in from the camera operators and director, because there are certain angles and shots that they have to catch in order for it to be successful.

Afterward, I did a thorough after-action review and determined that, ultimately, it was my fault. What I wanted to accomplish was too complicated, and I was being too clever. I should have simplified the trick and made it clearer. But I was both skilled and experienced enough to not let this mistake devastate me. Honestly, I had to silo myself for the next few days after the game, because I got so much hate from people online that had placed bets based on my mentalist prediction.

So. Much.

One guy was furious. He told me, "Buddy, you owe me $1,000."

I replied, "Buddy, why are you taking financial advice from a mentalist?"

When you get that kind of pushback, the only way through is to allow the hate and the bad feelings to fuel you. What I didn't do was relive that moment over and over, berating myself with "coulda, woulda, shoulda." I had to let it go. I didn't permit one single misstep to stop me. Instead, I doubled down on my work with the NFL and have since created some of my most spectacular and iconic moments with players, like when I stunned Dak Prescott, transforming a pack of playing cards held tightly in his hands into any animal called out at random.

So now when you google *Oz the Mentalist* and *football*, you don't see the trick that went afoul, because I didn't let that one bad moment impede my progress. Instead, you'll see me correctly predicting the first thirteen picks in the 2024 NFL Draft, including Michael Penix Jr, which absolutely no one saw coming, not even the owner of the team. Or you'll see me blowing the minds of every member of the Michigan Wolverines before they won the College Football Playoff National Championship, guessing which players Coach Jim Harbaugh would think of, predicting each of their jersey numbers, which, when flipped upside down, spelled out *Go Blue.* The stadium played that moment on the jumbotron as Michigan concluded their perfect season—going undefeated and then winning the National Championship. To have my history intertwined with such a pivotal moment for my alma mater is a memory I will always cherish.

Listen, I know rejection is no picnic. But if you don't try, you're never going to achieve more. You have to face down those disappointments, and you can't let them immobilize you. While it's painful, you have the power to shift that negative energy elsewhere. Learn how to separate yourself from the fear and pain of rejection, and watch the paradigm shift that occurs in your life and your ability to start achieving your biggest goals.

FOUR

Focus on Others

In 2006, the beer brand Dos Equis created an iconic advertising campaign called *The Most Interesting Man in the World*, starring a handsome, suave, and mysterious bearded actor named Jonathan Goldsmith. He was shown doing everything from exploring Egyptian tombs to arm-wrestling in South America to surfing killer waves. After the voiceover deemed him the most interesting man in the world, he'd raise a bottle of Dos Equis and say, "I don't always drink beer, but when I do, I prefer Dos Equis." The campaign was a huge hit for the decade it ran, and it increased the brand's market share by 22 percent.[1]

Of course, that man was fictional and the product of a marketing firm. Also, the idea of being the most interesting person in the world is a huge ask.

But what if I promised you could become the most interesting person *in the room*?

If you want to be the most interesting person in the room, you don't have to be the second incarnation of Ernest Hemingway. You don't have to run with the bulls in Pamplona or survive back-to-back plane crashes. You definitely don't need to write the Great American Novel or build a boxing ring so you can spar with your guests. You never have to go fishing.

The only thing you have to do to be the most interesting person in the room is to be *the most interested* person in the room. If you want to be fascinating, be fascinated by others.

One of the fundamentals of finding your inner mentalist is to know that it's never about you. Whatever you do and wherever you go, it should always be about *them*. I'm talking about your family, your clients, your coworkers, your community, your club, your audience, etc., because when you make the interaction about them, you make them look and feel good.

In much the same way that a rising tide lifts all boats, your ability to cast your light on others to make them shine will be the secret to your success. That means connecting with everyone—and never putting your baggage on them. People want to be seen. In our heads, we're all the stars in our own movies, but to everyone else, we're just supporting characters. If you want to feel like a star, make it all about *them*.

Mentalism is a finite series of tricks. What makes a performance legendary is being a storyteller and tapping into people's emotions with genuine interest. In this chapter, I'll teach you how to make whoever is in front of you feel like the most important and interesting person in the room, and it starts with kicking away the pedestal. I will break down the steps for transforming zero-sum game situations into win-wins for everyone, and also how to apply the showbiz rule "Always leave the audience wanting more" to your everyday life.

I'll also show how to turn the mirror around so that it no longer faces you but reflects the best parts of those around you, because that adds to them wanting more. This is exactly what happened when I spent half an hour with my childhood idol, Steven Spielberg. Only it was *he* who held up that mirror to *me*.

Use your inner mentalist to try to guess how many questions I was able to ask about him.

Kick Away That Pedestal

If you want to make people look good, then you've got to level the playing field, especially when there's a power imbalance. You can't put yourself on a pedestal, and expect others to feel comfortable around you. Let's take what I've been doing with ESPN as an example. I visit a lot of NFL training camps in the preseason, and although it might look as if I'm just performing tricks—like reading Josh Allen's mind or figuring out the play fake that Joe Burrow tried to fool me with—that's not my real intent. I'm there to help build team unity. The coaches, owners, and general managers aren't just looking for a magic show, they want a morale boost. They want their team to walk out of my show feeling more connected and cohesive, which often translates into better performance on the field.

This starts with making everyone feel equal. The "pedestal effect" is a cognitive bias. What this means is, in our minds, we've created an idealized version of who someone is, especially when they're in a position of power, authority, or leadership. By default, they often make us feel "less than," even if it's not their intention. The act of taking someone off the pedestal means that we're actively trying to humanize them, because the notion of someone being on a higher level than us inherently makes us feel insecure and disempowers us.

You've got to remember that even though these men are on the same team, it doesn't always *feel* like they're on the same team, especially when the other guys are earning more, getting more attention, and simply playing more. When the second-string quarterback sees the star player laughing and being equally as amazed as he is, the invisible wall starts to come down. What I'm doing in that room removes some of that underlying tension by humanizing the superstars and coaches, making them more accessible.

Now, for some teams, this is not as much of a factor. But a few years ago, one of the teams I visited had a new coach. Everyone was on edge. It felt like I was in an army barracks during basic training. I tried to get the coach involved, to get him to relax a bit so we could have some fun at his expense. The emotional temperature in the room was significantly warmer by the time I was done. This quest to humanize others is the same exact reason I decided to freak Aaron Rodgers out so completely by making a live goldfish appear in his otherwise empty hands. (And for the record, don't blame me for the season-ending injury on the first drive of his first game with the Jets!)

A lot of times, when we elevate someone because of their position, it can bring out the worst in ourselves. I like to call this the "compare and despair" mentality. But when we're able to find a way to make it feel like we're on the same level, when we're able to make them more relatable, when we can look them in the eye instead of gazing up at them, we perceive them as less intimidating. This is why certain celebrities are wildly popular on social media, even if they're not marquee names. While it's interesting to see these icons live glamorous lives on private planes or behind the velvet rope at exclusive events, it's so much more relatable when they show themselves getting a parking ticket or spilling coffee on their pants or cheering along in sweats while they watch the Olympics. (Celebrities: They're just like us!) When you can see yourself in someone else, the gap is bridged.

When I perform at corporate events, I often provide a social context that helps promote bonding and creates an environment conducive to business. Given the power dynamics within large organizations, access to the upper echelon is a very valuable commodity, and having people at the top of the food chain know who you are as an employee is a big deal. I always make it a point to include the CEO or other senior leaders, with the goal of demystifying them. I'll either reveal something very funny about them, such as the name of their first crush in elementary school, or have them serve as my mind-reading protégé and guess something impossible to know about a colleague.

When I do this, the CEO is no longer above everyone else; they're just a woman or man like any other, who appears equally as blown away as their colleagues. This creates a bonding moment for everyone involved, and suddenly someone who'd be too afraid to even look the CEO in the eyes is their partner in crime—they're high-fiving each other in front of the crowd—and it aligns everyone to the same level. This experience serves to unite the team, creating a memorable moment that they've shared and can therefore readily reference next time they see each other.

One company I recently worked for had just gone through a big merger. Now, I've been a part of corporate America, having started my career on Wall Street. (More on that in a later chapter.) That's why I knew firsthand that mergers are inherently scary, no matter the industry. There's always uncertainty and the fear of redundancy. Everyone's on guard and they all think they're getting fired, right? So this is the perfect scenario in which to put everyone on an even footing.

I asked the event coordinator about the state of affairs, and she was a little cagey, but I insisted, "Give me the honest truth." She explained that everyone was borderline panicky and that morale was way down. I told her, "Great, good to know, I get it. And the CEO is probably in a situation where nobody wants to give them bad news, right?" She said that the company just wanted to warm up the room, to de-escalate all those bad feelings, as things truly were on an upswing and jobs were safe.

When I did the trick for the CEO, I pulled in a personal assistant, someone who'd never get face time with the CEO, and yet my trick put them on the same team. It made them equals, collaborators, coconspirators. Later, the CEO wrote to me and said, "Hey, your performance was great, but the real magic was the way you had me integrate with the team. This led to an entirely different atmosphere after the show, where people were fearlessly approaching me to laugh and joke about what just took place. The ice was broken, that glass ceiling which normally separates us shattered. I'd say that close to a hundred people, who would have been completely nervous to talk to me, walked up and said, 'Did you really guess that? How did you know their pet's name?' It was transformational and went a long way to turning things around. So thank you."

If you can find a way to put everyone on the same footing, things change for the better. It's kind of like if you get stuck in an elevator with a bunch of strangers. Five minutes in, you're all cracking jokes and full of gallows humor. You're going to get to know those people. That's the same exact mentality. The shared experience causes a shift in your brain; suddenly you can open up to others that you would've never even acknowledged otherwise.

One of the reasons I've been invited back to the *Today* show so many times isn't just because I deliver on camera (though that's important, too). The producers have told me it goes deeper than that—my repeat visits are because I bring joy to everyone on set, from the security team to craft services, makeup to wardrobe. That positive energy creates a kind of home field advantage, with the whole crew rooting for me. And here's the thing: This is something anyone can practice. When you go through life trying to make someone's day a little brighter, you'll find that people naturally want to be in your corner.

Take Note

An easy and economical way to make people look and feel good is to remember what's important to them. Doesn't cost you a penny! If you're in sales or a position where you have to influence people, and you're not doing this, you are missing a tremendous opportunity. Start to write everything down. Taking notes is so simple, and leads to such powerful results. Each note translates to a memory for that person, and there's nothing anyone likes more than being remembered. This is something I've been doing for years, as it was born out of necessity.

Much of my business involves repeat clients; if you do great work, then hopefully your clients will want you back again and again. When I head into a show, I don't want to perform the same act this audience saw the year before—in much the same way a joke doesn't hit as hard if you've already heard the punch line, the element of surprise is incredibly important to my craft. So I started writing down everything that happened at my shows to help keep track of things.

To prep for repeat performances, reviewing those notes is like studying for a midterm exam. I'd always rather be overprepared than under. I'll look up the names of the people I met and who I called onstage. I'll also have jotted down the interesting information they gave me, like their childhood dog was named Tripod because she only had three legs (that's actually true!).

When I do the next show, I'll either read their name tags, if they have them, or I'll say, "So great to see you again. Please remind me of your name." In either of those instances, I'll get the name and I'll remember where I saw that name in my notes. Let's say I was talking to John last year. And because I've looked at what I recorded last year, I'll remember that I guessed John's banking PIN.

John will often say, "That was so much fun last year!" While we're talking, I will find the right moment, usually layered with what magicians call "misdirection" (controlling where your audience members look), to check my phone and get a reminder of the info I know about John, if I don't have it memorized. When I turn back to him, I'll say, "John, I hope you've changed your PIN since last year. It's not still 2472, is it?" Even though his PIN was already revealed a year ago today, it's almost more amazing for him to perceive that I retained that info all this time.

Whether I figured out his PIN again or memorized it in the past, my knowing it still makes him feel so special. But this isn't witchcraft, it's just paying attention and taking notes. It's one tiny step that can make a huge difference. You can do this yourself in any part of your life. Let's say you meet a potential business contact at a gathering. When it's over, you jot down a note or leave yourself a voice memo about who you met and what you discussed. If and when you bump into that person again, you are ready to go, you can ask them, "Hey, how'd your kid do in the spelling bee? I know she won last year. Did she win again this year?"

People are genuinely touched when you remember something important to them. Don't underestimate how impactful these small touches can be. Even if you're not pretending to be a mentalist, you can still generate that same level of amazement by simply recalling and reflecting back information people once shared with you. Most assume that their details will have been forgotten, so when you remember, it's a moment of shock and delight. It's like getting points for free. Just remembering something about somebody, honestly, is a magic trick in many ways, and shows you care.

The first thing I do when I complete an event is log everything that happened while it's still fresh in my mind. When you do this, your notes don't have to be elaborate, just use whatever shorthand works for you. It can be as simple as, "Rhonda, blonde woman, patent attorney, friends with Louie's mom, kids go to such and such camp." This is super useful information for you to have. It's useful for connections in the future, where it's not *what* you know, it's *who* you know. For example, let's say you end up needing a patent attorney, or you want to send your kids to a tennis camp. You don't know anyone there, but suddenly that person you talked to does.

In another example, one of the ways I promote my business is by sending quarterly email blasts to past clients. Each time I do this, I receive at least 150 emails back. Most of them say things like, "Hey, congrats on the fourth kid," or "Loved your TV appearance with Tom Brady!" If I remember something about that person or have access to what we spoke about, I can write back and say, "How's Victoria doing?" or "How are your kids' costumes coming along for Halloween? Are they all still dressing up as M&M'S?" I make sure that if someone is in touch, I reach back out in a way that makes that person feel special again. And how much better is that than an auto-reply, especially when AI is making it all the easier to pretend to be personal? If I make someone else's day better, it brings mine up as well.

That little bit of effort pays dividends in the long run. What's funny is just that you're getting extra credit for the same things I do as a mentalist. And all it takes is giving people back the information that they already told you. That's the unbelievable thing. No bells, no whistles, no hidden gimmicks or difficult instructions to remember. Hell, you don't even need a good memory, simply cheat and write it down right away! People assume you've forgotten, so when you later bring it up, it makes a big impact. Of course, we remember important things about our families and friends—like birthdays—but when you're able to pull up that information about someone you don't know well, it instantly makes them feel more connected to you. That feeling builds trust and rapport, both of which are the cornerstones of strong personal and professional relationships.

My job is creating the illusion that I can read the minds of audience members, even though I go onstage and literally tell them the truth: "I don't read minds, I read people." The whole game is knowing how to reveal seemingly secret information in an entertaining fashion. And this is one of those life hacks that you can do today and start reaping the rewards from immediately.

Just imagine how useful it could be if you are just starting out in an entry level position: You're brand-new in your career, but you were savvy enough to take notes about the people at your potential new company. Maybe during your interview, the HR rep mentioned that the big boss who'd give the final approval on your hire was out of town watching his kid compete in a sport. When you later run into that executive at lunch and mention, "Hey, I saw that your son's team won the state lacrosse championship. Congratulations, you must be so proud of him!" that simple gesture sets you apart. It opens up conversation, shows attention to detail and makes you seem fascinating—because you're making it about them.

Once you start doing this, it will become almost second nature, but let me offer you this bit of advice: Exercise a little restraint. If you start rattling off details like you have a photographic memory, it might come off as a bit much. No one wants to feel like they're being stalked.

Remember, everything that might be important to others is fair game. I'm talking kids' birthdays, interesting vacations, anything that's given to you, that's been revealed, don't just let that go. Information is a commodity; it's kind of like getting a coupon that only expires if you forget it. And the longer you hold on to what you know, the more valuable it becomes.

For example, a guy texted me the other day. I performed at his son's bar mitzvah fourteen years ago, which is wild. (I was huge on the bar mitzvah circuit.) When I used to do small private parties, I'd take a photo with the kid or the guest of honor at every gig. After each of these gigs, I would send out a custom printed thank-you card within one day of their event. If I'd do the party on Saturday, they'd get the card around Tuesday or Wednesday. The parents were always so busy hosting that, most of the time, they didn't get the chance to actually see me in action firsthand, but rather just heard about me from their guests. I quickly figured out that what mattered most to them was that their son or daughter and their guests had an unforgettable experience. They had invested a lot of money into this party, and hoped their circle would remember it for the rest of their lives. So I'd always get a photo of me with their child holding a deck of cards, or in the middle of a trick, both of us smiling and engaged. This would serve as the cover of the card I'd send out. And I'd thank them, mentioning one special and specific thing about their child, like, "Wow, what a funny kid Aaron is, so well-spoken, poised, and mature for his age. What impeccable comedic timing he has!" I'd thank them for trusting me to be a part of their celebration, which is making it about them. So this guy who texted me had just come across that card. His son is twenty-seven now, but seeing it brought back a flood of memories from that special day, and he reached out to let me know.

How great is that?

Lead with Empathy

If you want to truly make others feel seen and heard, you've got to keep empathy at the heart of your interaction. Empathy goes beyond just recognizing what someone's going through; it's about tuning in and sharing that feeling with them, even if only briefly. Unlike sympathy, which is *your* reaction to someone's situation, empathy keeps the focus on *them*. Sympathy is feeling for someone, whereas empathy is feeling with someone, putting yourself in their shoes and responding from a deeper place.

Now, here's what you may not know about empathy: When you witness someone else's emotion, whether it's joy or excitement or sadness—your brain is wired to mirror that emotion. You feel it, too. How cool is that? You're predisposed to want to relate to that person; it's in your DNA, and that impulse dates back to our survival as a species. What's so powerful about this is that our empathy really enables us to feel those emotions alongside others. Empathy is the glue that binds us, that makes us feel connected.

If our current political climate feels like we're not leading with empathy . . . well, you're not mistaken. As a society, over the last four decades, we've begun to lose what they call the "empathy bone," and research has found that the average person in 2009 was 75 percent less empathetic than people were in 1979.[2] Some research shows that this stems from how much we're exposed to technology and social media, largely because social media causes us to compare and despair.[3] Even I had a couple years where my social media was a very negative influence in my life, because all I did was hyperfixate on the handful of people in my profession who I perceived were doing better than me. I had to take a step back and tell myself, *That's an insane way to go about tracking down success, because everyone in the world thinks there's someone richer, faster, better looking, stronger, more successful . . . you name it, they got it! You have to celebrate who you are and what you bring to the table.* I instead started to focus on the other side of that coin: gratitude—realizing that there are likely billions of people that would give anything to have what I have. Health, family, being my own boss, success, fulfillment, and the list goes on and on for me, but also for you! The key is hyperfocusing on the positive.

You might think that having the shared experience of social media would increase our ability to be empathetic, because we're reaching people we'd never have reached before, but you'd be wrong. Instead, witnessing the same experiences over and over again, especially in crisis, causes a phenomenon called compassion fatigue that actually numbs us to tragic incidents.[4]

Whoa.

The good news is that empathy is a skill you can cultivate. So let's bring it back! The first and best way you can cultivate empathy—especially in a world as divided as ours—is to seek out what you have in common with others, instead of your differences. I'd wager this is one of the reasons everyone loves cheering on Olympians—we all get to put aside what divides us and root for a common cause. I challenge you today to step outside your comfort zone and ask someone whom you normally wouldn't think twice about a deeper question about their life, like maybe what your Uber driver's favorite playlist is, or what the woman making your sandwich at the deli would order. See what makes them tick and give them your undivided attention while they respond without any thought to what you will say back.

If you want to be more empathetic—and you do—start with active listening. When you're just a bystander in a conversation, waiting to jump in and talk about yourself or, worse, interrupting, you're approaching the situation wrong. By actively listening, you'll make everyone feel heard and understood, especially if you're paraphrasing back what the other person has said, to demonstrate that you've been listening. Someone who's great at this is my wife. When we were interviewing at schools for my oldest son, she would take everything the administrator said, rephrase it, and repeat it. I swear, I thought she was doing a bit at first, but her way ended up being super effective, and we got our kid into the school we wanted. She showed this person that they were truly being "heard," and also demonstrated shared values that resonated most strongly with our family.

To up your empathy, actively put yourself in the other person's shoes. Sure, for example, you may be upset that your flight has been delayed again, but yelling at the gate agent is not going to change anything. Venting your frustration isn't going to clear the skies or bring in a replacement flight crew for the one that just timed out. Try to see things from that poor gate agent's perspective. He or she has probably been standing for hours. Because of storms in the area, it's been chaos for the gate agents all week. When they look up from the desk, there's just a sea of mean travelers waiting to yell at them for circumstances beyond their control. That must feel awful.

Acknowledge this to them. Make them feel seen and heard.

In fact, when you take that agent's feelings into account, understanding that you're the hundredth upset person they've dealt with in the past hour, you'll change your tone and realize it's not a me-against-you scenario, but a how-can-we-get-through-this-together situation. No one wants to be stuck at the gate, so try leaning into kindness. Smile. Make a joke. Tell them this must be a nightmare and that they're doing a great job keeping their cool. And don't be surprised when your seat is upgraded on the next flight because you're the only person who wasn't a jerk to the person assigning the seats.

To help grow your empathy, you also have to look inside yourself. How are you reacting to something external? How are you feeling? How are you expressing yourself? Is this a situation where you're expecting respect but not reciprocating? Remember, unless you're all alone in a room, your emotions don't happen in a vacuum.

Bottom line, if your feelings are going to spill out onto others, make them positive so they will lift up everyone.

Tap Into Their Emotions

I can't say this enough—mentalism offers a limited number of options. A big part of the secret sauce of what I do is having multiple methods to get the same result. I then analyze how you think I did it and reveal why your assumption isn't the correct solution, presenting an alternate method, and upping the ante yet again. It is a game of cat and mouse. Each time I do this with a greater element of surprise, and I generate greater amazement. This method is like tying the brains of the audience into pretzels, with seemingly no explanation for what they are witnessing. But what sets my performance apart, from simply being a puzzle that you cannot put together, is tapping into people's emotions by telling a story.

For example, some of my tricks include guessing a person's childhood phone number, the name of their fifth-grade best friend, or the first girl they ever kissed. I don't just say, "Think of the person who was your first kiss." There's no buildup, there's no story, the question doesn't evoke any emotion. Recognizing and tapping into emotions is critical when you want to influence others, because that emotional intimacy builds excitement and anticipation.

Instead, I go for the slow build. I help paint the picture before I guess. I want to take you back there to that sacred moment in time, because when I re-create the scene, it stirs an emotion that you can't get by just guessing a name like a carnival trick. I want you to reinhabit your nerdy fourteen-year-old self, coming home with the rest of the marching band after a regional competition. You stopped at Pizza Hut on the way, filling yourself to the brim with pepperoni and root beer. I want you to feel that awkward excitement again, the sugar and carb high you're riding, the smell of that girl's lip balm, the cacophony of your bandmates singing along to Third Eye Blind's "Semi-Charmed Life" (and it's clear why you guys were in marching band and not chorus).

I figured out how to do this because I noticed my peers were really straightforward. I realized I could differentiate myself by tying a trick to an emotion. Any good mentalist can tell you to pick a color, and then guess it. But my approach is to say, "Think back to when you were seven years old and you wanted your room to be a certain color. You drove your parents crazy about it, what was it like for you at that moment?" Creating that emotional hook is a way to package myself, to market myself differently. I learned that what truly matters is the story that person will tell about *you* in the future, and what they remember from your experience together. Some companies have figured out how to make a billion dollars just selling bottled water. What did they do? They took water, which was a cheap commodity, and they created an ultra-premium experience by packaging it in a square bottle instead of a round one, and slapped a label with a beautiful beach vista on it, which looks exotic. Now they charge you five dollars—while every other bottle of water costs two—and when you drink it, it feels like an experience because it's evocative. That's what emotion can do for you.

Mentalism is magic of the mind and there is a "trick" to everything I do, but most of what you're witnessing has taken decades to perfect. It's a skill, but nobody cares about the time I've put in. My audience cares only about the result of all that work. But what makes the trick phenomenal, what makes it memorable for the audience, is bringing everyone along as we travel back in time together. Painting that picture to create a feeling is the *real* magic, because I used that story to make it about *them*.

Early in my professional career, before I concentrated on mentalism, I was very big on learning rope tricks. There was a magician named Tabary who won the "Olympics of Magic" (yes that really exists and is held every three years in various spots around the world and is known as FISM) with a spectacular rope routine that was one of the most beautiful things I'd ever seen in my life. This ten-minute routine involved nearly a hundred moves and sleights of hand, each of which was smooth as silk and completely deceptive when deployed by the creator's hands. I spent hours every single day in front of a mirror studying where each finger should go. I was obsessed with perfecting and emulating what I saw on the video. Fast-forward to a year later, after putting my heart and soul into this routine, I finally started testing it out in front of audiences. And guess what? The rope routine just didn't connect with them the way it did with me. No matter how much I tried to get them to care, they simply did not. It was a painful lesson to learn, but the fact was that the trick was all about *me* and not *them*. Sometimes you have to kill your darlings—because the audience doesn't care about what you like. Remember this, the audience is always right. I discovered that I needed to make my performance about *them*.

(My rope tricks really were incredible, though!)

One of the tricks I performed for the New York Jets on HBO's *Hard Knocks* involved a football being thrown randomly around the room. I closed my eyes, threw it over my shoulder, and said, "Someone, catch it!" That player threw it to another player who in turn threw it to another player. Thousands upon thousands of combinations and permutations were possible for how that could have played out in a room with over eighty men, all of whom were about double or triple my size! Saying this was beyond random is overstating the obvious.

The climax of this trick involved me guessing the name of someone famous that the last player to catch the ball would think of. On the surface, this trick could be very plain and vanilla. What elevated it to another level was the story and the feeling along the way as the decision was being made, an emotional experience that was both motivated and organic. I began to paint a picture for them. I leaned into the story and truly made it about them. I said, "Imagine you catch the football and you're in the end zone. It's the Super Bowl. You just won the game and you're on cloud nine. You have all this joy in your heart and your teammates are going crazy because you guys did it, you won. All that work, all that blood, sweat, and tears. You did it. Everyone's crying and dumping that freezing cooler of Gatorade on the coach."

And I know the player could picture that whole thing in his mind, because I guarantee he's visualized this scenario a thousand times before.

I set the scene, "Look out at this crowd, they're all so happy. Your family is there, your friends are there—they're all celebrating. You notice that when you look into the stands, the front row is all celebrities. You lock eyes with a random celebrity at this moment." Then I asked that player, "You picked that person right this second, yeah?" And he laughed, saying, "Yeah," while deeply disturbed by where this could possibly be going. In his mind, he knew it was impossible for me to pull this off, but in his heart that, somehow, I still would.

Then I added, "There's no way I can know who you would've picked, or that the guy before you would've caught the ball and thrown it to you, or that the guy before him would've caught the ball and thrown it to him. Do you agree?" The player replied, "Yeah. I had no idea." And that's when I said, "I'm not gonna get inside your head, no, that's what you expect. I'm gonna get inside THAT BALL!"

I flip open a sharp pocket knife, startling several players, and plunge the blade deep into the football and saw side to side to form a large hole as it deflates. I ask him to reach in and take out what's inside, which appears to be a folded-up photo. The tension is so thick you could cut it with my knife. I look the player in the eyes and slowly ask, "Who are you thinking about?" And then he replies, "It's Kevin Hart." I point at his hands and mouth the words "open it." There it is, a gleaming headshot of Kevin Hart and the entire team unleashes a series of whoops, screams, swear words, and laughs!

Of course, when I do this, a little piece is about me, too, because my hope is that the clip will go viral. That the player will absolutely freak out, that he'll be like, "How in the . . ." and then everyone in the room will just erupt.

There are multiple methods at play when designing a trick of this sort. There are all these things that I'm anticipating along the way. A lot of times the audience is saying, "Well, you set it up with this person." No I didn't, because we threw the ball randomly around the room. Or they'll say, "Well, you stuck the picture inside the football when you were putting your hand in." No, because I made sure my hands were seen as being empty the whole time.

A lot of the time, I build these layers by using a different trick for each portion of the setup. Each portion is being done differently to make sure the audience doesn't keep up with how I'm actually pulling the whole trick off. If you saw this play out, you might actually get one of the methods. But when I change things up a second later, you'll think, *Well, that couldn't have been it*, because I've done something to exclude that method.

The point is that I'm constantly pulling from the same limited playbook. I have only so many tricks. I'm telling you: finite. And I did some version of this at every training camp. But each one felt different to the people who were witnessing it because I'd tell a different story each time and I'd home in on their feelings, making them the star of my show. Imagine how much less dramatic it would have been if I'd just said, "Think of a celebrity," and then pulled out the photo. That simple trick lacks all the buildup and it doesn't tap into that player's emotions.

Not only did I amaze them, but I evoked those feelings by making them verbalize the scene that likely plays in their head every day. I became special to these players because I made *them* feel special, and there's no reason you can't do the same when you put emotion into your stories, no card tricks required. Maybe you're in a pitch meeting and you're evoking nostalgia. (If you're a *Mad Men* fan, think of that Don Draper scene with the Hershey's bar.) Or maybe you're telling your kids why the Grand Canyon is so much cooler than Grand Cayman because it's been around since the Ice Age, and you spend all of dinnertime speculating how different your lives are from ancient humankind.

The more you pull at heartstrings—even your own—the more effective you'll be.

Leave Them Wanting More

Like nearly every kid, I was a massive Steven Spielberg fan. Who didn't grow up on *Jurassic Park*, *Jaws*, *Raiders of the Lost Ark*, and *E.T.*? He was a huge part of my childhood and his movies have stayed with me to this day.

So imagine how I felt when I got a call to perform at the ninety-ninth birthday of Steven Spielberg's dad. I was over the moon. I spent weeks thinking of everything I wanted to ask him, all the things I wanted to know. I could not believe my luck.

I kept my emotions in check and performed the show with this amazing milestone as my focus, surrounded by family and friends that adored the guest of honor. At the end of the show, Steven makes a bee-line straight for me to thank me for making this day so special. And I wait for him to take a breath, to give me the pause I crave so that I can jump in organically with my one thousand questions. We did end up having a twenty-five-minute conversation . . . but I asked him precisely zero questions.

Not a single one.

I went in wanting all the highlights, like, How did you build this? and How did that work in *Close Encounters*? and How did you manage to train all those dinosaurs? But no. Not a single question. I did learn that the reason he is "Steven Spielberg" is because he's a person who is able to turn the mirror around and reflect his light back onto you. He must know that every person he crosses paths with is likely to talk about their encounter for the rest of their lives.

What's so fascinating about him is that he's naturally curious, he just has this passion for all the people around him. What's created his suc-cess is the fact that he can get completely absorbed in asking me all these questions about myself. And in my head, I'm like, *You're Steven f*ing *Spielberg! Right now, I want to ask* you *things.*

His home run swing was getting me to talk about myself, getting me to open up and share about what I do. Despite having every reason to talk about his own achievements, he chose to focus on me. He held up a metaphorical mirror that made me see my worth, and feel like a star. That day I learned what a superpower that kind of attentiveness can be, and it's something every single one of us can do. Steven gave me 100 percent of his focus, 100 percent of his energy, and made me an even bigger fan of his while doing so.

When he walked away to rejoin the party, all I wanted to do was chase after him like that magician on the cruise ship. He left me wanting so much more. That was his gift, too, understanding the timing of it all. Understanding why it's important not to overstay. Had he stuck around, it might have diminished how special the interaction was for me. I got a taste, but not a whole meal, and I bet I'll spend the rest of my life savoring the bites that I had. Because he made me feel like the magician on that ship, like I was the most interesting man in the world.

You don't have to be Steven Spielberg to develop this set of skills. All you need is a genuine interest in the people around you. Be radically curious; ask questions beyond the generic small talk we all dread. Instead of "What do you do?" try "What's something most people don't know about you?" Practice active listening—don't just wait to interject but really give people your undivided attention. Notice things that make others special out loud, like, "You have great comedic timing."

Regardless of what we do in life, each of us only has a limited tool kit from which we can draw. There's only so many skills we can master, things we can accomplish, or know. What makes us truly memorable is how we make others feel.

When you help others kick away that pedestal, when you demonstrate how they're special and memorable, when you make it about them, when you cast your light on others, it all reflects back on you twice as strongly.

FIVE

Forget Tomorrow, Start Today

A few years ago, another mentalist asked me how I was able to book appearances on TV so frequently and consistently. I turned the question around and asked him, "Well, what have you tried doing?" He was taken aback, almost surprised by my question, and stammered, "Well . . . I haven't." I swear to you, nine times out of ten when I ask this question, I get a blank stare in return. Like it never even occurred to them to try, to be proactive, to log every producer they ever met and continue to circle back. If you meet someone while at a gig or a party that offhandedly mentions a friend who works in TV, you take their info and follow up. Never leave the ball in someone else's court when it is your future that hangs in the balance. I got the ESPN gig because I cultivated a relationship and spent over a decade keeping in touch, waiting to pounce on the opportunity when the timing was finally right.

That's the whole secret. If you want to win the lottery, you need to buy a ticket!

In this chapter, I'll cover buying that ticket—that is, what it takes to move toward any goal. I'll discuss how to end procrastination, then get through the horrible first two weeks of taking action, during which habits start to form and the dread melts away. And I'll show you how momentum always begets momentum—it's *literally* physics—by explaining how, as an adult, I went from being not very good at running to regularly winning races and setting ultramarathon world records.

Achieving goals is all about working backward from the desired outcome, whether it's personal or professional, and this starts with learning how to define and quantify them. The chapter wouldn't be complete if I didn't also give advice on how to be brutally honest with yourself and not lose sight of taking joy when you actually achieve the goals and success you've been chasing. I learned that lesson the hard way the day I ran my fastest marathon ever, a personal best of 2:23:52, but could only focus on the fact I didn't run as fast as I had hoped.

Sometimes you just have to let what wasn't perfectly on plan go and appreciate the moment.

Now, Not Later

You may not believe it, but I'm an expert-level procrastinator. This is not because I'm lazy, but because I'm most motivated and inspired by a sense of urgency. In college, I learned to procrastinate very effectively, mastering the art of cramming, pulling all-nighters to make it through. It is a bad habit to get into because you'll tell yourself that doing an hour or two of work daily seems like so much more effort than just two sleepless nights at the library immediately prior to the assignment due date or exam.

For the longest time, I believed my best work came when I was under the gun. If you told me I'd have a TV appearance in six months . . .

forget it. But if you told me I had a massive appearance in just six days, my synapses would start firing. The urgency and panic, the sense of being backed into a corner—that's when I'd lock in and come up with something incredible.

Guess what?

I'm the first to admit this approach wasn't healthy, so it's something that I've had to actively work on. I finally figured out that when I leave everything to the last minute over and over, I don't feel as good about the results and that ultimately more things are likely to go wrong.

Turns out, we're genetically predisposed to procrastination because there are two opposing forces in our brains and they are locked in battle. We all have a limbic system, which is responsible for regulating our emotions, our behavior, our motivation (that's a biggie), our autonomic nervous system, and our memory.[1] The limbic system is similar to our most hedonistic friend, the one who wants only fun, pleasure, and immediate gratification.

Our limbic system is pitted against our prefrontal cortex, which mimics our most responsible buddy. You know, the one who prints up itineraries for everyone at the bachelor party and packs a first aid kit. While our prefrontal cortex is equally as important, that bossy little voice often gets drowned out by the more dynamic and fun limbic system, especially when something is challenging or unpleasant, and this is why almost all of us procrastinate.[2]

It's not just our brain chemistry at work that causes us to put off today what we could do tomorrow. We can be paralyzed by our fear of failure, causing us to avoid trying new things and taking risks.[3] This fear can keep us safely cocooned inside our comfort zones, where we're never challenged—and we never grow, as we discussed earlier. Sometimes we procrastinate because we lack time management skills, and sometimes it's a matter of confidence.

Fortunately, whatever your issue is, it's fixable if you take a new perspective on procrastination.

The key to adopting a do-it-now mentality is to break your goal down into smaller parts and make one of them something that you absolutely do immediately. You need that spark, that initial momentum, that snowball you roll down a mountain so it grows. The resulting dopamine hit will overcome your brain's tendencies toward inertia because our brains remember incomplete tasks with far more clarity than those we've completed, and that creates stress and unease.[4] This is called the Zeigarnik effect and it means that what remains incomplete haunts our memories.[5] In our minds, an incomplete task feels like an untied shoe. If we want to move around freely, to really use our brains at their full capacity, we have to lace up that sneaker. We have to stop procrastinating.

After a lifetime of being a procrastinator, I decided to figure out how to get things done sooner rather than later (even when I don't feel tremendous, overwhelming pressure). In retraining myself, I realized I needed to change my perspective, to value getting the chore done early, rather than at the last minute, because giving myself space took a lot of unnecessary stress off me—and my wife.

We procrastinate because certain tasks seem so daunting and our brain wants the easy way out. Where do we even begin? But every marathon starts with one step, and starting small was how I shifted my perspective. For example, several years ago when I landed the gig with ESPN, I had about three weeks to plan, which is very little time to come up with somewhere between nine and twelve new tricks. (I only want to perform the latest and greatest custom content when I'm on TV.)

Not only do these concepts have many intricate machinations that take a lot of time to ideate, I also have to make sure they're going to work. While I've said that mentalism entails a limited number of tricks, the tools I have at my disposal will often mirror the common ingredients a chef might use, such as sauces and proteins. You put a dash of this and a splash of that, and the combination creates something entirely different and new. Similar to when you go to Chipotle and there are maybe twenty ingredients on the steam trays: You can combine them into hundreds of different creations with different flavor profiles. I have endless permutations when it comes to creating these tricks; plus, I have to present them in a way that feels seamless and entertaining, and I must adapt the reveals to be appropriate for the audience. I can't deliver them looking like they're still wearing training wheels. I can't come across as if I'm thinking of the lines when I say them. If I'm onstage, it's imperative that my act feels natural to everyone watching. Otherwise, it's just bad acting.

When those initial videos aired throughout the football season, I immediately got to work ideating for the following summer training camp. Had ESPN confirmed that we would be doing it again? Absolutely not, but always assume the close and be ready and overprepared when the moment you are hoping for arrives. I decided to be proactive and break the planning down into more manageable chunks. And I said to myself, *One new trick a month nets me twelve new tricks by next year.* Not only would that lower my stress level, it would also allow me to be more present with my family leading up to the events. And if I could get two tricks in a month? Even better. I'd be so ahead of the game.

By starting now, you're on your way to being more creative and a better problem solver, which in turn will benefit your overall well-being. Win-win.

Be Specific

When I mentor other mentalists, one thing they always ask is, "How do I take my career to the next level?" Now, that's a daunting question with no set answer because there's a million different ways to move forward and also my definition of *forward* might differ greatly from yours.

I'll reply with probing questions like: "What does the next level mean to *you*? Do you want to perform for more people? Are you trying to make more money?" To determine what it is that they really want, I make them hone and re-hone their answers. And then most of the time they'll figure out their bottom line, which is: "I just want a steady gig somewhere."

Now, *that's* an easy fix.

I'll say, "Great, let's look up your geographical area right now. Go to Google Maps and pull up country clubs. Look up restaurants. Let's identify places where there's a precedent for hiring a magician or mentalist. And if there isn't, we're going to invent one and we'll show them why you're such a value-add that they'd be foolish not to take you."

So often, we already know what we need to do, which is what my mentees often say when I tell them what to do. With all the information that's at our fingertips, most of the time it's just a matter of defining A and B and then drawing a line from A to B and figuring out that first step to take. The way I approach everything, whether it's coming up with a new trick or prepping for a race, is to design my plan of attack from the end and work backward. The start and the end are more important than everything else. Getting to the starting line is always the most difficult part for people. And when you get there that day, there's the dread, the fear, the trepidation. But if you can get yourself to the beginning, then you can more clearly visualize the finish and rely on your preparation to get you there. Once you begin moving your feet, it's kind of easy from there, because you're over the mental block of having started. You might still suffer, but you're past the hardest part, as starting is very often overwhelming. And remember, you can't buy achievement; you have to earn it.

I do a lot of speaking engagements and whenever I talk to sales teams, I say, "There's only one person in this room who's your top seller. I can tell you for a fact that person has had doubts creep into their mind, just like all of us do. But that person believed to their core that they would be the top salesperson for this organization. Because if you don't believe that, you will never achieve it. Some of you will believe it but not achieve it, but without that belief in your own ability, you'll never get there. The top salesperson isn't the best because of luck; They didn't stumble into it by accident. They are hypercompetitive. They're willing to battle. They say to themselves, 'Why can't it be me?'" That's how I feel when I'm at the starting line of a race. I tell myself, *I'm gonna finish this thing.* The option to give up simply does not exist in my mind. And for the people who do finish the race, they must have believed that they could do it. So you have to think that you can do it—whatever your "it" might be.

Back to my mentees—the reason I ask them those specific questions is that I'm looking for something measurable. *Next level* is too amorphous. That's like if you were to tell me you want to experience "more career progression at work," or that you want to be "happier at home." What does that mean? What are the parameters that define progression or happiness? But, if you were to say, "I want to make X dollars, get promoted to X position, buy my family a boat that costs X," I can work with that.

Often, people think of something they want from a reflex perspective, like, "I want to be successful." But if you truly look inward, you'll realize that to you, success means earning X on a weekly basis because it enables you to cover your bills without sacrificing your personal life. That's a number. We can work with a number because it's tangible. There's an end point. When you say something elusive like *happiness*, there's no hard stop, there's no finish line. It's a moving target. Having worked in finance, there's a point where making more money doesn't bring additional happiness, so it's key to drill down to what *your* definition of success is. It may have nothing to do with finances and everything to do with being able to pick your kids up from school every day and take one amazing vacation per year.

If you want a garden, it doesn't just grow—you have to plant the seeds, water them, fertilize them, till the soil, etc. You have to get your hands dirty . . . and probably sling a little manure. That's why I say, "buy the ticket." Think of it like this—how could you win the lottery without buying a ticket? One isn't going to fall magically out of the sky and land in your hands. Even if it did, it's still a lottery ticket, with only a chance of winning. One hundred percent of lottery winners took the chance. The point is, if you don't "buy the ticket," you're never going to win—100 percent of the time.

You buy the ticket by starting to make moves. (Your first move was picking up this book, so you're already on your way!) Then it's time to self-assess. Lay out the top three things that you want to see a change in, and then figure out exactly what those changes are. Then break those large changes into smaller bits.

For example, let's say your goal is to be healthier. Well, what does that mean? Let's be specific. Do you want to lower your blood pressure? Reduce your cholesterol? Build up your stamina enough that you can run a race? Or do you just want to foster the kind of endurance that lets you carry your kids on your shoulders at the Fourth of July parade because last year they couldn't see anything (and you hurt your back when you tried to lift them)? "Healthy" is amorphous. Maybe you really mean you're trying to lower your average blood sugar levels because your doctor says you're borderline diabetic, and you're terrified of having to give yourself insulin. Getting an A1C test result under 5.7 percent is measurable and specific, and you get there by upping your protein intake, eating fewer grams of sugar, and exercising regularly. When you don't break down what it is you're really seeking, you can get frustrated and fall apart because it seems too overwhelming.

Let's figure out how you can buy your ticket today.

Say you've determined your goal is to run a marathon by your fortieth birthday. Does it seem impossible? Well, if you tried to run 26.2 miles today with no conditioning and no training, it probably is. After all, the courier who ran from Marathon to Athens to share the good news that the Greeks had beaten the Persians, did drop dead at the end of his journey.

But what if you started right now by running around the block? That's it, just once around the block. You can do that, right? You may find yourself sucking wind, but you will get through it. If that's too much, start by walking, with an eye toward building up to running. And forget that it's cold out. Forget that you really need better sneakers. Forget that you don't have the right running clothes. Just get out there and do it today. Take that first step, whatever it is, like buying the URL for that business you're looking to start. The hardest part is beginning . . . yet that's also where the magic lives.

When you set a goal in motion, the neuroscience of this pursuit is called the "productive struggle." When you task yourself with something challenging, your brain starts to produce myelin as it creates a new neural pathway.[6] Myelin is a protective substance that coats your neurons to speed the path of transmission, making your nervous system quicker and more efficient.[7] (In nonscientific terms, this is totally a good thing and absolutely what you want.)

The more you challenge yourself, the more connectivity you're creating between those neurons. I know that description is sort of vague, so imagine it like this: There's three feet of snow between you and what you need in your mailbox at the end of the driveway. The first time you try to trudge through that snow, it's going to be brutal. You're going to be sweating and swearing by the time you reach your mailbox, cursing winter and your decision to live in the Midwest. But every subsequent time you head to that mailbox, you're creating a path through the snow, and it's going to be easier to get back and forth.

Metaphorically, walking through that snow, you're creating what's called "synaptic plasticity," which means that by confronting this challenge (making the trek), you're creating or strengthening new synapses (a more efficient pathway).[8] When you tamp down the snow enough, you're not even going to have to put on boots to grab the mail, because you'll have made it so much easier. You made yourself a cheat code. Your reward? Dopamine. Also known as the feel-good chemical, it's basically candy for your brain. That brain-candy reward is going to reinforce this behavior and motivate you. And who doesn't want a treat?

Define Your Goals

When I'm creating a new trick, the secret sauce is determining how to make it crescendo, each phase stronger than the last, culminating in a surprise ending with an emotional hook that truly connects with the audience. To get there, I have to analyze the trick from the audience's perspective—not only what they will see and hear, but also what they will feel and, most important, the story they will tell others afterward. A lot of people who do what I do start with a tool, like a hammer. They'll swing that hammer around and say, "I know how to use this thing, so what can I build?" I never do that. I start with the house that's already built. Then I work backward and figure out the tools that I'll need to construct it. The final product informs every creative decision I make along the way.

Previously, I explained that my television appearances go well because I plan for every eventuality, stuff that most would never even imagine. I have thought through exactly what my plans A, B, and C are, all the way to Z. That's what is required with mentalism, because I'm reverse engineering the most complicated computer that's ever existed— the human mind. I'm thinking about what you (the audience) will do at every given moment. How can I influence what you'll do? How can I guide you through a maze so that when you ask yourself, *Am I going left, right, or forward?* you choose *left*, not realizing I've gotten you there through subtlety, persuasion, timing, and a multitude of other techniques. (That's the *real* secret sauce.) It's like a chess game where you feel like you're making your own moves, only I have already planned ten steps ahead. When you see a trick executed effectively, it's particularly mind-blowing, because everything about it feels like a free choice, *yet it's all planned by me.* Mentalism is just a magic trick with no props where I'm able to guide your thoughts.

I've spent over twenty-five years learning how to reverse engineer the human mind. And I do it to entertain people all over the world and bring joy. I want to teach you some of those same skills so that you can use them to gain an edge in your everyday life, to unlock your potential and attain the goals you thought were impossible. While I can't give you superpowers, what I can provide are tools, so that when you hit a speed bump, you know you can get through it. One of the first tools is developing an understanding of what goals you want to achieve.

The oft-used mnemonic for goals is that they should be SMART, meaning Specific, Measurable, Achievable, Relevant, and Time-bound[9]

Let's say you just had your annual physical and your doctor tsk-tsks you as he reviews your chart, saying, "I want you to work on your health."

Yeah, thanks a lot, Doc, but what does that mean?

Well, that's for *you* to define.

In your head, maybe it means you should lose those fifty pounds that crept up on you these last few years. And you want to do that before your next physical in a year. So already we have a *specific* end result. We can *measure* it because fifty pounds is something tangible. You know that regardless of excuses, it can be *achieved* because you were at that weight at one point in time. Plus, you're not tasking yourself with becoming a supermodel, of whom there are only a few.

Having the sum of fifty pounds in your head is *relevant* because that number will improve your overall health, as weight loss will lower your blood pressure and your risk for heart disease and stroke, as well as positively impact your joints. (Having your knees hurt less will be an added benefit.) And it's *time-bound* because you want to do this in twelve months so you can come back and show your smug physician that you were taking his advice seriously.

To be fifty pounds lighter, let's work backward. That's only about a pound a week, or roughly a 3,500-calorie weekly deficit, equal to burning 500 calories a day more than you've taken in. What can you do to achieve that caloric deficit? Well, you can improve your diet by adding in five servings of fruit and vegetables. You can be mindful about portion control, limiting yourself to four to six ounces of protein per serving. You can decide to stop eating after 7:00 p.m. You can make sure to consume thirty grams of fiber each day. Or you can burn those 500 calories by getting a fitness tracker and figuring out how many steps gets you into that deficit. You can build muscle so your body's metabolism improves, measuring it on one of those biometric scales that are all over social media. And you can even make attaining this goal social by joining a group of friends for X number of walks a week, or X number of games of pickleball. Every one of these suggestions comes with a smaller goal, whether it's getting in a certain number of steps or tracking and maintaining your macros.

A major goal for me when I got into running was to one day run a sub-2:30 marathon, and I worked for years to achieve this by creating a series of smaller goals. What truly helped me along was folding science into my workouts, so I purchased a heart rate monitor for my training. This taught me to pace myself, because if I was going too fast and the monitor started beeping, it would alert me to the fact that I was going anaerobic. This is similar to redlining a car engine: okay for a short period, but do it too long and you'll overheat and gas out. This helped me become more efficient—and patient. The changes didn't happen overnight, but over time. With a great deal of training over the next few years, I saw my times drop from 3:21 to 2:57, then into the 2:40s and 2:30s and finally in Tallahassee I did what I thought was the impossible and nabbed a 2:29. I have since managed to run ten sub-2:30 marathons and prove to myself that it was no fluke.

The more you break down your greater goals after working backward from the end result, the easier you'll find it to move forward, especially if you're receiving feedback. Every small win feeds into the outcome. Remember, you set the importance of the goal, and it only matters how *you* define it. So let's get started already!

Make It a Habit

I said starting is the hardest part of forming a new habit, but a close second is maintaining that change and converting it into your new status quo. This can be particularly difficult if you beat yourself up when things don't go your way in those first weeks.

As my marathon times started to improve with better training, I came to realize that an even more important factor was my weight. If I could lose some pesky extra pounds, my times would get even faster. Think how much slower you'd run carrying a backpack with five bricks weighing a couple pounds each, except in this case those ten pounds might be spread out all over your body. I would implement several rules to stay healthy, while also reducing my calorie intake. These consisted of eliminating late-night snacking, setting a firm deadline to brush my teeth and be done eating by 8:00 p.m. (similar in a sense to intermittent fasting), and cutting out fried foods, sweets, and other culprits that I tended to overindulge in. After the first few days of this regimen, I would begin to fall apart. There would be an emotional induced tantrum where I'd tell myself, *This is such BS! I'm just going to pound some cake and a burrito. I don't care about any of this.* But I knew I had to be in top form to race if I wanted to be at my best and beat my previous time, so I learned to trick myself, to overcome those moments when I wanted to give up, because I can't buy achievement. I have to earn it.

Know this: Your brain will lie to you as you try to form a habit. For me, my brain will say, "Hey, I don't want to do this, I'm done." So I have to do with myself what I'd do with my three-year-old. It's Misdirection 101. I will fool myself, *Here's what I'll do. I am 100 percent going to eat that burrito and I am 100 percent going to eat that cake. But not right this minute. First, I'm going to eat a banana. Then, I'm going to drink a big glass of water and I'm going to set a ten minute timer. If I still feel this strongly about the burrito and cake when the timer goes off, then I'm eating them.* The funny thing is that as I watch those minutes and then seconds tick down, the impulsiveness and the emotional trigger, both of which are at the core of what makes me want to "break," start to melt away entirely. I am able to trick my own mind and body with simple "time misdirection"—as it is known in my business.

I started to understand the control my mind had over my body, my emotions would try to fool me into quitting a race despite still being physically capable of finishing. In the darkest parts of those extremely long runs, my mind would start shutting down and telling me, *This sucks. This is horrible. Stop. Throw your sneakers in the trash. Go back to the hotel and watch Netflix.* A lot of times, that destructive self-talk would start up because my blood sugar had dropped, and that was directly impacting my frustration tolerance. Your mood is connected to what you eat, how much you've slept, and a multitude of other factors. I found that if I could just repair that blood sugar discrepancy, my mood would lift, I could realign myself, and I'd realize my goal was more important than that quick emotional outburst. I created a mental checklist of all the systems that I thought could be causing my issues, ranging from self-doubt to exhaustion to sheer annoyance, and almost all could be readily deduced from a simple list.

This example is a direct parallel to so many things that we try, where we might commit for a day or two, and then we accidentally blow it and give up before the habit is formed. Then we beat ourselves up. Our inner monologue says, *Hey, we're not good enough to do this and it was never going to happen anyway.*

Instead, try giving yourself some space, *You know what? Today's tough. I'm putting it aside for today; tomorrow we restart the clock and we're back at it.* We live in such an all or nothing society that this kind of grace can be a challenging thing. Remember that it's okay to have a good day, a bad day, followed by three good days. It's what you do 90 percent of the time that really matters. The 10 percent isn't going to kill you.

Frequently, we get off track and we don't allow the habit to form because we're not really paying attention to our goal. How often do you stop and check in with yourself? The frequency with which you do so isn't nearly as important as the consistency over time. You have to be the chief strategy officer of your life, thinking not just about today but also next week, next month, and next year. Look at the big picture and set yourself reminders, like: Once every two weeks, you sit down for an hour and think about where you are and what you could do differently.

Most people I know—myself included—are often just treading water to get through the day. It's like we're all trying to stay afloat. We're so caught up in the day-to-day that we don't really ask big-picture questions, we're not stopping to assess ourselves. We're just plodding ahead, even when our heart's not in it, because we're wired with an autopilot we didn't thoughtfully create. We're not mindful of what we're doing or why we're doing it, so we have to create a plan to prioritize what we want to achieve, and hold ourselves accountable. So often, we think, *One day*, but what if you made "one day" today? Start right now and create the steps that will get you over that first hurdle.

You can only begin to build when you commit your mind and body to whatever it is you're seeking out. You have to make the pursuit of what you want its own habit. It's got to happen like clockwork. Once you do this, you'll start seeing positive effects. Whenever you start something new, creating change is going to be hard because you're not used to integrating the goal, so I want you to keep the "two-week rule" at the front of your mind.

What do I mean by that? Well, the hardest part of a new routine is the first two weeks. I swear. Okay? The first two weeks are everything. If I train for a marathon, I cut out crappy foods. I mean no ice cream, no eating late at night, and no alcohol. And the first two weeks are brutal because my body is rebelling and saying no, and I have emotional outbursts; that's when I have to actively trick myself with the water and the banana.

When we want something that isn't good for us—emotionally, spiritually, physically, whatever—our knee-jerk reaction is to just give into ourselves. When I'm training, it's about not scarfing down all the ice cream. My ten-minute time misdirection trick allows me to distance my mind from that emotional trigger. Often, I find that once I give it a little bit of time, I don't go for the ice cream. So I want you to figure out what *your* banana is. What do you need to do in those moments when you just want to give up? The banana works because willpower and motivation alone can't always do it for you. You need something that will help you trick your own mind long enough that you stay on track.

There's a lot of neuroscience behind what it takes to make something into a habit. For example, let's say you move a trash can under your desk from the left to right side. For the first fourteen to sixteen days, you're going to drive yourself mad by instinctively throwing your trash in the wrong direction.

Somehow, about two weeks later, something clicks. Your brain finally rewires itself and you'll notice when you get the trash in the can the first time, and you'll think, *Finally!* Be aware that it's not your fault if getting things right takes a while. There's nothing wrong with you; that's just how we're hardwired. Now that you know your limitations, you have to trick your own mind and say, *I know you're going to screw me over these first two weeks. I know it, I know going in that you're going to be my enemy. So if I can just get through this day, if something goes wrong, tomorrow is a new day, I'm going to keep going and within two weeks, the new routine will be solidified.* But the clock only starts ticking once you first move the trash can. We have to be cognizant that we're not so on autopilot that we never even move the can in the first place.

You don't have to beat yourself up forever—this kind of failure is short term. Just get through the first two weeks and you'll have created whatever habit you need to meet your goal. That's when discipline comes into play. The time it takes to create that habit is much shorter than most people expect, and yet they still give up so soon. This all goes back to having to rewire our brain with those neural pathways. As Dr. Sanam Hafeez says, "Any habit we develop is because our brain is designed to pick up on things that reward us and punish us."[10] In layman's terms from *Atomic Habits* author James Clear, "What gets rewarded is repeated. What gets punished, gets avoided."[11]

My friend David Goggins, a retired Navy SEAL and author, says that to create a habit, you've just got to clamp down on your mind. He says there's no puppy love, no simple approach, there's no motivational this or that. He went from three hundred pounds to being a chiseled ultramarathon runner by force of will alone. His approach is truly empowering, and his philosophy is that you don't stop when you're tired, you stop when you're done, although that's not a one-size-fits-all solution. You may respond better to your inner supportive friend than an inner drill sergeant; everyone is different. But the method is always the same: Define your goals and the small steps along the way to get there, and *do not give up.*

Charles Duhigg wrote a book called *The Power of Habit*, in which he discusses what he calls the "habit loop," the neurological process that causes habits to develop and take hold.[12] Habitual actions start with a "cue," which is what prompts the habit; a cue can be internal (like a feeling or a thought) or external (such as an environmental factor). The next step is the "routine," the action that happens automatically once your brain is activated by the cue. The last step is the "reward," which is the immediate sensation your brain gives you for acting on the routine.

Let's use social media as an example. The cue could be your phone pinging, alerting you to a text from your friend. The routine is to open your phone and read the text. The reward is that good feeling you get from having heard from your friend. If you want to actively develop a habit, the most surefire way to go about it is to create that loop.

What I do know is this: The hardest part of forming a habit is the start and the following two weeks, so if tricking your brain helps, then by all means do it!

Hold Yourself Accountable

This is where the rubber meets the road. It's not enough to establish that you need to start today. It's not enough to buy the ticket and work backward from a quantifiable goal. It's not even enough to make it a habit. The final step to turning your goals into reality is to hold yourself accountable toward them. And that takes discipline.

Discipline is a tough one because nobody wants to do something that they don't like. My wife loves high-intensity interval workouts and for years tried to persuade me to try them. I finally caved the week before my bachelor party and did a session with her trainer. He had me swinging thick ropes, throwing medicine balls, doing burpees, and putting me through absolute hell. I could run one hundred miles no problem, but this was way outside my wheelhouse. When I got to my party, I was so sore that I couldn't raise my arms above my shoulders. My future wife didn't have to worry about me misbehaving because I could barely move. Come to think of it, she might be a better mentalist than me!

People assume I'm so disciplined because I run a hundred or more miles a week. But that's not it—I'm just doing something I've come to enjoy. Running provides value in my life because it gives me time to focus, a form of meditation with more cardio benefits. The difficulty is in how you trick your mind into creating and following that discipline.

In the beginning, there was a point where I didn't enjoy running. It was hard. It hurt. I was slow. The key to creating discipline is to find the things that are good for you, then convince yourself you want to do them more. With running, I found that I enjoyed it at a certain point because it allowed me to quiet my mind, even though I was slow and it was difficult and painful. For me, running helped me solve a greater problem. Ironically, I'd tried running in high school and hated it. I was bar none the slowest person on the cross-country team, hated it and gave up after one season. But when I revisited running as an adult, I was working a day job on Wall Street. While I was doing well professionally, and I had all my needs met and some material success, I couldn't stop myself from thinking, *So this is it? Global IT infrastructure? This is what I'm just gonna keep doing until I die?* I felt stuck in my life. I found myself wanting something different, something unique, something that excited me in my soul.

I found out the cure for what ailed my psyche was not just running, but racing. Even though it was painful—during my first race, I was crying for a mile or two—I kept going. There was something about it that made me feel alive in a way that a lot of other things didn't. So when you say to me, "Is it discipline?" I don't know that I'm disciplined, because I *for sure* did not want to do the awful workouts my wife did. In a perfect world, I would've said, "Hey, this bootcamp session is pure misery. So I'm going to do more of this." I've instead tried to seek out the things that will help me and that I also actually enjoy doing. Unfortunately for a lot of us, the things we enjoy are often wanting to sit and scroll while watching TV. I'm not judging that, because I do a lot of it, too. But I run much more than I would if it was all punishment, because of the benefits I get from it—both the pleasure and the physical health. I can't say if my joy is due to discipline, or if I just tricked myself into being accountable by telling myself I enjoyed it. By the way, I didn't immediately start running ultramarathons. The process involved creating a number of smaller goals, and chipping away until I felt ready to take on bigger challenges. (And yes, I absolutely wrote to my old high school coach when I won my first marathon—he was shocked!)

When you find yourself going off track from your goal, give yourself space for a day or so, but then revisit your plan and recommit to something quantifiable. Tell yourself, *I'm going to do X, Y, Z in the first month. I'm going to do this once per day, five days a week. I have no excuse not to.* Then whatever it is you've committed yourself to, whether it's sending résumés or getting to the gym or making calls to potential clients for the small business you want to create, just do it. The doing is typically where a lot of people falter because they don't hold themselves accountable for what they committed to.

If you're not at the point where you can trick yourself into accountability or force discipline on yourself, look externally. Communicate your goal to others so that they get on board. I think sometimes being a little bombastic and excited will motivate you. Make a bold claim and then put in the work to live up to it.

A lot of people confess to me they want to run a marathon. I tell them, "External accountability is an excellent motivator. Everyone's got social media now. Call your shot and make your friends hold you to it." A great way to stay on track with training for a 10K race three months from now is to post it all over your socials, even make some bets with friends, so that you're willing to do whatever it takes to maintain motivation and avoid embarrassment. Now you've got skin in the game. You've got people who are going to ask you about your training, and if you don't follow through, you're going to eat some humble pie.

You'll find that people are drawn to passion and goals, and you'll be shocked by how many support you. It's not just a good idea to involve others—there's science behind it. When you share your goals, your brain becomes like a kid in a candy store, as you'll trigger not just dopamine hits from the positive engagement, but likely also chemicals such as oxytocin (often called the "love hormone"), which are released during social interactions, and endorphins, which reduce stress and increase your feelings of well-being.[13] You'll become addicted to all that good chemistry.

Regardless of how you get there, whether it's internal or external accountability, remember that action leads to motivation (not vice versa) because it triggers a positive feedback loop. And momentum is a self-perpetuating cycle. In physics, *momentum = mass × velocity*, which means that momentum is something we control, whether we're talking about the physical act of rolling a snowball down a hill or creating a social movement.[14] To throw a little more physics at you, a body in motion will remain in motion unless acted upon by a force—so you'll keep moving unless you stop yourself. What I'm saying is, the more we put in, the more we get out.

The Final Caveat

We've covered getting past procrastination and why it's so important to start now, not later. We've shed light on how nothing will happen until you decide to buy that ticket. And once that ticket is purchased, you've got to be determined to plow through those difficult first two weeks as you form new, better habits to support you in attaining the goals you never before imagined you might achieve. Let momentum carry you as you drill down on your goals, working backward and making them SMART. And, of course, we've talked about the importance of accountability.

I'd be remiss, however, if I didn't end this chapter with a reminder to value not only your own achievements, but also the effort you put in to reach them. In this respect, enjoy the ride and not just the destination.

Don't be like me when I ran my fastest race ever at the Philadelphia Marathon. By pure chance, that was the same city I ran my first marathon in and clocked 3:21. The difference being that after the first marathon I was so thrilled at the results that I was instantly hooked on the sport that would change my life. Flash forward to the 2:23 race and I couldn't even enjoy having a new personal best time because I was so focused on getting under 2:20. Those four stupid minutes were viewed as total failure in my eyes.

Don't become so focused on where you might go that you end up stealing rewarding moments from yourself. Have gratitude for what you've been able to do.

SIX

Stack the Deck in Your Favor

Betting on yourself isn't a gamble; it's the smartest move you can make. The trick is learning to stack the deck in your favor and choosing the right moments to make your move, because timing is, indeed, everything in life. Remember, bad timing can often be a by-product of your own impatience, so I'll show you how to most effectively play the long game. For example, I didn't even make it onto *America's Got Talent* until my third try. I'll also cover the psychological impact of a growth mindset and what can happen when you effectively advocate for yourself.

Sometimes, the best way to set yourself up for the future is to pounce on an opportunity when it presents itself. I'll get into how timing led to the creation of my college side hustle. What I couldn't know then was that the savings from this little seasonal business would later give me the option to transition from Wall Street to my dream job as a performer.

Quiet Your Mind

One of the best ways to stack the deck in your favor is to learn how to quiet your mind at the right times. This is another trick used by professional and

Olympic athletes, who say the key to achieving peak performance is by turning off their inner monologue and letting muscle memory and training fully take over. When prompting themselves to swing harder or jump higher, the voice in their head goes quiet and allows them to focus 100 percent on the task at hand. Remember, the foundation of autopilot is the hundreds of times they've visualized themselves in that competition before. Two Japanese neuroscientists conducted a study in 2014 on the famous Brazilian soccer player Neymar. They compared his brain capacity to those of a whole group of second-division players. By measuring neuron signals, they found that Neymar used 90 percent less of his brain capacity than the players in the other group, the less-talented and less-experienced players.[1] Neymar was able to get himself easily into what's called a "flow state."

When competing, being in a flow state means these athletes are frequently thinking of nothing, instead of running through the aforementioned internal monologue. I realize this advice sounds contradictory to what I said earlier about shifting out of autopilot, but athletic and creative endeavors are actually instances we *want* our self-driving controls to take over.

Harvard psychologist Michael Hollander noted this difference in regard to Simone Biles withdrawing from the Tokyo Olympics when she got a case of "the twisties." He explained, "Your cortisol levels go up and your entire body is now hypervigilant to the point where you're actually making mistakes because you're hyperfocused on things. Your body is saying 'There's danger.' In a way you can think of that as you now have two tasks. One is managing the danger that's in your mind, and the other is doing your triple twist off the floor mat. And trying to do two things at once rarely, rarely works. Your focus is gone, and you stumble."[2]

How do we tap into that flow state? How do we know when to turn off our brain and when to turn it on? Researchers John Kounios and David S. Rosen, at Drexel University's Creativity Research Lab, studied jazz musicians and improvisation and they found that "it seems that creative flow can occur when two conditions are met. First, one has to gain expertise by practicing the task enough to develop, or 'bake in,' a specialized brain network for performing that task. Second, one must release conscious control so the specialized network can take over and produce ideas on autopilot, without the performer overthinking what they are doing or becoming overly self-conscious."[3]

The bottom line is, if you want to position yourself for peak performance, it's crucial to set yourself up to attain that flow state. What I want you to know is that the ingredients of preparation and visualization add up to something so much more than being ready: Putting in that time, taking no shortcuts, wires your brain to execute seamlessly when you get your big break. Being ready to access flow is key—it quiets the sections of our brains that are self-critical and allows us to be our best selves and to operate at our fullest potentials.[4]

Take the Leap

It never occurred to me that I could be a professional magician or mentalist. I certainly didn't plan for this, at least not consciously. I've met teenagers who tell me, without a moment's hesitation and with total confidence, that they plan to do this for a living. And I'll go, "How do you know that!?" I admire their determination and self-awareness.

At that age, I had no clue this profession was even an option.

When I started college, I was like one of those windup toys when it came to performing . . . once you turned the crank, I'd just go and go. From the time I was about fifteen years old, my default setting was to constantly chase the next gig. Whenever I found an opportunity, I'd take it; I never let it slip by. Let's say I met someone at a restaurant and they said to their friends, "Wouldn't this be so great at a Christmas party?" I would never, ever just reply, "Here's my card." Instead, I'd jump in with, "Amazing, I do Christmas parties all the time. What's your name and number? Someone from my team will reach out." (Spoiler alert: My "team" consisted of me, myself, and I! But saying that made people feel more secure—like I was part of a team, and therefore more legit. But never rely on someone else to get in touch if you don't have to. You need to take charge so you can own the outcome.)

My motto has always been "Do not wait for others to call you." You act, always. So even though by the end of college I was working on Wall Street with an enviable day job, on weeknights I had gigs at restaurants all across New York City, including T Bar, a steakhouse on the Upper East Side where all of Bravo's Real Housewives dined regularly, and Nino's, which served up delicious Italian fare and was a known mob hotspot. Suffice it to say I had leveled up from my Zia's days. Those restaurant performances led to parties. At those parties, I met event planners who'd book me for other events. I always took their business card and followed up early the next week saying something like, "Why don't I come by your office? Let me know a slow day. How about Tuesday at lunch?" It was a win-win, and I'd always bring something with me— pastries or donuts. Delicious treats went a long way and showed that I'd put in extra effort to make the interaction fun. These weren't just "meetings"—they were opportunities to deliver an experience to the planner's team. I loved being able to connect human to human. I always walked in knowing that they already had a roster of trusted magicians and mentalists, but knew I could prove to them that I could offer something unique to their clients.

Rather than beat around the bush, I would try to be direct and find out where I could add value and differentiate myself. I wanted to go the extra mile for them, to be memorable. I acknowledged that they surely worked with top-notch magicians already and showed respect for that, while simultaneously building the case for why I was worth a shot. It was all about getting that first gig, then proving myself and earning their trust. How could I get my foot in the door? By listening to what they said in those moments and taking action. Then once I established those relationships, momentum would build and my business would grow.

I learned that I couldn't be impatient, that I had to put in the work. For years, I was performing on the side, never really believing I would do it professionally. It always felt like a side hustle, because, in my mind, the formula was simple: you go to school, you get a job, that's how the world works. That's what my parents had taught me, that's what you see in the media and movies. That's the American Dream. In many ways, mine was the opposite of a growth mindset back then.

But two things happened that completely changed my trajectory. First, there was a magician who used to give me a lot of his overflow work. That meant gigs on nights when he was already booked, typically the most popular for private parties. Friday and Saturday nights are when most people host milestone birthdays and anniversaries, galas and similar social events. If he got calls for four different parties on a Saturday night, he'd tell his clients, "You know what? I'm not available, but I've got somebody great for you." And then he'd book someone like me, an up-and-comer. These heavy hitters acted as unofficial agents, getting us new performers new opportunities.

Getting those calls is the hard part, as is getting people to trust your recommendation over Yelp or Google. The folks who farm out their extra events either make a percentage of those gigs or they negotiate the deal and get a piece of the pie up front. This is just how it's done in the magic world.

I used to do a lot of this guy's overflow work. One day, we were hanging out—and I should point out that he was not exactly the warm and fuzzy type. He wasn't the kind of person who dished out words of encouragement or pep talks, which is why what he said next was particularly poignant. He looked at me and asked, "Why are you still working at Merrill Lynch?" I was caught off guard. "What do you mean?" I asked. Nobody had ever put it to me that directly before. His question went against everything I'd heard up to that point. Everyone else saw magic as a fun hobby, whereas working on Wall Street was viewed as the safe, respectable path.

I told him, "Well, I have a great job."

He was the kind of guy who challenged everything, so he wasn't going to concede a point. He asked me, "Do you love it?"

I had to think about that, because it had never occurred to me to consider whether or not I loved my day job before. I was just doing what I was supposed to do, and I didn't have an inkling that there were other options. I gave him an honest answer and said, "It's okay."

He continued, "Do you want to do it forever?"

That felt like a punch to the gut, imagining myself in this boring job forever. "No, not really."

He kept peppering me with very pointed questions, and every one of them demanded a yes or no answer. He wasn't trying to be nurturing or paternal, as that was not his brand.

Finally, he got to the point. "What do you need to do to perform full time?"

I totally panicked and I made up a number. No one had ever asked me anything like this before. I thought about my rent, my bills, my student loans, etc. "I've got to make $100,000 a year doing magic."

He wasn't going to let me off the hook just because I threw up such a pie-in-the-sky number. He pressed on. "How much are you making now?" And I told him. In his aggressive line of questioning, he took all these obstacles and barriers, all this baggage I had in my mind, pushed it all away and said, "Get rid of all that crap. Let's talk numbers." I saw it so clearly, for the very first time. He knew what I was making on the side, as those jobs were often funneled through him. He said, "You make this much doing magic when you do this many shows. Can you land one extra show a week for the next year? That's fifty more shows a year. And what if you charge 20 percent more? How's that math working for you?"

Everything he said made me think, *Yeah, if I wasn't at work* . . . A light bulb went off in my mind—one that should have always been on. But it took someone who was already doing magic professionally to lay it out for me and push me to think, *Holy shit, yeah, it's possible.*

That's when I blurted out, "Oh my God, I could do that."

It's so silly that I didn't realize it before, but that was an epiphany moment. I didn't quit right away, but that conversation got me thinking about an actual escape path. I needed that goal. It's like an ultramarathon; if you're going to run a hundred miles, you don't run a hundred miles all at once. I wasn't going to become the most famous mentalist in the world overnight. There are so many little steps, and they can seem absolutely overwhelming, but you've got to start by running the first mile. Most people can run one mile. I needed to just take where I was and think, *What's the next step?* For me, that was getting just one more show a week.

I had to start thinking, *Let's work a little harder and then I'm going to raise my rates this percent.* To work the system, I had to come up with realistic small goals that I could achieve, actionable bite-size things, one step, followed by another, followed by another.

Two months after this conversation, I performed for the CFO of my company at an internal event. Event planners within Merrill Lynch would hire me for shows because I had a bit of a reputation within the company, as a novelty, but also as someone who did a great job. They brought me in to perform for an intimate group of twenty top execs, bankers and their clients. I was in a beautiful office on one of the top floors of the World Financial Center, interacting with CFO James Gorman and his people. I performed one of my favorite tricks at the time, turning a stack of one-dollar bills into hundreds with the snap of my fingers and in the blink of an eye, perfect for the Wall Street crowd.

It was an amazing sleight of hand trick and the crowd was enamored. James looked at me and joked, "Oh my God, we've got to get you working here," which is what every Wall Street guy would say upon seeing that trick. I laughed and replied, "I do work here." He clearly thought I was joking as he continued to laugh. But then I paused, maintaining eye contact, and said "No, really, I do work here."

That stopped him in his tracks. He looked at me with confusion in his eyes and exclaimed, "What do you mean?" He didn't even understand what I was saying.

I confirmed, "I actually work in your global technology services department at 95 Greene Street." It was so out of character, but I broke the fourth wall, and maybe his brain a little bit, when I spouted all the corporate lingo from my group and he finally realized, *Wait, this guy actually works at Merrill Lynch.*

He looked me up and down and, in all seriousness, he said, "What the hell are you doing working here?" That was it, that was the final nail in the coffin, and I immediately asked myself, *What* am *I doing working here? This guy is the second in command at the company. If he doesn't understand why I'm here, neither do I.*

I put in my two weeks' notice less than a month later. What's so great is that everyone I worked with was genuinely happy for me; they all said some version of, "This is your calling, this is what you were meant to do."

I had inadvertently put all the pieces into place to make the seamless move into pursuing my dream. I wasn't married and I didn't have kids to send to college yet. I had plenty of savings as I built my magic business, thanks to Wolverine Spartan, which I'll explain shortly.

But what's most important is I was finally ready to go all in and bet on myself.

Learn from Every Setback

When I talk about my time on *America's Got Talent*, I refer to it as the rocket fuel that propelled my mentalism career. They say it takes ten years to become an overnight success and funny enough, it was exactly a decade after quitting my job in finance that I landed *AGT*. But by no means was this actually overnight success, especially because it took me three tries to even get on the show.

For my first audition, I had an *in*. I'd gotten a call from a producer, which is the best-case scenario because it meant I didn't have to wait for hours and hours for my turn. Think walking up to a club, skipping the line, and having the velvet rope opened for you by a smiling bouncer.

The process is pretty straightforward: You show up at an appointed time, go in and perform. In theory, this should have been way better because I didn't have to wait around with thousands of other hopefuls. The bad news was that they didn't factor in that my act is interactive, and stuck me in front of a camera with a microphone. Great setup for a singer . . . not so great for a mind reader when there's no mind available to read! I timidly explained the situation to a PA (production assistant), and let's just say this kind of troubleshooting was a few notches above his pay grade. He ran my situation up the food chain through his head-set and was told to fill in as my "audience." Unfortunately, he was mildly irritated and very distracted—not exactly a recipe for success when your goal is amazement. Still, I rolled with it to show that I was adaptable. No one wants to work with a diva, right?

I tried to explain the trick I was doing and what I needed from him, but the PA kept saying things like, "Wait, sorry, what was that?" be-cause he was half-focused on his walkie-talkie. There was no way I could pull this performance together; the cards were stacked against me.

Guess what?

It went terribly! I mean downright awful and no way to sugarcoat it. Before the audition even started, I was dead in the water. So I did the trick, and the PA was like, "Okay, cool, we done? Gotta get back to work now." There was no sense of wonder, no magic, no "Mind blown!" reaction. Immediately I realized I should have been much more of an activist for myself. I should have said, "Nope, listen, this won't work. I need somebody who's fully committed." I didn't push, I didn't advocate for myself effectively, and I allowed my audition to get steamrolled, rather than saying to myself, "Hey, this is my big shot. I'm going to do everything in my power to set myself up for success."

The mystical thing about our brains is that they are wired to help us succeed. They are on our team. Our brains have our backs. It's hard-wired into our DNA to learn from our mistakes—evolution at its fin-est, survival of the fittest. Mistakes trigger our neurons to self-correct. In fact, the brain normally recognizes an error within one second and then continues to process after the mistake, insulating itself from mak-ing that error again.[5] My brain sent me back to the drawing board, al-ready figuring out what I could do differently as I walked—dejected, Charlie Brown–style—out of the building. I knew the next time I got this opportunity, I'd give the producers a lot more advance notice about exactly what I needed, and I'd hold them to it.

The best advice I can offer is, if you've got your one shot, make it truly count and don't compromise when your future is on the line. Try to place all those dominoes in a row so they fall in the pattern you want. When I was setting up my audition the first time, and those producers pointed to a PA running around and said, "We have someone for you," I should have been more forceful and said, "No, I need somebody who can focus the entire time." I should have been more assertive, and more direct. I should have taken a breather, rescheduled, *something* instead of accepting a bad position. But I was so anxious to get in there and do my thing that I allowed unfavorable circumstances to crater my chances.

Please note that sometimes, even if it all goes right, the timing can still throw everything off. People will often reach out to me now, saying, "I'm trying out for the show," and I'll always lead with, "Hey, guess what? First time I didn't get on." I'm not trying to discourage them; in fact, it's just the opposite. I want to give them a dose of reality: One year you don't even make the show and the next your standing in the top three. Often, success boils down to timing, a little bit of luck, and not knowing at that moment that the producer may have already found somebody for your slot. This is why persistence and the ability to keep going is crucial, which is why we've already covered how to handle the pain of rejection. It's hard to do, separating yourself from the person being rebuffed. I didn't take the turndown personally that first time, because I know how crippling that could be. Instead, I looked at what I could have done to stack the deck more in my favor.

For the second audition, I didn't have the same *in*, probably because the first one had gone so poorly. This time I was part of the more traditional "cattle call," with thousands of people waiting long hours to get their shot. A lot of the wait took place outside, and it was a particularly bone-chilling January day in New York, with wind chills well below freezing. I stood around for almost six hours, turning into a human popsicle and then had to leave to perform a gig. I didn't realize the time commitment required and had not planned accordingly, so yet again it was not meant to be. There I was, ready to advocate for myself, and an entirely different factor stole my chance. I would not make that mistake again.

What's funny is that by that point, I was working at about 250 private parties each year. I'd developed a very thick skin from doing so many bar and bat mitzvahs in restaurants and banquet halls. In so many ways, I was already set up for success as a performer. I'd developed bulletproof strategies to win people over who were reluctant or not necessarily welcoming. Sure, the hosts wanted me there—they hired me. But the other people at the event had no idea who I was . . . and often didn't care.

If I was working at a bar mitzvah, the hosts are the parents. Teenagers, as you might well know, don't typically care about your feelings and will eviscerate you. Well, multiply that by a hundred if you're a strolling magician and they sense any weakness. Worst of all was when I'd realize that I was working my way through one segment of a social stratum across several bat or bar mitzvahs—like all the kids were in the same school, so the same group might end up seeing me three, four, or five weeks in a row, and I'd already burned through most of my repertoire. Nothing was more devastating than hearing, "Oh, I saw this last week, do something different." And some of them I couldn't shake off. They were like a rottweiler that grabs your leg, following me from group to group. My set was organized in such a way that I was repeating tricks, like a band playing their greatest hits. I wasn't set up to perform three hours of different material; there weren't songs to debut from a new album, if you know what I mean. I needed to either face the wrath and humiliation of getting called out, or pull material that wasn't my best.

When you know what's about to happen at the big reveal of the trick, then it's much, much easier to figure out, because you're watching it differently. First time around, when the rabbit comes out of the hat, your mind is blown. The second time, you're a little more wary. You'll just stare at one hand waiting for the next pivot, and you're less likely to be misdirected by that rabbit squirming around in my breast pocket, when I try to make you look away at the right moment. And when you're watching for the third time, the trick just doesn't work anymore. The secret sauce is gone. And those kids would be like, "Ha, ha, I figured out what you just did. And I'm gonna tell everybody!" (Yes, I recognize the irony of thirteen-year-olds following around the magician. I'd come full circle in life.)

The bar mitzvah circuit was not sustainable for my mental well-being. That's the reason I was more than a little anxious for the career boost I thought *AGT* could give me, especially because I was sure it would enable me to segue into more corporate gigs and away from the teen set. Again and again, I worked through every scenario of my audition, visualizing it all, to ensure this time I'd come in with the deck stacked in my favor and flow on my side, and I'd earn a spot on the show.

Answer the Door When Opportunity Knocks

I'd never have had the chance to pursue my dreams on *AGT* if it weren't for a somewhat miserable opportunity that serendipitously presented itself when I was in college. As I've mentioned, I'm from Michigan. My buddy Mark Wachsberg's parents became empty nesters when he went off to college and decided to move to a house on a lake, so we'd spend a lot of time on the water in the summer. If you know anything about lakes and cold weather, it's that every house has a boat dock that has to be installed in the spring and removed in the fall. In cold climates, the lakes freeze and you have to take the docks out or ice will destroy the structure.

If you're familiar with boat docks, then you've also encountered the guys who install and remove boat docks. Boat dock guys are not exactly known for their customer service, to put it politely. They might show up when they're scheduled and they might not; you never know. They tend to be a hard drinking, hard smoking type and leave your waterfront littered with Marlboro Reds . . . if they even show up at all. (I hate to generalize, but in our area, these were the facts.)

Dock work is a seasonal business where everybody wants their boat dock installed at the same time, so these guys were (and still are) in high demand but the work is quite miserable. When the season starts, you'll get a beautiful day in late April or early May, and everyone will want their boats out *right now* because they have spring fever.

Mark's parents got tired of waiting for the unreliable boat dock guys and said, "Guess what? You kids are about to earn your keep around here," and had us install the dock in freezing-cold water. We put on waders, which are rubberized overalls that are supposed to keep out the water. They do work . . . until the moment you step in too deep and that ice-cold water goes directly down your butt crack and fills the legs of the pants. It's the coldest, worst feeling in the world. Meanwhile, I'd be holding this heavy dock over my head while my buddy was screwing it together, and we were freezing and swearing, and his parents were just sitting on their patio with friends having drinks, all laughing at us. This was not the type of entertainment I was used to providing at my other job.

It was misery.

It was also an untapped opportunity.

Mark and I realized that installing boat docks could be very lucrative if we were also able to provide excellent customer service. We saw an opening in the market. At the time, I was attending the University of Michigan, home of the Wolverines. Mark was at Michigan State and their mascot is the Spartan. We couldn't figure out what to name our nascent company, but then we realized that 90 percent of the homes on the lake had an affiliation with one of those two schools.

My nights performing magic at restaurants taught me how critical it is to have a great icebreaker, and I thought humor would be the ticket for this type of business. We named our company Wolverine Spartan Boat Docks because it gave us a great joke right off the jump. People would look us both over and ask which one is the Wolverine (or Spartan depending on their alma mater or allegiance). One of us would answer, "That's me, sir." And you could time your watch to them replying, "Well, I'll work with you, but I don't know about this guy," and we laughed wholeheartedly and unabashedly, as if we hadn't heard the exact same joke a hundred times before. But guess what, we just landed another deal!

We established ourselves as clean-cut college kids earning money for our future, which most people respected and wanted to support. Our company took off like wildfire because we didn't worry about failing, we didn't overthink it, and we didn't procrastinate. We hit the hardware store for two ratchets and Kinko's for flyers and business cards, the latter of which I was a pro at since age fourteen as a magician. We spent our weekends dropping off flyers in each and every lake house mailbox within a half-hour drive, while telling dirty jokes, making fun of each other, and having an overall great time.

We were so successful that we could barely handle all the business that came in. Because it was so explosive—customers hated the other providers with a passion—we ended up making tens of thousands of dollars in a short amount of time every year.

Why is this story relevant?

Because I saved all that money and it's why I had the safety net to quit my job on Wall Street less than five years later to pursue magic full time. I had no idea that I was giving myself an edge with the boat dock business; I thought I was just goofing around with my friend.

Maybe you've been waiting for your sign to stop working for The Man, but you haven't known what business to start. If you want to find what's likely a profitable enterprise, begin looking around at the pain points in your life and the lives of people around you. What is that business? Can you make money? Is there something you like to do that everybody else hates? Or maybe you hate doing something, but other people hate it too, and you hate it a little bit less? Spend five minutes on social media and you'll find something, like the Dallas woman who makes hundreds of thousands of dollars a year putting out and then cleaning up autumn pumpkin displays. Be creative and be relentless.

I will never forget the feeling of ice-cold water shooting down my back and trickling all the way down to my toes in those waders, but I'll also never forget how that frigid water led to the comfort of financial security at a time when I needed the courage to strike out on my own.

If you wait for the perfect moment to do something, odds are you're going to wait a long time. There are moments when you should act first and ask questions later. With the clarity of hindsight, you can always look back and see how the events of your life fit together like interlocking puzzle pieces. But it's harder to look at what's happening in the present and know that you have that next perfect puzzle piece in hand. There's always going to be an excuse available, like, "I don't have an idea for a business," but you can achieve greatness if you stay focused and keep pushing forward. Odds are you have your phone at hand this very moment and the full breadth of human knowledge available just a tap away. The world is at your fingertips and there are no excuses not to pursue your passion. All you do is type in "How do I do X?" and thousands of videos and articles will explain it in great detail. So, my goal here isn't to teach you how to install and remove boat docks, or how to become a mentalist for that matter.

Instead, I want to impress upon you the importance of taking those swings.

If you just keep doing the same thing over and over, it's like putting money under your mattress rather than investing it. Instead of growing in value, inflation keeps chipping away at it; the same thing applies to my profession, to any profession where you've got to challenge yourself and be willing to step outside your comfort zone to advance. It's not easy, but it's necessary if you want to take that leap—and hopefully reap big rewards. So when opportunity knocks, throw open that door—even if you're still wearing your pajamas.

There are pivotal moments in everyone's lives. Now, we've all heard about entrepreneurs like Sara Blakely betting it all on Spanx, or how Fred Smith, the founder of FedEx, went to Vegas and put all the money he had on the roulette wheel in order to make payroll. You hear about people who max out all their credit cards as they pursue their goals, and I can't deny that these are powerful stories and we eat them up. Nearly everyone wants a Susan Boyle moment—one minute she's a quiet, unassuming librarian, and the next she is discovered by the world, a superstar with the voice of an angel—but we all know that is more of a fairy tale and definitely not how things usually happen.

In real life, you have to stack the cards in your favor. For me, I had businesses since I was fourteen and I had been saving money diligently. I didn't have a fancy car or a flashy watch, like so many of my colleagues. I lived below my means and would always delay gratification. I was never ordering dessert, literally or figuratively.

That's why, when it came time to choose whether to quit my job and become a professional magician, I thought, *I'm giving myself a year to do this and I have the runway to do it.* I was lucky that timing was on my side. Wall Street was booming with a roaring bull market, and firms were hiring left and right. I told myself that the worst-case scenario was landing another corporate job in a year if this didn't pan out. Had this exact same scenario played out a few years later during the Great Recession, with widespread layoffs and uncertainty, I probably would not have gone for it. Fear would likely have held me back and made me cling to the security of my stable job.

Don't be too hard on yourself, because sometimes the timing is not right to take that leap. I saved up a bunch of money, and when I quit, I knew I could handle it for a year. Not everyone is in that position. I didn't have kids or a stack of bills to pay. Health insurance wasn't a concern because I had COBRA. Mine is not a fairy tale, but the story of all the things I'd put in place over years, so that when the moment came to make that decision, I knew where the card I needed was stacked in the deck.

Prepare for Success

I believe you're going to succeed. Still, sometimes when everything starts going your way, you can find yourself overwhelmed by free-floating anxiety. In fact, this is a common occurrence.

Psychologist Carla Marie Manly, author of *Joy from Fear*, says, "The brain's fear circuit works very quickly, and it doesn't always pause to differentiate between good anxiety and bad."[6] This is why we often feel tense and unsettled after we reach a goal or achieve an accomplishment, even though whatever happened is inarguably a good thing, whether it's a promotion or a degree or a move. Happiness can be overwhelming to some. According to Manly, for people who suffer from anxiety, the physiological change felt after something great occurs can trigger an automatic response in the body that something has gone off the rails, largely because you're not used to feeling good. It's like your system is expecting the other shoe to drop, and this feeling keeps you from enjoying your legitimate victory. There's actually a word for the irrational fear of being happy—it's called *cherophobia* and it often stems from childhood experiences where pleasure (like delighting in eating a stolen candy bar) was followed by pain (getting in trouble for stealing that candy bar).[7]

As you learn to read your own mind, better things will start happening, and that may well lead to anxiety. You can fight this phenomenon by recognizing and acknowledging it. The goal here is to force yourself out of the danger zone—to kick your autonomic nervous system out of overdrive. Clinical psychologist Alicia Clark, author of *Hack Your Anxiety*, says that one of the best tactics is to face this distress head on.[8] Acknowledge it. Allow yourself to think through all the scenarios that could happen when your dream comes true, like dealing with your snarky aunt's judgment when you're finally able to buy that lake home. Walk through how you'd handle that chatter, because the more strategies you have (such as inviting her to spend the holidays with you there), the more you'll give those unfounded worries a place to be put to rest.

Another hack when you're overwhelmed by the good (that makes you feel bad) is to intentionally try to relax yourself. Try taking deep breaths, practicing mindfulness, meditating, getting in some light exercise, or sitting under a weighted blanket.[9] One of the very best ways to de-stress is to just step outside and get yourself some fresh-air therapy. The quicker you can calm and center yourself, the better you'll feel.

If, regardless of what you try, you can't stop worrying, take that energy and use it for planning. Instead of ruminating about what happens if you get that executive level job, try to figure out how you'll tackle those new responsibilities. If you're about to live your wildest dream, create contingency plans beforehand so you can enjoy your time instead of fearing the unknown.

Remember, the world is not an either-or scenario. Something good happening to you is not going to automatically trigger something bad happening. You're not jinxing yourself by being happy.

Try to strike a balance between enjoying the present and still planning for your future. So often, we only chase short-term comfort and instant gratification because they are the path of least resistance. And I can assure you there were times when my friends went on vacations that their parents paid for and I'd say, "You know what? I can't. My parents unfortunately aren't supporting me, so I'm going to keep that $800 just in case." The sacrifices I made back then are what allowed me to now live my dream.

I'll never forget the morning after I left Wall Street, parked on the couch, still in pajamas, with a bowl of cereal in hand, watching daytime TV. I had this realization of, *Holy shit, I don't have a job and if I wanted to just veg out and watch TV all day, I could.* The weight of that thought hit me like a ton of bricks as I turned the TV off. I told myself, *I don't have a boss anymore, so I have to be the boss. This is day one, and there is no playbook for how to be successful at what I do. The phone isn't about to ring with some agent saying, "Hey kid, let me make you a star!" I need to define my goals. I need to find people that have done it and learn from them, and I need to start working. I have to make this happen because no one's going to make it happen for me.*

Which is exactly what I did.

Develop a Growth Mindset

The third time I tried out for *AGT*, I waited again for a very long time, probably six or seven hours, because I showed up to another open casting call. Here's when having some self-awareness comes in handy: I knew I was good because I was already making a living as a professional mentalist, one rowdy group of thirteen-year-olds at a time. I had a level of confidence that could only be acquired over thousands of performances for paying audiences and I understood what I had to offer.

The third time was the charm. I finally made it onto *AGT* because I incorporated what I had learned from the first audition and had the participant entirely focused on what I was doing, so I could properly showcase my talent. There was a sense of peace that came from knowing I didn't need the show to validate me, as I was doing well already. This gave me a calm demeanor and reduced any nerves that would have haunted me after my first two tries. The producers in the room absolutely loved my act and even asked me if I had any other tricks I wanted to show them after my audition set was complete. I punched my ticket to the televised shows and was ready to go! This was my chance to perform in front of Howard Stern, Heidi Klum, Howie Mandel, Mel B, and all of America. They each gave me a yes and my career would never be the same again.

Mind you I was still working the bar mitzvah circuit at this time. What's funny is, even if you're on people's living room TV every week, they don't necessarily recognize you in real life. The same week that my episode aired for judge cuts—the second round after the initial auditions—I was hired for a party in Rockville, Maryland. I was doing tricks for a small group of family members when the bar mitzvah boy's great aunt said, "Oh my God, I've got to tell you about this guy we saw on *America's Got Talent* this week." She was raving, going on and on about how great he was.

Brimming with pride, I replied, "Yeah, that's me."

She laughed at me and said, "No, it's not you."

Wait, *what*? More emphatically, I let her know, "Yes, that was definitely me. The trick you just saw? I did that trick Tuesday night on *AGT.* I assure you, it's me."

She was absolutely not having it and she went to get her husband to come back and confront me. She pointed in my face and said, "Why are you lying?"

How awkward was this?! I calmly explained, "I don't know what to tell you right now, but that was me. I'm Oz Pearlman. I'm the guy you saw. I'm Oz the Mentalist. I think I'm even wearing the same suit."

She was resolute. "No, no, this guy was hysterical," which was sort of insulting because I'd just done the same trick . . . and delivered the same joke! Then, right in front of me, she proceeded to have a full discussion with her husband about whether it was me she'd seen on television the night before! Eventually, the dad came over and confirmed that they'd booked me about eight months before I'd landed the show and that they had gotten very lucky with their timing. But that aunt could not comprehend that she'd just seen me on TV and then met me at the party.

Finally, she said, "You don't look like your picture on TV." That was it. No apology. It was the biggest inspiration yet to keep giving the show my best . . . I really had to get off the bar mitzvah circuit.

When you're looking to level up, the best practice is to adopt a growth mindset. To me, that means believing in yourself and your abilities, facing challenges, and combining hard work, learning, and dedication to create the outcome you most desire. A growth mindset is seeing a challenge and digging in with delight, confident that you'll come out better for it on the other side. It's about picking yourself back up when you fail and trying again, using the lessons you learned on the initial stumble. It's about seeking feedback and then applying it to constantly refine, hone, and improve yourself. It's about being proud of the sweat on your brow, because that exertion is propelling you closer to your goal. The best part is, with every step forward, you're making positive changes to your brain's neuroplasticity. You're clearing that smooth walkway from your front door to your mailbox.

America's Got Talent is comprised of a number of rounds. First there's the audition, then the second round, and afterward the live performances begin. With each round, more contestants got cut, narrowing the field from thousands of folks auditioning to less than one hundred who make it to TV. Every stage filtered out more people. The quarterfinals and semifinals are live, as are the finals. The pressure is intense, which I loved because I operate best when I'm backed into a corner. Reaching the finals comes with an extra performance, and that was one of my favorites. It was short—less than a minute. It felt like putting a cherry on an ice-cream sundae. That round changed the way I view TV, because up until that point, I thought that the longer the performance, the better it would be. Turns out the world was changing. This was 2015, right as social media was becoming really big (and attention spans were shrinking really small). My routine for Heidi Klum involved having her imagine an invisible deck of cards in her hand and asking her to choose any card she wanted; I even asked if she wanted to change her mind. Not only did I seemingly make a card appear in her hand out of thin air, but it was the very one she had just thought of . . . on live national TV with more than fifteen million people watching. Quick, direct, and to the point, with a palpable sense of risk and danger; I had found my sweet spot.

Going into *AGT*, I knew I didn't need to win to benefit, especially because the experience taught me so much. For example, I learned to be more creative, and that there's nothing like a deadline to get your butt in gear. Necessity is truly the mother of invention! If you have to come up with something great, and there's no timeline, you'll do it eventually, right? But if you have it forced upon you, there's no backing out or procrastinating.

The format of the show involves performing Tuesday nights live on national TV, with millions watching. Then America has twenty-four hours to vote, and the results are revealed live on TV the following night. I'd stand on the stage at Radio City Music Hall, alongside my competition, knowing full well that half of us were going home that night. With six thousand people in the audience and pin-drop-quiet atmosphere, host Nick Cannon would slowly open up the envelope, look at the results, and wait what felt like an eternity to build the tension as we each hoped to hear our name called. Then, like music to my ears, he announced, "It's Oz the Mentalist!" I'd be moving on to the next round. The timelines on the show are tight and people are chosen to perform in Week One or Week Two. I got Week Two both times. That meant as soon as I was done that night, I'd have to talk to a producer and tell them what I was planning to do the following week.

In this position, a lot of people might think, *I'm going to save my biggest and best trick for the finale*, but that's not what I did. The finale is never guaranteed, so I knew my best bet was to raise the stakes and go bigger every week, basically buying myself a fresh lottery ticket each time to stay in the game.

Ultimately, I placed third, and I was thrilled because the exposure did exactly what I'd envisioned it would do: It set me on a path to success—which meant way fewer bar mitzvahs.

I'm not much of a Vegas guy, but when it comes to gambling, I will always bet on myself. You have to play the hand that you were dealt in life and all of us have different circumstances to contend with, but stacking the deck means no more excuses. Having that positive growth mindset will help, as will self-advocating and never letting an opportunity slip through your fingers. You are in control of your destiny.

SEVEN

Don't Be Your Own Worst Enemy

Stop right now and look around. Are you at home? Are you sitting in a coffee shop? Are there other people there? Then here's something you don't know: Right now, every single man, woman, and child in your line of sight is the lead actor in their own movie in their head. They're *it*, they're the A-lister, everything in their orbit revolves around *them*. Those of us in their peripheral vision? We're just the extras with non-speaking roles, the non-player characters. We fade into their background. We may as well be wallpaper. Yet that's fine, because we're all so busy being the stars of our *own* movies.

The downside of having this main character energy is that we're also our own worst critics, harsher to ourselves than any high school bully could ever be. No online troll could poke our raw nerves and tender spots like we do when it's us trolling ourselves.

Our natural inclination is to allow our inner monologue to reinforce the negative, so in this chapter, I'll show you the important work of turning the tables on negativity, assuming the best, and treating yourself gently. We'll talk about how to quiet that inner critic for good.

I'll show how I shut down my inner critic by delving into my story of running Spartathlon, one of the hardest ultramarathons on the planet. I will walk you through my failed first attempt at this race, when my mind collapsed and gave up long before my body did. The biggest mistake of all was mentally writing my DNF (did not finish) speech and listing out all the excuses in my head for why I couldn't do it, rather than focusing on the task at hand. I soon learned the physical pain of pressing on would have faded far faster than the long-lasting inner turmoil of quitting. This was a valuable experience, as it taught me to throw everything plus the kitchen sink at problems, rather than allowing them to overtake my goals. And I'll explain how the next year, during the hottest day in race history, with the lowest finisher percentage ever, I changed my approach . . . and my outcome.

I'll also break down how to properly value yourself and your time. I'll teach you the greatest negotiation advice I've ever learned. Following my own negotiation advice led to me breaking a world record and raising six figures for Save the Children's Ukraine Relief Fund; I learned that when you do good, you're not just paying it forward for others.

Ultimately, when you learn to value yourself, you become invaluable to yourself, and it all starts with learning not to be your own worst enemy.

Time to Take Charge

The fastest way to silence your inner critic is to remember that just because you're the headliner in your own mind doesn't mean others perceive you that way. Not being the star of their show has nothing to do with you and everything to do with them . . . and there's nothing wrong with that. Except when we allow ourselves to stew about it. For example, when the lack of a timely response from someone else causes us to fabricate unpleasant stories, especially when we then project our un-kind judgments on others and we get angry.

I'm not immune to negative self-talk. For example, recently I was waiting to hear back from a big podcast that I've been dying to be a guest on. When I didn't hear back from them immediately, my thoughts began to race about having been blown off. I let myself feel hurt and insulted, regardless of that not being anyone's intent.

Instead of just being logical, I began to beat myself up about why I hadn't made the cut and I shame-spiraled. *Where was I lacking? Was I not funny enough? Not clever enough?* Then my self-protection instinct kicked in and I started to get mad at *them.* Nothing about this was mentally healthy. I found myself complaining to my wife, who had the sense to laugh and reply, "I don't want to hear about this anymore. It's not about you, Oz. You have no idea what's happening in that producer's world. Why don't you assume the best, assume they really want you? Right now, they're probably slammed with production on other stuff and they just need a nice, friendly reminder in a week." (Yes, my wife is often more clearheaded than me.)

If you find yourself mired in negative self-talk, guess what? You're not only human, but you're an *evolved* human. This is a function of *survival.* If thousands of years ago, our ancestors hadn't allowed themselves to anticipate danger and threats, and hadn't allowed themselves the opportunity to stew, we'd have gone the way of the dinosaur.

Our prehistoric kinfolk likely sat around their caves, thinking, *You know, I don't feel fast enough to outrun that saber-toothed tiger. I guess I'll just stay in today and stare at the ceiling and eat these stupid berries instead.* They weren't depressed; they were preserving our species! And there are times your inner critic is right. If it's telling you that you're not twenty-two anymore and you don't recover like you used to in college, and refusing to be goaded into taking tequila shots out of some stranger's boot in a weird Tijuana bar means that you're lame, embrace it. Listen to that critic and be lame. Bask in your lameness when you're not crying on the toilet twelve hours later with the rest of the bachelor party. You just saved yourself a world of hurt.

The caution here is to not let your inner critic negative-self-talk you out of feeling your own worth, because that will limit your potential and can lead to anxiety, depression, and a host of other feelings.

When it comes to someone not getting back to me, my solution is normally to be proactive and to try to take the onus off them. I didn't in this situation, probably because I was too excited and the stakes felt so high. If I were coaching myself, I should have said to the producer, "I'm going to keep this date on hold for you. I'm sure you're slammed, so I'll make sure to follow up with you in a few weeks." This is effective because I'm front-loading the fact that I'm assigning them as busy. This affords them some grace and they don't have to say, "You know, I've been really swamped," especially if they've just been busy enjoying their summer break and I inadvertently make them feel guilty for the audacity of needing downtime. Then I put the job of reminding them onto myself by saying, "I'll make sure to check in with you in a couple weeks."

When I do check in, I'll say, "Hey, I promised to follow up. Let me know what's going on." Or if we're still in the planning stages, I'll tell them that I'll circle back again on X date. So I'm creating this dynamic where somebody doesn't have to make an excuse or feel as if they've been rude to me. I'm extending that extra bit of grace and runway, and people really appreciate it. Plus, assigning myself action gives me a feeling of control in the situation, which makes me less likely to turn my frustration outward and blurt out career-limiting statements to soothe my own ego.

Of course, there have been instances before where my gut tells me I need to act out, say to write a nasty email. I've learned over the last few years that it's okay to draft the email, to get it out of my system. The anger I might feel is real and I don't want to bottle it up. So I write the email. The rage channels through me and directly into my fingertips as they loudly slam each letter on the keyboard, and damn, does it feel good. I make sure to leave the address line blank, lest I accidentally hit send! And now I let that emotional brain dump sit and stew in my drafts folder, my mind free and clear. I set an alarm for the next day, and tell myself that if I still feel the same way in, say, twenty-four hours, then I'm going to send my missive. (I'm a big fan of timers and alarms to keep me on task.) And guess what happens, ninety-nine times out of a hundred? The delay has healed—or at the very least reduced—those red-hot initial feelings. I go from boiling to either simmering or luke-warm, and end up deleting the email. I've taught my kids the same move: If they're mad, they should wait a ten-count to react. You wouldn't believe how much less chaos this contributes to our house-hold, where my wife and I are outnumbered by five kids under the age of nine.

Still, there are times I want to be petulant, like, "Hey man, I deserve more respect than this." I have to tell myself, *Stop it. Stop it right now.* The issue is that I'm just assuming that something's going wrong and it's my fault. But in reality, it's likely that whatever is happening has nothing to do with me. This is an example where creating a silo to separate myself, Oz Pearlman, from Oz the Mentalist and the associated frustration that I'm taking quite personally, is extremely beneficial. The issue is I'm one person, but if I can trick myself into two separate personalities, then I avoid anger, feelings of inadequacy, and potentially lashing out or being petty. Any of these overreactions are more likely to hurt my chances of getting what I actually want rather than help.

Try to separate a piece of yourself that can act as an agent who represents you. The best part about an agent is that during negotiations they won't take unpleasant situations as personally. Find a way to create your own good cop and bad cop in one person, so that you can extricate yourself and not feel that stress, that anxiety, those feelings that wear all of us down in our day-to-day, in both our business and our personal lives. I tell myself, *This isn't about Oz Pearlman; this is about Oz the Mentalist.* Be your own alter ego.

A good way of siloing and tricking yourself into better humor is to "Fake it till you make it." This expression is an example of "behavioral activation." According to behavioral therapist Rachel Thomasian, "Behavioral activation is a concept and intervention frequently used in cognitive behavioral therapy that utilizes behaviors to influence emotions, thoughts and mood. In other words, a therapist will often prescribe behaviors for their client to take part in, with the expectation that it will modify or ease some painful emotion they might be experiencing, such as anxiety or depression."[1]

In my case, that means if I'm feeling down because the podcast I've been obsessing over still hasn't invited me on, I let myself sit with that feeling. Rather than wallowing in self-pity, I use this no (or this "not yet") as fuel to strengthen my inner resolve and promote even greater focus on my goal.

Another important thing to consider is that sometimes you just need to take a breather. As counterintuitive as it may seem, waiting patiently can be the best course of action. The expression "a watched pot never boils" has proven true in my life so many times. So let it go, let that pot burble without you. You'll often get better results by shifting your energy to something enjoyable, like being around friends or playing a game with your kids. It helps trick your brain into a lighter, more upbeat mood. And when you're in that headspace, you're far less likely to get resentful when someone forgets that you're supposed to star in *their* movie, too.

Positive Self-Talk

No matter what the circumstance, I want you to consciously decide to be kind to yourself. Treat yourself gently. Say things to yourself that lift you up, not bring you down, because kind self-talk makes a world of difference. Maybe you think repeating positive affirmations feels silly—but they work because they rewire your brain when you say them enough.

S. J. White said in an article for the *American Journal of Health-System Pharmacy*, "The human mind seems to focus on the negative, and we tend to berate ourselves in ways we would never tolerate from a boss, spouse, or anyone else."[2]

Again, this isn't just advice I offer, it's advice I follow. I aim for an ever-running chyron of happy thoughts and positive affirmations in my head. I maintain a sense of humor about what I do as a mentalist because let's be real here, I'm not a brain surgeon or fighter pilot. My decisions and performances aren't life or death; they're purely for entertainment. I have a weird job and it's odd to me when my peers are overly solemn about the tricks we perform. Like actors, we're all effectively playing make believe. And people pay us for it! I've fed, clothed, and sheltered my family by being one or two rungs above a clown in the hierarchy of showbiz—trust me, I'm not complaining!

While it may feel temporarily indulgent to wallow in that negative self-talk, it's actually toxic and something you should avoid. When you berate and belittle yourself, you're essentially activating the "threat system" of your brain, so you feel under attack and become defensive and risk-averse.³

What does that mean? It means *moping doesn't help.*

You end up feeling way more stressed and this depletes you both mentally and physically. Even worse? There's a phenomenon called "emotional contagion," meaning all the negative stuff you're thinking and feeling leeches out to those around you and brings them down, too. This is exhausting for everyone!

For the longest time, before I learned to have a sense of humor about what I couldn't control, and before I really clued into the power of positive self-talk, I'd hold myself up to some of my peers and I'd give in to the compare and despair mentality. I'd watch what these guys were doing, and instead of being inspired, I'd look at myself and wonder why I wasn't at that level, too. I wasn't necessarily rooting for them to do worse, but I would feel bad about not personally doing better. Every time I looked at their success, it was a mirror revealing my own insecurities. So I'd think, *Oh man, I'm not doing enough. I'm not doing enough.* (What's ironic is that when we're on an upswing, we think nothing of others, so it's smart to remind yourself of how you felt on the downswings.)

This is another example of learning when to shift out of autopilot. My default setting was to base self-worth on how I ranked subjectively to others, and that typically sent me spiraling into a negative feedback loop. Sometimes shifting to a better state of mind is just a matter of stopping and taking stock from a different perspective. For me, I had to remind myself that I was making a living pursuing my dream and that I was doing exceptionally well. I'd certainly escaped the drudgery of global technology infrastructure, and now when I wear a suit to work, it's by choice. I have an incredible wife who loves me, five healthy, happy children who bring me tremendous joy, none of whom care what TV show I was just on or if I made as much money as a mentalist halfway around the world. I taught myself to *decide* to be happy, and if I were bound and determined to compare, to look at past versions of myself to see how far I've come. So whenever I'm tempted to start complaining or feel like crap when things aren't going exactly the way I want, I check in with myself, asking, *Are you doing better than you were a year or two ago?* That's what matters. And if I'm not doing better for some reason, *How do I try to catch up with where I think I should be? What tangible actions can I take?* In situations like this, we need to give ourselves a road map and a pep talk, not a beatdown.

How do we stop this negative-self-talk cycle? Well, there's an easy way to go about this with the clever name of Catch It, Check It, Change It, which comes from cognitive behavioral therapy.[4] This method requires you shifting out of autopilot and catching yourself in the act of thinking negative or anxious thoughts. So, let's say you're trying and failing at something, like making pad Thai from scratch. The kitchen's a mess and the dish looks terrible . . . and that's before you even taste it. And why isn't the recipe working?

Maybe you catch yourself thinking, *I was dumb to think I could do this.* In this instance, I want you to stop and examine the thought behind that feeling. Maybe it's *I'm a terrible cook.* Now, take a step back and look at the situation objectively. Ask yourself if that thought is helpful, accurate, and useful to the situation.[5] That's the Check It portion.

When you realize that thought is neither useful nor accurate, then it's time to Change It. What could you replace it with that would be accurate and useful? How about, *I make a mean lasagna that everyone loves,* or *My kids say my chocolate chip cookies are better than store-bought.* So you objectively know you're not a terrible cook. Also, pad Thai is incredibly difficult to make at home. You spend fifty dollars on ingredients you'll never use again (unless you don't give up) to make something that isn't nearly as tasty as the divine fifteen-dollar stuff from the Thai place around the corner. Don't beat yourself up; Catch It, Check It, Change It, and then hop on Grubhub or Uber Eats.

Remember, when you're trying something new or different, producing less than favorable results doesn't define you. Remind yourself of that. Because you might be killing it on other fronts. Your business might not be thriving, but business can be cyclical. You're still doing great on the home front, or your friendships are rock-solid, or you found a new hobby or something else that fulfills you. Downturns happen to everyone, but what makes the difference is how you weather those storms.

What helped me change myself and my poor attitude was, instead of comparing and despairing, I made the conscious choice to use others' success to light a fire under my own butt. When I was a little kid, I loved the movie *Rocky IV*. I thought it was so cool that Rocky kept a picture of Drago on his mirror and every day he looked at it and let that image reignite his focus. Eventually, I took that lesson to heart. Let other people fuel the fire for you, not because you want what they have, but because they inspire you to work harder. That's what I've tried to do. It's taken some growth to realize that's the case rather than just bringing myself down. I no longer view the world as a zero-sum game. Now, I let my competitors' success fuel my own ambitions. *Hey, if they can do it, so can I. What's the difference between us? Nothing. Nothing. There's nothing that's stopping me from doing what they're doing.* But real talk, my wife definitely found it a bit weird I was hanging up photos of other dudes on my bathroom mirror.

I won't sugarcoat it and say it isn't challenging to get over the hump with a new endeavor. You have to put in a great deal of work to get through said challenge. A lot of people just don't believe they can do stuff, so they half-ass their attempt in an effort to get the failure over with. By not believing in themselves from the jump, they end up self-sabotaging and reinforcing the belief that it was never going to work, so why even try? And then they feel far worse.

This is where treating ourselves kindly and offering up positive self-talk becomes so important. I'll remind you again of the snowy drive-way between you and the mailbox. When you speak kindly to yourself, or when you repeat positive affirmations, you're carving a path in the snow, meaning you're stimulating those neural pathways that are a shortcut to making your brain happier and more positive. Giving your-self a positive affirmation like, "I'm a great salesperson" (or whatever affirmation you prefer), means you're actively decreasing your stress levels and you're lighting up those reward centers in your brain.[6] And that feels like a win.

This Is Sparta

I want to talk about the Spartathlon because it's one of the best exam-ples I can share about being my own worst enemy—and what can be learned from the experience. But first, I should explain what the event entails. It is a 153-mile ultramarathon (not a typo!) with a strict 36-hour time cutoff that takes place every year in Greece. It re-creates the path, from Athens to Sparta, taken by a foot messenger in order to deliver a critical message to King Leonidas, which many believe changed the course of history. The very existence of our current civilization today can be traced back to a small band of Spartans defending a mountain pass against a massive Persian army, as depicted in the Frank Miller graphic novel *300* and the movie based on it, starring a shirtless and ripped Gerard Butler.

In 480 BCE, during the Greco-Persian Wars, the Persian armies assembled to invade Greece, which had very little time to recruit an army to repel them. In order to buy more time, a messenger name Pheidippides was sent to deliver a message to King Leonidas of Sparta. As the legend goes, he ran from Athens to Sparta in exactly thirty-six hours and instructed the Spartans to gather in a mountain pass at Thermopylae where the Persian armies couldn't attack en masse, as they would encounter a bottleneck. Three hundred Spartans defended against what they estimated were tens of thousands of Persians. Every single Spartan died, but they fought for days, which enabled the Greek army to assemble and beat back the enemy. This is considered a turning point in world history, because otherwise, civilization wouldn't be what we know it today.

The idea of the Spartathlon is to honor the memory of this one person, running this specific route in a day and a half, to deliver a message that changed the course of history as we know it. It's such an epic story. So five members of the British Royal Air Force decided to re-create the course in 1982 (the year of my birth, in an interesting twist), and the Spartathlon was born. At 153 miles, which is 246 kilometers, the race is the equivalent of almost six consecutive marathons—it's *a lot*.

There's a marble obelisk in the center of Sparta with the names of the Spartans who won medals in the Olympics, from the very first event up to modern day. And then on one side of it, for the last forty years, they've engraved the names of those who won the Spartathlon.

This is without a doubt the most iconic race I've ever participated in. When you get into town at the end, local kids ride bikes alongside you for the last few miles. Everyone in the cafés is cheering, and the cars are honking as you get closer because they all know the historical significance of this race and how hard every runner has pushed to make it this far. At the finish, there's a huge statue of King Leonidas. You bow

before him and deliver a ceremonial message, receiving a hero's welcome. Race officials dressed in togas greet each finisher with a glass of
water from a local river and place laurel wreaths on their head. Most
runners carry a personal message—often a hope or a wish—to leave at
the King's knees. (I had mine on a piece of paper, wrapped in a plastic
bag.) It's an incredibly moving moment, shaped by the rich history of
the race, the meaning behind the journey, and the extreme difficulty
involved in finishing it.

Suffice it to say, I wanted this. I wanted this so badly . . . but apparently not badly enough.

The race proved much more mentally grueling than I could anticipate and I got in my own head. I knew I was done for when I began
mentally composing what I'd tell my friends and family about why I
quit. Instead of visualizing myself succeeding and focusing on how to
never give up, all I could visualize was my DNF speech, and that is
what did me in.

Most ultramarathoners find themselves quitting at some point. If
you told me you had a gun to my kid's head, and said, "Can you keep
running?" the answer is always, "Yes, of course." So you learn to look
inside yourself and dig deeper. But that first year, I couldn't imagine
what running 153 miles would be like. It was just unfathomable to me;
I couldn't wrap my mind around it. If the race were in America, that's
roughly the distance from Times Square to Albany, or Philadelphia to
Washington DC.

That first year, 2011, I was running the race with my friend Michael
Arnstein, and at mile 54 I was a train wreck. I'd been puking nonstop
for hours, captured in all my glory in a video that has since gone viral.
In a bid to uplift my spirit, he says, "We have less than a hundred miles
to go!" I wanted to murder him, and on the video you hear me huffing
out, "Stop talking, just stop talking right now!"

After vomiting more than eighty times, my body was in bad shape, but that's not what did me in. The issue was my mind. Rather than staying focused on the next step, the next energy gel, the here and now, I became obsessed with the daunting and overwhelming task ahead of me. There was simply *no way* I could run ninety-nine more miles feeling like this.

Therein was my fatal mistake . . . my mind was fixated on how I felt *right now and how much more I had to go.*

What I should have been telling myself is, *Things will get better, just don't stop moving.* But I had decided that I was toast and now it was just a matter of pulling the rip cord. Once I made the decision, I still had a whole lot of walking and shuffling to do before the chance would present itself to actually drop out, and by then it was the middle of the night. In the midst of this slog, I met a guy at one of the aid stations who barely spoke a lick of English. He saw my face and how I looked; he could see I wasn't going to make it. I'll never forget the way his face animated or the look in his eyes. He was like a man possessed by a demon. In halting English, he said to me, "If you cannot run, then you walk. If you cannot walk, then you crawl. Never NEVER give up!" But his pep talk came too late—I was already too checked out. I quit.

Then I sat on a bus for more than three hours, which was picking up the others who couldn't gut it out, who'd cried uncle like me. We looked at each other with varying degrees of shame in our eyes, all of us broken in one way or another. I eventually arrived at the hotel in the wee hours of night, slept in a bed, woke up, waited, and watched all the people who had been behind me finish, my heart in my mouth the entire time.

As I saw those competitors cross the finish line, I felt far more pain than I'd have felt if I'd just stuck with it. I was so mad at myself. I'm not even sure I can describe how I felt on an emotional level; I was almost crying watching people get their cold river water and leafy crowns. I was just so blown away by what they could do and I could not. (Not a single American completed the race that year, FYI.)

By Saturday of that week, I told myself, *I'm coming back.* I kept thinking about that guy I met in the night, that wild look in his eyes . . . he haunted me.

While his words didn't work in the moment, I let that man's attitude work its way into my DNA. I thought about the race every single day and I channeled him when I returned the following year. Physically, I was in approximately the same shape, but mentally, I was so much more fit. I said, *There's nothing that will keep me from finishing this time,* and I meant it.

The race the second year was two weeks after my wedding, yet I still came back. I returned again with Michael, who DNF'ed with me in 2011. (We have the YouTube documentaries to catalog the good, the bad, and the ugly from both races). If I'm being real here, I knew that first time I wasn't going to finish. If I were to have looked at myself in the mirror that day and asked, *Am I going to do this today?* Had I simply been honest with myself, the voice in my head would have said no. That voice was just overwhelming me, creating endless reasons why I could quit if I wanted to. Had I approached the race with the mindset that I was going to finish no matter what, the day would have gone so differently. You can lie to the people around you, but it is very hard to lie to yourself. I should have gone into the race with a different mindset. When quitting is not an option, everything that gets in the way is a speed bump, not a stop sign.

As I started the course in 2012, that man with his wild eyes was with me in my head for every stride. He set my cadence. On my forearms, I'd written in Sharpie, *Pain Is Temporary, Glory Is Forever* as a reminder of what these 153 miles meant to me. That became my mantra. I went into this race pumped up on positive self-talk, saying that I was going to enjoy myself and enjoy this race.

It was the hottest year on record in the history of the race, and I knew there would be no ice or outside assistance for the first fifty miles. At one hundred miles, roughly twenty hours into the race for me at 2:00 a.m., there's a 3,600-foot climb up a mountain. My brain gets loopy at night without sleep and all my ultramarathon friends make fun of me for being such a baby, but truly, I cannot function effectively with zero sleep.

I arrived at an aid station on the side of that mountain in the middle of the night. I asked someone in broken Greek to wake me in five minutes, then I proceeded to collapse onto the rocky shoulder of the dirt road. Instantly, the volunteer shook me awake. I said, "Why didn't you let me sleep?" She replied, "Five minutes, five minutes," with her palm splayed. I looked at my watch and, holy crap, she was right! It had been five minutes. I'd fallen asleep before my body hit the rocks. That was the deepest sleep of my life. But like blowing on a Nintendo game cartridge (you might be too young for this reference), the pause worked to give me the necessary reset. When my circadian rhythm kicked in during the sunrise, I shockingly felt good again.

I can't tell you how many times between 2011 and 2012 I'd visualized myself running this race, crossing the finish line, and kissing the feet of King Leonidas before drinking from the chalice of Eurotas River water. This is one of those races where the best years have maybe a 35 percent finish rate. The second year when I did it was the lowest rate in history. It was 19 percent. Only sixty-five people finished out of hundreds that year.

I was so proud to have been one of them.

I was sobbing as I ran those last few miles—it was all so emotional. But I had validated the mantra I'd etched onto my skin.

The next day, everyone who finishes is invited to a huge festival and awards dinner with around twenty thousand people packing the town squares. It's unlike any other race I've run; the history, the passion, the energy of the Greek people who embrace us like warriors. People attend from countries around the world, and the Japanese and Korean contingents all came over and bowed to us. They couldn't believe anyone had finished, given the heat. For the next two days, kids asked for my autograph as I walked through town, recovering and taking it all in.

There's no question that, before I die, I'm going to go back and run that race once again. It was both the hardest race I've ever done and the most fulfilling. When I watch Michael's 2011 and 2012 Spartathlon documentaries, I now notice that I was full of bravado in the first one, all "Let's do this!" But I knew inside that I'd likely bitten off more than I could chew.

When I decided to not finish, I fed myself lines like, "It's better to play it safe than not," and "I'm going to grow from this." But ultimately, that was all bullshit. It was me giving up before I even started. Every one of us has been guilty of this at a certain point, when we write whatever our version of a DNF speech is. When you've already thought of all the reasons you can't do it—why you should give up, why this won't work, why somebody else is better or more deserving than you—it creates an endless feedback loop of negativity. You will start to question whether your goal is even worth trying.

Instead, write the speech that you'll deliver at the finish line.

Your mindset going into a challenge shapes your results. How do you prepare for the things that might go wrong? How do you anticipate obstacles? Push through when every ounce of your being is telling you to quit? These aren't rhetorical questions and they apply far beyond the realm of ultramarathon running. You need to find the answers to them in your life and use that as fuel to achieve your goals.

I've said it before—when there's a problem, throw the kitchen sink at it. Give everything you've got. This works for anything: Let's say you're starting a new business and it's going poorly. You're not selling anything. You're not getting calls back. You're thinking of giving up. This is when you must dig deep and ask yourself, *What can I still put into this? What do I still have?* More often than not, challenging yourself can provide a fresh perspective, and maybe that's part of your solution.

Remember, whatever your Spartathlon is, if you can't run, walk. And if you can't walk, crawl. You might progress more slowly than you want, but you'll still get there.

The Price Is Right

Another way to prevent yourself from being your own worst enemy is to understand your own value. This is crucial when it comes to negotiation. When I started performing professionally early on, the biggest challenge wasn't learning the tricks. Instead, it was figuring out how I should price myself.

We know the prices of lots of things. When you go to the store, you know what the price of milk is, you know what the price of eggs is, but what in the world is the price of a magic show? This business is so niche and there are so few of us that there is no rubric for competitive pricing. This isn't like a commodity where you can go to three shops to find the best deal. I didn't know how to price myself effectively, because I didn't know the law of supply and demand.

Here's an easy hack—you keep going till people say no. When I was a kid and I walked into Zia's for the first time, I got paid fifty dollars for two hours and thought that making twenty-five dollars an hour was insanity. I mean, I was fourteen! It didn't occur to me to even wonder if I was undercharging or overcharging, because I was thrilled with what I got.

When I quit my job on Wall Street, I loved performing magic. It's a passion that became a profession. I landed my absolute dream job and it was my favorite thing to do. If you're lucky enough to work at something you love, how do you assign a value to it when you would effectively be okay doing it for free if there weren't bills to pay?

When this is the case, you have to consider opportunity cost. Think, *Hey, if I'm doing this for free for you, I can't be somewhere else doing this for money.* That's how you must value to your services. And when you have a family, the math becomes, *I'm giving you my time instead of spending it with my wife or my kids, or traveling or a vacation.* There's a finite pool of resources. I was my own worst enemy because I took every no personally. If somebody called me for a party and they turned me down directly, or tried to spare my feelings with the old "we went in another direction" excuse, it would honestly bring me down. If I got two or three no's in a week, I thought the world was ending and I'd never do another show again.

So, I would underprice myself all the time and also be very negotiable because I didn't assign myself enough value—and couldn't face those no's. At some point, you have to say to yourself, *Here's what I'm worth.* And a lot of that is confidence that builds over time. But it's very difficult early on. I was doing hundreds of shows a year for far too little money. I loved it because I liked being busy. But once I got married, I had somebody who I loved spending time with, and all those gigs now came with a cost. Parties and weekend outings that I could not attend, vacations that were impossible to book because of my performance schedule. Suddenly, I wanted some of my time back, and taking a gig became a very difficult choice, especially when I was on *America's Got Talent* and finally decided to have someone else handle my bookings.

That was a rough handoff. It felt akin to saying, "Oh, you're gonna take care of my baby," with no transition time; handing off the reins was no easy task for me after years of being a control freak. Now I have a manager who books my gigs. You have to be cognizant that it doesn't matter how much your clients love you, they will take advantage of you if you allow it. If they can get something cheaper, they will. That's the nature of the beast. That's what any of us would do. Let's say you own a market or a small mom-and-pop shop, someone walks in and says, "I want to buy that item right there." You say, "Great! It's twenty dollars." But then they say, "Eh, I'll give you fifteen." They'll want to argue that, because it's your store, you should be negotiable. But if you go to Walmart, you can't say, "I'm gonna pay you fifteen bucks." The cashier will be like, "Dude, it's Walmart. Do I need to call security?"

This is why I mentioned the concept of separating your sense of self from what you hope to accomplish. In entertainment, there are intermediaries like agents and managers, but for most people in their day-to-day lives, there is no one else representing you. The closest thing you can do is to take yourself out of the equation and become your own agent, because without that mindset shift you probably won't ask for what you actually need. But think of your agent as a cutthroat shark who believes that you are the best thing since sliced bread—and that you deserve every penny and then some. Find a way to silo yourself into Regular You and Agent You so you don't undersell your services and talents, especially because Agent You wants his or her 15 percent.

Ultimately, I'm a people pleaser. My whole job is to bring others joy and wonder. I'm there to make sure you have an incredible experience and want to generate good feelings from the moment you reach out to me until I leave the show . . . and even afterward in your memories. That's why it's imperative that I separate myself from the less enjoyable aspects of my job, parts that every profession has. You know what I mean—the awkward moments, the hard asks, the negotiations. I'm talking about when to say that things aren't right, when to say no to events, when you're not being valued properly, or when agreements aren't being honored.

If you're selling a service, you're not hired because somebody likes your smile. You're providing real value, whether for their business, pleasure, or life. You're working. So understand that you can ask for things and you can stick to your guns on certain standards. When it comes to determining a dollar amount, the only rule that matters is: You can always come down in price; you can never go up. That's not just in negotiations, it's everything in life. Whatever you want, start by asking much higher than your bottom line. Set the anchor high. Then if you negotiate down to what you really want or need, everyone feels great. You got what you wanted, they got a deal, and both of you walked away happy from this interaction.

Decide what you want, start higher, and give yourself the option to lower your price to where both people can win. Sometimes you'll be shocked by what you can get. You begin high, and some people will just say yes right away. You both feel great about what just happened. This applies to situations outside of money as well. The same rules of negotiation apply to your time, your energy, your plans, your thoughtfulness. Set yourself up to always exceed expectations and overdeliver on your promises. Let's say you're a tailor and you know you can have those pants hemmed by Wednesday. Tell your client you'll have them ready by Friday, then they're pleasantly surprised when they get that call from you on Wednesday. And they're going to tell all their friends.

When you learn to price yourself right and to leave room in the negotiations, everyone wins.

Setting the World Record

By now, you've gathered that I get a little obsessive about racing. For me it's about pushing myself as far as I can possibly go, past what I thought was my breaking point, not just physically but also mentally. Ultramarathons teach you that when you feel you have absolutely nothing left, not one drop of gas in the tank, your mind is almost always lying to you. Your mind controls your body, and in there I see a direct parallel to what I do for a living: Learning how to trick the minds of others is what I do to myself when running extreme distances. Chasing those dramatic highs and lows is intoxicating and in many ways addictive. You learn so much about who you really are when facing tremendous adversity and being able to battle through it. It's not unusual for people who have jobs that challenge their bodies to seek out hobbies that are more cerebral, and vice versa.

Running allows me to heighten my mental acuity. In fact, exercise is known to provide a litany of benefits, from aerobic fitness to improving nervous system plasticity, which helps you adapt, rewire, and learn in response to experiences, stimuli, injuries, etc.[7] My moods are more stabilized thanks to exercise. A good exercise regimen is tantamount to mental health, so if you're feeling down, go exercise. Runner's high is *real* and it will up your endorphins and lower your stress. Way to not be your own worst enemy, right?

Physical activity isn't just important for your body, but also your mind because raising your heart rate increases blood flow to the brain. You want this extra blood flow because it increases the molecules that spur the formation of new synapses, improving how sharp your mind and memory are, particularly long-term memory.[8] Now, am I suggesting you train for an ultramarathon? Ha, no. You really have to want to embrace that degree of suffering. But if you've been on the fence about starting to take walks after dinner or finally try your hand at pickleball, consider this your sign to do it. Challenge yourself, set a goal, and see it through to completion.

In early 2022, I'd spent months training for the Umstead 100 Mile Endurance Run in North Carolina. Right before I was set to travel to the race, a very successful client of mine, who happens to be a billionaire, asked me to change my plans and perform at his wife's birthday party on race day. He'd hired me a couple weeks prior and said it was so much fun that he needed me back to amaze a different set of guests. My manager declined on my behalf and explained that I had a personal obligation. I'd trained hard, sacrificed, and was super excited to run this ultramarathon. On top of that, the race was supposed to have taken place the year before, but got canceled due to COVID-19. Once it was finally rescheduled, two high school friends planned to fly in and help crew me at the race. We were all excited to get together again after many years. And my running one hundred miles provided the excuse we needed to make it happen. There are some things you can't put a price on. I did not forgo all that cake and all those burritos to change my plans at the last moment. But alas, everyone has a number.

Let me clue you in on a little secret . . . billionaires aren't fans of the word *no*. It's not even in their vocabulary. This guy was insistent that I be there, and again, I said no. But he kept asking. So I finally told my manager to quote an outrageous number that I had basically pulled out of thin air, and she said, "Whoa, I think that's going to ruin the relationship." I was absolutely fine with walking away from this gig and running my race, which is the strongest position to be in when it came to a negotiation.

Still, I persuaded my manager to throw out this ridiculous figure. (If fourteen-year-old Oz was bowled over by twenty-five dollars an hour, the sum adult Oz demanded would have *put him in the ground*.) Remember, I can read people and knew that within thirty seconds, my client would text back with a yes because he'd already heard no from us four times, which was four times too many in his book. It was all about winning.

Lo and behold, the mentalist was right and he said yes. So . . . I wasn't going to run that race in North Carolina after all. It's a weird feeling to simultaneously be furious while also trying to wrap your mind around the biggest payday you've ever gotten for taking a twenty-two-dollar Uber ride from your home.

I was in amazing shape and didn't want to waste my fitness or the long hours spent getting there. I looked for something else I could do and decided to run one hundred miles around Central Park. Totally normal and sane right? This is hallowed ground for me, the holiest of the holy: That 6.1-mile loop is my favorite place on the planet to run, and trust me, I've been to a lot of places. If I was going to do this, I decided that the run should have a purpose and be for the greater good. The world was reeling from the recent Russian invasion of Ukraine, and I saw horrific images and videos each day on TV, so I wanted to try to make a difference.

During this run, I'd raise money for children in Ukraine. I was out for a run the next morning with my training partner Tom Knight and told him about my idea, to which he replied, "Hey, last year a guy named Robbie Balenger broke the record for the most loops ever run. And it's all over the press. It was in *Men's Health*, it was in *GQ*." And then the idea became *very* interesting to me because it wasn't going to just be me competing against myself.

It's funny how ideas that are almost nonsensical can turn into something tangible. Especially if you're passionate and if there's some element of your goal that's good and selfless. I set up a page for donations and the whole thing caught fire. People heard about it and shared with others, and interest started to grow. Luckily, I'd also landed in a good news cycle, and it took off from there.

I ended up breaking the record, raising $116,000 and running 116 miles. No one's broken my record yet. Of course, when I finished, I felt I could have done a twentieth lap, which would've gotten me to 122 miles. The goal was to break the record. This is a great example of defining your goals effectively and then being relentless in your pursuit of them. I could have gotten one more loop in, but I had a small injury and I knew that if I didn't complete the whole loop, there would've been a whole lot of suffering for naught. My crew was tired and I had achieved what we set out to do, so they didn't push me to keep going. Plus it was midnight, and the next morning, I had to fly to Augusta, Georgia, to perform a show at The Masters. To do one more loop, I would have had to take a bunch more caffeine to gut it out; I likely wouldn't have fallen asleep until 6:00 a.m. and would have been a wreck the next day at my show. But I never forget the lessons of Spartathlon: Pain is temporary, glory is forever! I'm pretty good at letting things go, but there's a tiny piece of real estate in my brain that tells me I'm going to try to better that record at some point.

What's ironic is that I just wanted to do something good for humanity to balance out a healthy payday. My thinking wasn't transactional—my hope was to give back in some way while chasing a personal goal. Yet I found myself on the front cover of *The New York Times*, with a full two-page insert inside. I couldn't pay a publicist hundreds of thousands of dollars to get that kind of great press. Reuters picked up the story and it went global! This wasn't premeditated or part of some big idea. I took the initiative and went for it, the entire plan came together in ten days as I tried to turn lemons into lemonade, and all because I knew my worth.

I want you to ask yourself, *What can I accomplish when I come to terms with my own worth? What happens when I silence my inner critic and stop being my own worst enemy? How can my life change for the better when the voice in my head starts to dish out positive self-talk consistently?*

If I hadn't made changes, I'd never have learned to ask for what I'm worth. I'd never have completed the Spartathlon. And I'd certainly never have set a world record.

Never forget that a brighter, happier, more successful future awaits you, and it starts the moment you realize you deserve to be the star of your own movie.

By the way, I never slept on the goal of being on that podcast—I thought about it every day, wondering how I could get a toe in the door. I listened for years and saw where my network overlapped with past guests and close friends of the host. Then I would ensure that I found a way to amaze them and that word would slowly but surely trickle back. I played the long game, stayed patient, and never took my eyes off the prize. My persistence was dogged and my progress wasn't linear. Sometimes it would be two steps forward and one back, but I was perpetually focused and in pursuit of that goal—and I finally got on! By the time this book is in your hands, I'll have been on *The Joe Rogan Experience* and those years of planning and converting *no* to *not yet* worked! It was an amazing achievement and one that left me feeling truly fulfilled.

EIGHT

Ask for Help

We often shy away from reaching out for help when we need something because we're worried that being open and appearing vulnerable will be mistaken for weakness. This has been a particular struggle of mine because I hate the idea of being a burden. I know I'm not alone in previously having taken on more than I could handle because I wanted to be able to be self-contained . . . and doing so was often to my detriment.

One of the most powerful lessons I've learned comes from running, but it applies to all of life: If you want to be great, you have to push yourself out of your comfort zone because that's where the change happens. But what you must realize is that *you don't have to go it alone*. I'll walk you through not only how to ask for help, but also finding the right person to ask. Your best bet is seeking out someone who is currently where you want to be in five years. Even in a niche profession like mine, there are those who've done it before. I'll share the story of learning with my mentor, Bruce Kessler, who's one of the reasons I've reached the level I am at today.

The secret formula for getting a mentor's buy-in is simple: Be of value to them. Find out what you can do for them and then do it. Think like they think and make them see themselves in you. When there's a give-and-take, people are much more likely to give. When you find the right mentor, they'll ask you the questions you should be asking yourself—and that's the fast track to success. The converse here is that if you're asking for help, you should just as freely be giving it. Paying it forward is one of the best investments you can ever make, as its returns are often exponential and can be deeply impactful.

In this chapter, I'll talk about learning to let go of that need for control, to grip the steering wheel a little less tightly, or even better, to give someone else the chance to drive. Remember, you're not failing if you can't juggle every single thing—you're overwhelmed. I'll cover how to off-load what isn't mission critical.

Tear Down Your Walls

I was not good at asking for help for the longest time. I would try to shoulder as much as I could, and in many instances, took on more than I could handle, because in my head I was Superman, and as everyone knows, he has no sidekick. We think we're heroes when we try to do it all: so strong, so competent, women and men of steel. Yet when operating at the I-alone-can-fix-it level, things often end up falling apart. Right? We'll say, "Nah, I've got this handled. First, I'm gonna do this and then I'm gonna do this," despite the fact that there are only twenty-four hours in a day, forgetting that we need to sleep, shower, and eat lunch.

When we try to be a jack-of-all-trades, we inevitably become a master of none. Over the years and with a lot of trial and error, I've learned what I'm really good at and where I'm lacking. To be our most successful, we have to focus on the unique skills that set us apart and delegate the other tasks if possible. That can be a difficult realization, but recognizing this was both smart and healthy because it allowed me to reclaim my time and energy. When I finally made the decision to off-load responsibilities where I don't excel to people who are better at them than me, everything changed.

Let's be clear—asking for help can feel hard, but you have to remember that vulnerability is not a weakness. Let me say it louder for those who are trying to carry the whole world on their shoulders like Atlas: *Vulnerability isn't weakness.* Dr. Brené Brown, one of the foremost experts on vulnerability, says, "The difficult thing is that vulnerability is the first thing I look for in you and the last thing I'm willing to show you. In you, it's courage and daring. In me, it's weakness. This is where shame comes into play. Vulnerability is about showing up and being seen. It's tough to do that when we're terrified about what people might see or think. When we're fueled by the fear of what other people think or that gremlin that's constantly whispering, 'You're not good enough,' in our ear, it's tough to show up. We end up hustling for our worthiness rather than standing in it."[1]

The hard truth is that the more vulnerable and open we are, the better off we become, even though showing vulnerability can crack the door to potential rejection and pain. Still, the benefits far outweigh the costs when you look at the science behind it.

Our brains are programmed for us to be a part of the collective. We aren't meant to be lone wolves. When we're able to lower our guard and connect with others, we trigger the neurotransmitter that releases that sweet brain candy called dopamine. When dopamine is released, whatever the behaviors are that triggered it are reinforced to create a positive feedback loop.

When we allow ourselves to be vulnerable, to let others in, there's the potential to release oxytocin. Oxytocin is triggered by physical touch, acts of kindness, and positive social interactions. It's produced in the hypothalamus and it gets distributed into our bloodstream via the pituitary gland.[2] While oxytocin is most often associated with facilitating childbirth, men produce it as well. Basically, it's a love hormone, and who doesn't want a hit of the love hormone?

Also, allowing ourselves to be vulnerable can impact the anterior cingulate cortex, because when we share our feelings of pain or we empathize with someone else, we trigger this region. What I mean by that is, when we let down our guard and connect on an emotional level—whether we're expressing our own hurt feeling or someone else's—we're engaging a part of the brain that's wired for deep human connection, understanding, and even suffering. This confirms that vulnerability isn't a weakness. Instead, it's neurologically tied to empathy and shared experience.

Essentially, vulnerability lights up our neurotransmitters like a Christmas tree. The more we allow ourselves to be vulnerable, the more likely we are to build healthy relationships based on trust, mutual respect, and intimacy. You might think that being vulnerable would cause us to feel weakened and compromised, but actually, the opposite happens. Vulnerability helps us manage our emotions, makes us more resilient, and can improve our self-esteem because it leads to a more positive self-image.[3]

There are a few different strategies you can use when it comes to embracing vulnerability. Just recognizing that you're afraid to allow yourself to be vulnerable is a step in the right direction. Another strategy is to not accept your own negative thoughts as fact. We've talked at length about that snowy driveway analogy. The more you're offering yourself positive self-talk, the more you'll create that neural pathway. And you don't have to start big by sharing your every truth—you could (and maybe even should) start small by, say, asking a coworker to walk you through the new sales reporting tool because you didn't quite grasp the nuances the first time. That will build your relationship because it will create trust and good feelings between you. As always, you have to give yourself some grace when you start this process, because we're working to change long-ingrained patterns. Learning to read your own mind and tap into your greatness does take effort.

Let Go of the Wheel

I'm not saying that relinquishing control is easy, but I am saying it's necessary, so let's take some steps right now to put you on the right track. I want you to stand back and assess where you are in your life. Ask yourself, *What's bogging me down? What's keeping me from firing on every piston? What am I good at? What am I not good at? Do I even need to improve what I'm not good at? What's my highest and best use?*

The answers to these questions will help you determine what tasks and responsibilities might not need to be on your plate.

I'll give a tangible example here. Maybe you're like me and you're not good at managing your bookkeeping and calculating your taxes. First, let's recognize that this is not a personal flaw, okay? Not enjoying organizing receipts and keeping a spreadsheet is not a character defect. Poor knowledge of the tax code doesn't mean you're a bad person, in fact it likely suggests you're more fun to be around. I imagine your taxes are not something you enjoy doing or want to work on getting better at. (They certainly weren't for me.) The computations are nothing but a necessary evil . . . and a civic duty. I mean, who doesn't want roads, schools, and firefighters?

In a case like this, most likely it's time to get an accountant and say, "The money I'm spending, it gets repurposed into time. And what I'm doing with that time could yield a lot more value than sitting around for a few hours each month, bookkeeping and figuring out my deductions." I'd say this is a silly example, but it's something that every one of us has to do if we'd like to avoid jail time.

I was terrible about trying to do it all myself for a long, long time. But now I've started asking for help, even going so far as to rely on a crew (more on that shortly). I realized that time is a nonrenewable resource and becomes more finite the older we get. So I had to force myself to start spending my time more wisely and not get hung up on the things that were outside my control.

A chore that's oddly specific to what I do is creating the materials that are used in my shows. For example, I have these envelopes that have to be sealed in a specific way. In a given week, I have a bunch of things that need to be stapled or glued. My act is pretty minimalist, but there are things that I've had to make for years. I used to just sit in front of the TV for hours, doing arts and crafts until my hands started feeling arthritic, yet I felt that paying these dues were necessary for my craft. This was the very definition of labor that could be outsourced, and my stubbornness was getting in the way of enjoying my life. As my wife pointed out, I could literally train a monkey to do the same thing in twenty minutes. Let's just say the incessant hammering of the stapler while watching our favorite show wasn't exactly an aphrodisiac . . . shocker! I had to recognize that there are people on Craigslist who are very driven, ambitious, and hardworking and who want to work from home with a minimum of interaction from a boss-type. This was the perfect task to off-load . . . even though I resisted for years.

Eventually, I realized I had to hand the wheel over to them, so I did so with the caveat, "Here's what I need you to make, following these exact specifications. I'm going to reward you handsomely if you do a great job." Even though it went against every fiber of my being, I outsourced the making of those materials to others. What I never expected was that delegating this seemingly little task would be such a weight off my shoulders. I had to get past the voice in my head that kept telling me, "Wait, are they going to do as good a job as me?"

Guess what? They did. Then all of a sudden, hours in my day opened up and I realized, "Wow, that was so worth it." It's no different than fighting against, say, hiring a landscaper to cut your grass, and then finally giving in and finding yourself with an expanse of weekend.

Consider areas in your own life that you could pare down. We hire other people all the time to do jobs for us, whether it's Rick the Roofer or Pat the Plumber. While it might sound like a luxury, what if you decided to take a taxi to the office instead of driving yourself? You would buy yourself half an hour of uninterrupted time to answer your emails, and start your day ahead of the game.

An issue that gets in the way of delegating can sometimes be that we think of things too transactionally. We think, *I'm going to do this for them, which means they're going to do this for me.* We see a clear and distinct correlation, that if I take my hand off the wheel, then my expectation is that all of these other things will happen when someone else is allowed to drive. While that's often the case, it's worth noting that some of the best things that ever happen to us aren't transactional, especially when we relinquish some control. When we trust others to fill our shoes, we're afforded all sorts of new freedoms. Let's say you're organizing a large-scale event and instead of micromanaging every detail, you decide to hand off the planning to a pro. Not only can they do a fantastic job, but also they add thoughtful touches you'd never have expected or thought of. Delegating often pays off in ways you can't foresee.

Not everything has to be transactional. This is why any time somebody reaches out for an autograph, I mail them one. I don't charge; I don't need a self-addressed stamped envelope. I figure if someone is a big enough fan of me that they want a headshot or an autograph or a signed playing card, they're going to get one. You'd think I get nothing from this, but you'd be wrong. Every request galvanizes me, fills my tank, gives me a boost on the days when I might need it the most.

When I was a teenager, I would attend magic lectures, which are kind of like social hangout for magicians. Yes, there are conferences and conventions, but people really connect in their local magic shops. For me, that shop was Wunderground Magic in Royal Oak, Michigan. They hosted lectures where they brought in professional magicians. Those of us in the audience had maybe read their books or watched some of their videos; here was the chance to meet them in person and learn some behind-the-scenes material. The fun part was that afterward, people would hang out and talk shop. As a kid who was just starting out in magic, it was amazing.

Being treated like an adult by people I was a huge fan of, even though I was a teenager, meant everything to me. I've seen people nowadays who, when they meet a YouTuber, will melt into tears because of the intimacy involved, like, "Oh my God, I've been watching your videos!" To you, they might seem like a superstar, even though other people have no idea who they are. But value is all in the eye of the beholder. Having those people treat me with respect, having them say, "Come on, we're all going out," and then getting to sit down with them almost as an equal and absorb their advice was a feeling I recall fondly to this day. There was nothing really in it for them, yet they included me anyway and that just blew me away. This was a defining point for me, and it colored my whole understanding of how I should interact and connect with people in my own career. The concepts of paying it forward and having a seat at the table have stayed with me.

Here's a story that I recall far more fondly than my folks do. One night, I went out with a group of magicians after a lecture. It was 1996 so I didn't have a cell phone and ended up staying out until 2:30 a.m.

because I wasn't paying attention to the time; I was just too enamored with the company. I was fourteen years old and had never done anything like this before.

By this point, my parents had banded together, searched the neighborhood, and filed a missing person report. They were driving to every diner that was still open. When they finally found me, knee-deep in card tricks, coffee cups, and cheeseburgers, their reaction was a combination of relief that I was still alive and wanting to kill me at the same time. I was just hanging out with a bunch of magicians on a school night and never even considered going home or the time. I was sitting with magician Gregory Wilson, who may as well have been Paul McCartney to me, hanging on his every word. My parents basically had to wrestle me into the car.

Because of that experience, I've always tried to re-create it for others. We'll talk more about paying it forward later in this chapter.

Build Your Team

Becoming your best self sometimes requires recognizing that you need a team. You cannot always go it alone. When it comes to long races, crew members help get you across the finish line when you no longer believe you can do it or are an absolute physical disaster. In the ultramarathon space, *crewing* is a verb. The crew are effectively personal assistants in every regard. They're there to check on the runner's nutrition, their hydration, what they're wearing, and to be their strength when things start going wrong.

My chief crew member is Ryan Dexter, nickname "Iceman." Less *Top Gun*, more literal: He constantly dowses me in ice during hot races, ha! I like to say he is a certified badass in his own right. The man has run 150-mile races galore. We met while running 2.4-mile loops around Lake Nokomis in Minnesota for twenty-four hours straight at a race called FANS (totally normal, right?). We lost touch for about a decade or so and then reconnected. He's as selfless and loyal as it gets, and I'm honored to call him a friend. Michael Halovatch is another great friend who has been with me through thick and thin, through vomiting and you don't even wanna know what else. When I've been ready to quit, he has tough-talked me out of it more times than I care to admit. Michael Arnstein is a legendary ultramarathoner, and we go way, way back to my very first ultramarathon. And last, but certainly not least, is Dustin Emrani. An elite collegiate 800-meter runner who's now a distance athlete, he's the ultimate hype man and could get a smile and laugh out of anyone. Needless to say, it takes a village.

The thing about the ultramarathon community is there's maybe five to ten people who care about winning at any given race. Everybody else out there is on a personal mission against themselves to simply finish the race or battle the clock. Let's say you're on the road and someone's hurting and they need food, the other runners will stop without a second thought and attend to you, "How are you doing, man, take these gels. Let's get you back." They might slow down with you for the next ten miles to make sure you make it. It's such a selfless enterprise. We're all in it together, as opposed to cyclists and some triathletes (not all) who behave like scumbags. (If you know, you know. Sorry! Not sorry.)

When you're in an ultramarathon, you're battling demons. You are going to push your body in ways that somebody who's run a marathon can't even fathom. In a 100-miler or longer, you may find yourself walking for twelve hours straight while in the throes of terrible pain, GI distress, or hallucinations. It's like you're bringing a knife to a gunfight. It's a different beast. And you can always talk tough when you're sitting on the couch, but when you're out there and you're in it, it's a trial by fire where you figure out who you really are at your core when all the layers are peeled away. In this case, you cannot fake it till you make it. You can't buy the achievement; you have to *earn* it, and that is what makes it so fulfilling.

Generally speaking, in most of those races, you don't know what's going to happen. I can train for months, yet fall apart by mile 27 and not understand why. When things start to go downhill, the key is to quickly begin problem-solving. You reverse engineer the same way I do in mentalism: *Why am I not feeling well? Is this my mind tricking me? Do I have low blood sugar?* For example, when you have low blood sugar, you don't have an indicator light that blinks Low on Fuel; instead, you begin having negative thoughts.

You feel tired, you feel miserable, and you start thinking, *I have to quit*. That is the moment you need your crew. In races, as in life, having a crew makes it better, especially when you can be there for them, too. When you're part of a group you can trust, your performance improves. This is directly linked to the production of oxytocin. For example, studies have shown that when people build social ties at work, it's almost like taking a performance-enhancing drug, likely because that's what oxytocin is.[4]

Take, for example, Badwater, nicknamed "the world's toughest footrace." It is a 135-mile run from the lowest point in the Western Hemisphere to the base of Mount Whitney, the highest point in the contiguous United States. Oh wait, did I forget this is in Death Valley, the hottest place on earth . . . in the middle of July! At the start of the race, the first year I participated, it was a brisk 124 degrees Fahrenheit, or 51 degrees Celsius, with no shade anywhere in sight. One section is a seventeen-mile uphill with gusting headwinds that make you feel as if you're inside a convection oven with a hair dryer pointing at your face. My crew would dunk me in ice water every few miles, and by the next time I would see them, yup, you guessed it, I'd be bone dry. My hair would be brittle. In this setting, your crew can be the difference between life and death and are there to ensure that the goals you went in with remain the top priority, because during peak suffering you might want to give up. While the players might change up depending on who is free to lean into supporting me in a particular race, my crew is always made up of fellow nutcases who have seen and been through it all. They know all my excuses. A good crew won't let you quit if there's anything left inside of you. They do not allow you to give up on yourself unless medically necessary.

Look at your own life right now. Who do you have to cheer you on? Who's always in your corner pulling for you? Who inspires you to just keep going? These people are your crew, and if they're doing this for you, make sure you're returning the favor. Studies have shown that having a good friend literally gets into your blood: It makes changes for the better to every aspect of your health, from blood pressure to stress response to your immune system.[5] Having people you can rely on has been found to be as important a factor in your long-term health as exercise and not smoking.[6]

For running, my crew is there to remind me that I am comfort-driven and that if I want to be great, I have to break out of that zone. My crew are people I know who are going to raise me up, elevate my game. (The same should apply to your crew, whether they're in your personal or professional life.) They make it so that I can't quit, because if I did, I couldn't look them in the eye. Midrace, crewing becomes a thankless endeavor for them as I transform into a whiny prima donna. We have a running joke that at some point, usually around a hundred miles, I start getting annoyed at them. I can't even tell you why. And when I see them, I'll say, "How about some proactive crewing?" And we'll laugh because we all know they're literally about to kill me. These guys have been up since 5:00 a.m. and were organizing stuff the night before. They have no time to themselves. They're stopping every two or three miles and lathering sunblock on my legs, touching me in places they don't want to be near. They're cleaning me up, giving me food.

In addition to the crew, there are pacers who play an equally, and at times even more, important role. They run parts of the race with you. When I ran from Montauk to Manhattan in a day, I publicized what I was doing on my Instagram. And a lot of people saw that story and spontaneously decided to tag along for part of the journey. One guy was going to run with us for ten miles. He ended up running thirty-five miles that night. Wow. He was intoxicated by the experience. He kept saying, "Dude, I can't stop. It's just such a rush!" When I did the Central Park run, I only did one loop out of the nineteen alone because so many people knew about it. I even sent my plans to my client mailing list. Hundreds of people who came out had seen me on TV, and they wanted to witness the run. They brought signs and cheered. (Did it feel just like that running scene in *Rocky II*? Yes. Yes, it did.) They didn't know it, but they were absolutely my crew as well. We fed off each other's energy and it made the time absolutely fly by.

I'm always looking for opportunities to return the favor, because I get something out of it, too—it fills my cup. I like being able to help kids starting out fast-track past some of the mistakes I made, both in the world of running and mentalism. This brings me to a serendipitous meeting when I was nineteen years old with two college kids who had just started a company called Penguin Magic. They're a big part of my history. At the time, they were running the company out of their apartment at the University of Michigan, right where I happened to be going to school.

Acar Altinsel and Maxwell Murphy were hired to make a website for some Winklevoss-type investors, and once they got into it, they thought, *Why the heck are we making this for them instead of ourselves? We're the ones with the talent.* It's crucial to note here that this was in the early 2000s, when everyone still had dial-up. Broadband was just starting and streaming video was not yet a real thing. You could download music, but not video, and it took an hour. So, what these guys did was a paradigm shift.

Back then, buying magic tricks required going to a magic store and having someone demo the trick one on one. You'd point to something in a glass case and say, "That one." The magician working behind the counter would sell you the trick, then take you into a back room and teach it to you. And then you'd take the trick home with you, which was generally a gimmick or a specialty item, like a silk scarf on an invisible retractable filament, or lifelike pistachio nuts that were magnetized.

What the Penguin Magic guys did was a totally new. They started making demo videos of tricks. Their store had thousands of tricks, and they began performing the tricks on video instead of having to teach them in person in the store. This gave them so much scalability. Plus, the instructional videos were far superior to just sending you home with paper instructions. That was a huge value-add and it became a game changer.

The service altered the magic industry in the way that Uber has changed how we get rides now. By pure luck, I found out there was a magic store in Ann Arbor, which was unbelievable to me because I went to school there. What were the odds? Even better, my girlfriend's friend knew the guy who owned the shop. So I went to meet them one night after doing a restaurant gig, when I was all dressed up. I performed three tricks and they said, "Oh my God, will you do demo videos for us?" They saw potential that I didn't even know I had.

There was no money at first; I was just making their videos because

I got to learn a bunch of tricks without paying for them. I had no idea that having learned these tricks would be so important to me a few years later. (Put a pin in this because we'll get to that story in another chapter.) I was basically just giving them a hand because I loved it.

Their business grew quickly and they ended up moving to Las Vegas and getting a big warehouse in Sacramento. We made several videos together on DVD. One of the DVDs is called *Born to Perform Card Magic*, starring yours truly. This DVD is the equivalent of Britney Spears's debut album in the late nineties, as it was the highest-selling card-magic instructional DVD ever. I was twenty-one at the time this video came out in 2002 and not kidding when I say that nearly every magician on the planet between the ages of thirteen and thirty-five bought this thing. Around that time, I toured in Asia and saw a street vendor selling bootleg copies of my video, dubbed in Mandarin. My first taste of global success!

The success of these videos allowed me to travel the world. On the back of this wide recognition, I was invited to lecture in over forty countries. Magicians everywhere would say to me, "You're Oz Pearlman from Penguin Magic!" To me, that was priceless. Funny story: My wife one day invited our neighbor Karen over with her boyfriend Mike, and as I opened the door to meet them, he exclaimed "Holy f'ing s***, you're Oz Pearlman!" Turns out, he was a closeted magic nerd and had grown up with my videos. (His girlfriend, now wife, found this out at the same time as we did and had a lot of questions.)

Years and years later, a friend of mine in Israel did a trick that felt vaguely familiar. So I went to Penguin Magic's website and bought the instant download instructional video, because I wanted to understand how he did it. What happened next was like a *Black Mirror* episode, as I found that I was the one teaching the trick to myself.

What I can't get over is my own foresight. I want to say I had a master plan, but I truly just stumbled into it. If I hadn't been so willing to lend a hand in those early days, I'd probably still be working in global technology infrastructure. So if you're on the fence about lending a hand, keep in mind you never know where it might take you.

Find a Mentor

Ask yourself where you want to be five to ten years from now. The best advice I can give you is to then seek out someone who has already achieved a similar goal. For me, that person was Bruce Kessler.

After my folks got divorced, my grandma came to live with us because my mom was struggling. My escape was to perform tricks all the time so I never had to deal with all the pain. I thought maybe I could just be the dancing clown to take my mom's mind off things.

One day, my grandmother and I were at a Borders bookstore and I was playing with cards, because I was *always* playing with cards, with coins, doing moves all the time. A man in his early thirties noticed my sleight of hand and asked my grandmother about my interest in magic. Her eyes lit up knowing how excited I would be to meet a fellow magician and especially one with so much experience. He'd even been professional for a while before he went back to working a day job.

At my grandmother's behest, Bruce became my mentor and a father figure. No, it was more than that—he became my champion, my shaman. He did more than show me how to do new tricks. He taught me the value of questioning my own preconceived notions, like when he convinced me to try sushi for the first time. He helped condition me to think differently, to shift out of autopilot, and I owe him so much because of it.

Again, I met him because of dumb luck. There was no internet in

1995 and I'd have never found him if I'd gone looking on my own, especially without my grandmother's help. Bruce opened my eyes to all these new ways of thinking, and that gave me a lot more confidence. He helped me to start thinking in a more mature manner and treated me like an adult.

Basically, Bruce was the guy to give me that much needed push out of my very narrow comfort zone, saying, "I'm going to show you some new stuff. Maybe you like it. Maybe you don't."

At the time, I was very into what's called "gimmicks" in the magic world, basically props or specialty single-use items that allowed you to do one amazing trick reliably, like a modified card deck. It was like I just wanted to take a pill and get the results, instead of doing the hard work of learning. Bruce was instrumental because he made me step back and look at the bigger picture. Did I want to be a guy who bought tricks, or did I want to be a performer? He explained to me that I couldn't do a show with gimmicks alone; instead, I would have to do the legwork of reading books and learning how to do dozens of tricks with a single deck. He helped me see that I needed to build a foundation of solid skills, making mistakes along the way, rather than just going for what was quick and flashy. His lessons have stayed with me my entire life.

As important as he was to me during my formative years, eventually we lost touch when I moved away to college. But I always felt in a unique, New Agey way that when the time was right, we would reconnect because so much of who I'd become happened under his watch. His is one of the only phone numbers I have memorized to this day. Years later, I finally called him. I hadn't talked to him in more than a decade, but I'd been on *America's Got Talent* and I wanted him to know how he helped me get there. And he was just so proud of me; it was very fulfilling.

Having a mentor is important for learning to read your own mind because we often need an editor. We need someone to look at what we're doing with a critical eye toward improvement, because we're often too close to whatever the subject is.

We always consider how important mentorship is professionally, but it's rare that we delve into the neuroscience behind mentorship. Yet it's equally significant. The mentor/mentee relationship can generate far-reaching impact and results. UCLA social neuroscience professor Matthew Lieberman sums it up this way: "Being socially connected is our brain's lifelong passion."[7] Mentors fulfill so many functions that impact how we think and feel and act, from role-modeling behaviors to helping mentees develop skills and realize their aspirations.[8]

The bottom line is that effective mentoring leads directly to structural changes in the brain, with tangible improvements in productivity and goal attainment.[9]

But if you don't have a caring Israeli grandma to help you find a mentor, I'll share some strategies for seeking one in the next section.

Mentoring Is a Verb

I have five to ten people whom I mentor on a regular basis. Not daily given our busy schedules, but I have a touchpoint with them every couple of months. I think of myself almost like a Jedi sharing his knowledge of the Force, which is so nerdy and cheesy, but in some ways oddly true. I'm there at the right moment for a lot of these people, and vice versa. And more than anything else, I provide guidance, but not as some all-knowing being. Instead, I tell them what they need to hear, and what I think deep down they already know. I'm ruthlessly honest. So when somebody says to me, "I want to get on TV," I'll challenge them as to what's stopping them and to list for me all that they've done so far. I don't give them the answers; rather, I want them to figure it out on their own because then it clicks, like teaching someone how to fish rather than just buying them a fish dinner.

What's great about mentoring is that mentees reinvigorate us. We get to feel like we're helping others, and they have an effervescence that's exciting, especially when we are further in our career and it becomes easy to be a little bit jaded. Even though I'm the mentor, my mentees still call me on my crap. I might be complaining, "Ugh, I've gotta fly here, I've gotta fly there, and I have TV shoots." Meanwhile, my mentee is looking at me like, "Take it easy with your caviar problems, I would kill for a tenth of this." It gives me perspective and reminds me to have gratitude. Mentoring people helps me remain humble and grounded.

So, if you need a mentor, how do you get one?

I wish that everyone who's made it would welcome being a mentor, but that is rarely the case. Persistence is the key to recruiting one, with the caveat that there is a thin line between being persistent and annoying. A lot of those who've made it don't want to help others because they feel like success is a zero-sum game, especially if they came up without a mentor. There's an attitude of, *Why do I need to tell you what I've learned when you didn't earn it?* While that's not easy to work around, it's not impossible.

A great way to find a mentor is to make yourself of value to them. Bring something to the table. For example, a fellow performer who had been emailing me off and on for years decided he wanted to find a way to help me. He reached out saying, "I see that some of your photos on your website are out of date," because he'd taken the time (that I did not have) to sit down and analyze my social media presence, and he came up with a plan to make it all current. Not only that, he said, "Hey, let me take these things off your plate for you." It was so helpful to me that I suddenly couldn't wait to repay the favor.

It's kind of like if you buy somebody a gift: They always have to say thank you. Most people express appreciation, and that's not just manners, that's a part of the science of persuasion, according to social psychologist Robert Levine. He cites the example of charities giving you a free pen along with a request for a donation, because people are far more likely to give back if they get something. Per Levine, "Most of us are usually driven by a sense of equity and fairness. When someone does something for us, we feel obligated to do something for them in return."[10]

Getting that thank you back provides another touchpoint and chance to further the relationship. If there's a way to be of service, find it.

In every single industry, even one as niche as mentalism, there are mentors. Unlike teachers, mentors serve more as long-term advisers. You can attract mentors by asking the questions they might not even be thinking of asking themselves, and doing so will open their eyes.

As someone hoping to connect with a mentor, ask yourself, *What can I do to add value for them? What do I have to offer them that will make their life easier? How can I make an impression and create a mutually beneficial relationship?* Never be afraid to take that step, to be too scared to reach out.

If you do get an initial no, remember not to be your own worst enemy. Let it go, regroup, and try again. Turn the mirror on them. They're probably busy, they probably have a lot going on. How do you make yourself valuable to them? The truth is, it can be something as silly as inflating their ego and giving them compliments. Even better is asking if there's something you can do for them—adding value. I've had people who actually said to me, "What can I do to help you? Is there anything? Do you have emails that you need to write? Is there something menial on your website, like updating your links?" You may think this seems obvious, but I assure you that the overwhelming majority of people do not go that extra mile. Even if they think to offer that extra support, they don't execute on the intention consistently. Be the outlier, have the thick skin, and know that success is a numbers game.

Brainstorm things that you can provide, especially if they're free. If you're starting out, your time is less valuable than theirs because you're earlier in your career; you're not as busy. So offer up your time, proffer something to that person they will find valuable. The key is that once you unlock value for them, they'll often see something in you that reminds them of themselves years ago when they were still coming up.

At our core, most of us are happy to give to others. So figure out who the person who can guide you is, ask them thoughtful questions, demonstrate your interest and commitment, and find a way to get through to them. Be useful.

We're so quick to overcomplicate things in our mind to avoid doing hard things, but if you commit and follow these steps, you'll learn how to take a hand, and eventually you'll be ready to give one.

As you progress, you'll realize that to grow, you have to let go of some control, but you don't have to go it alone. Find your crew. Ultimately, the difference between success and stagnation is going to boil down to give-and-take, so be ready to give. And of course, whenever possible, pay it forward.

NINE

Turn Your Weaknesses into Your Strengths

Like most people, I struggle with areas where I feel weak or not as con-fident. Honestly, I'd rather just double down on my strengths and allow weaknesses to atrophy. For example, I will do almost anything to avoid a confrontation. I wish I were kidding. My aversion to conflict is a true shortcoming, to the point of being an Achilles' heel. So, in this chapter, I'll start by explaining how this limitation left me sitting, well past mid-night, on the floor of a Kurdish village home, trying to get paid after a disastrous gig I'd let my mother book for me. #NeverAgain.

But having a weakness should not be considered a character flaw or personal failing. Instead, I propose we consider your weak areas jumping-off points for improvement, which starts with being able to recognize where we're not as skilled. I'll detail how to assess where we may fall short.

For the longest time, my weakness was mentalism; I thought the practice was boring. There were no "moves," no flash, and very few props. Literally nothing up my sleeve. Plus, mentalism just didn't seem *fun*. Only once I worked with a mentor did I begin to understand where mentalism could take me, especially if I added in an emotional component and made it my own. By addressing the deficiency of not having an emotional hook, I changed my professional trajectory. Finding the discipline to pursue the uncomfortable is where growth begins—I know, I've lived it.

That's why I'm Oz the Mentalist and not just Oz the Magician.

From Magic to Mentalism

I hated mentalism as a teenager. But I loved *magic* and I used to practice sleight of hand moves with cards for twelve or more hours every day. Learning to control where each card was located in the deck, focusing my entire mind on the position of a finger during a split-second move, over and over *and over* again in front of a mirror. I had an attention to detail and an unwillingness to settle for anything less than perfection that bordered on the obsessive, but that's what was required to be a top-notch performer.

Practicing magic isn't any different than a soccer player learning to bounce a ball endlessly with their feet. They know how to place the ball in the corner of their neck, how to catch it on their head. Much like the way the player can control a ball, I can control cards. This also goes for coins, ropes, and close-up tricks, which involve random household items like rubber bands, matches, glasses, pretty much any common item you can think of. There are a few people who are the best in the world with each of these items. Silly as it may sound, I could list off the greatest rubber-band magicians in the world . . . yes, that is actually a real thing. They've dedicated their lives to magic with rubber bands, which sounds insane. They could probably do fifty rubber-band tricks for you in ten minutes. And you'd be blown away seeing them disappear, shrink, rip, restore, penetrate, and change colors.

Magicians have thousands and thousands of books written about their craft, the earliest of which date back more than ten centuries. It's fascinating how in-depth magic is, how far back it goes in history. Principles of magic have been around since way before Jesus Christ, and certain tricks can be traced back thousands of years.

I found this robust history and all the sleights associated with magic fascinating. In comparison, mentalism held little appeal and was far more limited in its literature, moves, and methods. And yet, now I perform mentalism for a living. I also hated running. And now I do it for pleasure and inspiration. Your weaknesses today can easily become your strengths tomorrow, but you must allow yourself to be open to those changes.

In both instances, I had mentors and people around me who opened my eyes to new possibilities. If you're interested in something that's not yet your forte, don't be scared to ask someone who knows what you're missing.

As for my getting into mentalism, it was a practical decision. When I finally made it onto *America's Got Talent* in 2015, I did a thorough assessment of how to best plan for this opportunity. Because it was a big opportunity indeed; a lot of people would see the show. I realized the scale and that I needed to make the absolute most of it.

So often, we try to swim against the tide, when we should just let the tide wash us along. Go with the flow if it pushes you in the direction you want to go. The key is to figure out what direction that is, so you know when to let the current take you. Just after I got married, I decided that what I really wanted was to be able to spend time with my wife. I didn't want to be gone every single Friday, Saturday, and Sunday, going from party to party. I planned to have a family, and being an absentee father every weekend wouldn't work long term.

When I got my big break with *AGT*, I thought that mentalism would parlay into booking more corporate events. From a material perspective, I knew these events could be very lucrative. Leaning into mentalism would give me options in other parts of my life. I decided to represent and brand myself accordingly when on the show, in every single instance, I'd be the guy wearing a suit and tie; I'd look clean-cut. I wanted my vibe to be different and to stand out from other mentalists, many of whom lean into an edgier, rockstar look. I was not going to put on guyliner and leather jackets. I wanted to be, for lack of a better term, square. I was squeaky clean when it came to both my image and the content of my act.

The year before, on *AGT*, a magician had won. He was a white guy in his late twenties. (Shout out to Mat Franco, who is amazing!) I was a white guy in his early thirties. We weren't different enough that people wouldn't do a head-to-head comparison of us. I didn't want to be compared or confused with someone else; I wanted to be distinct and unrivaled. To me, this was the chance to carve out my unique selling proposition: Either do something different than everyone else, or do something better than everyone else. Or thread the needle and do both! Those are your options. Because there are billions of people in the world and you must find a way to stand out. Carve out a little niche that makes you incomparable, different, or the best.

At that point, I was performing about 50 percent mentalism and 50 percent magic. The magic was a crutch that I leaned on to offset the fact that mentalism carries a much higher margin for error. It is far riskier in a lot of instances and there's simply no way to know if it's going to work every time. Hence the importance of learning to create backup plans, as I covered previously.

I made the decision to transition out of physical-trick-based magic even though it was an area where I was stronger at the time, which was frightening. While mentalism would set me apart from other contestants on the show, I was about to bet my career on it. But my plan worked: Mentalism made me stand out and took me much further in the competition. The audience perceived reading minds very differently from watching a magic trick, and mentalism captured their imaginations in a different way. Leaning into what was scary and embracing what wasn't my strength is how I was able to transcend the limits I saw around me.

While I'm not psychic, I can assure you that doing the same—taking stock of your weaknesses and letting them make you uncomfortable—will spur your ascent as well. If it was easy, everyone would be doing it already.

Half the Battle

Whether I was practicing magic or mentalism, my mom was (and continues to be) my biggest fan and cheerleader. She's been there from the very beginning, encouraging me to practice and perform. Her belief in me instilled confidence when, quite frankly, there shouldn't have been much, starting with my early days as a restaurant magician and kid's-birthday-party specialist. I'm grateful for the pushes she gave me and also owe much of my sense of humor to her. Yet as my number one fan, she sometimes wants to push me out of my comfort zone, and from time to time, acquiescing to her push is to my detriment. The promises of "Don't worry, it will be great!" aren't always necessarily true.

For a lot of us, particularly the conflict-averse, it's hard to say no to family. In fact, there's a scientific reason why it's especially difficult to say no to someone like your mother. The reason has to do with "asso-ciative learning," which is shorthand for the way the central nervous system classifies and encodes a situation as being either safe or threat-ening. Obeying our mothers is hardwired into our neural circuits, basi-cally because children need their parents in order to be able to survive.[1] So it's actually *science's* fault that I found myself agreeing to my mother's idea to perform in a Kurdish village.

Here's a quick history lesson if you're unfamiliar with the Kurds, like I was. The Kurds don't have their own state, as they are an indigenous people of the Mesopotamian plain and live across parts of Turkey, Syria, Iran, Iraq, and Armenia. While the Kurds have a united culture and language, there's no standard dialect or religion.[2] Put a pin in this fact, because it becomes important in a minute. The Kurds in *this* story—my mother's Kurds—happened to live in Israel, where they have their own religion. (FYI, they've been staunch US allies in the Middle East.) They serve in the military. They're not Jewish or Muslim, and again, they have their own language. They're a nomadic people, similar to Bedouins. Even up until recently, they'd travel in packs and not stay in one place. They're very unique in that they have their own little enclaves. Think of it like an SAT comparison—the Kurds are to the Middle East like the Amish are to America. If you hear about the Kurds, it's often in reference to how they've been oppressed. The Kurd-ish people in this story live outside of mainstream Israel. They're not integrated with the rest of society; they have their own insular commu-nities. A Kurdish village is probably the last place on earth where an outsider would consider going to perform mentalism. That's where the plot thickens.

One of my mom's colleagues at her job is a big fan of mine, likely because she forwards him every single one of my videos. He was con-vinced that my show would be a tremendous success at his village, even

though he'd never organized a similar event before and his primary oc-
cupation was making decorative glass plates at a factory.

As my mom explains all this to me, numerous alarm bells start going
off in my head, but she insists I don't need to worry. Upon my mother's
urging, I go to this village despite my many reservations. We're trying
to negotiate my getting paid to do a show, and also the ins and outs
of the fact that I perform primarily mentalism, not magic. Our glass
blower/artisan turned promoter promises that this is going to be a
huge hit and a major moneymaker for all of us. As we talk, he's telling
me, "I run big events in this community." In my head, I'm like, *Do you?*
My BS detector's going off like crazy, but my mom badgers me into
trusting him.

The pin I said to hold about the language? That comes into play at
the event. What I didn't know from the jump is that almost no one here
speaks Hebrew or English. My show requires some sort of communication; in fact, communication is the cornerstone. I'm not Charlie Chap-
lin and can't do a silent act. My words are my medium.

When I arrive at the venue, it turns out my mom's coworker has
oversold my appearance and there are dozens of people lined up outside, because they're already at capacity inside. This guy has chained the
doors against those who are trying to get in, which also *chains in* those
of us who are already here. All of these Kurds are running to different
windows to try to watch me, and the guys inside are trying to cover the
windows because they don't want the people who didn't pay to watch.
While I'm under lock and key, trying to do a show for an audience who
doesn't speak my language, other people keep running to different windows and banging on doors.

Total chaos.

I end up doing a trick called a "book test." It's kind of like a pick-a-
card, where the audience member picks a card and I find it. Along those

lines, a book test is where you open a book, select a word, and I figure out the word in your head. There are a hundred different versions and there are a hundred different methods, as this is a famous genre within the world of mentalism. Always smart to tilt the odds in your favor and be overprepared, so I've brought along books in both Hebrew and English

Now, my Hebrew comprehension isn't the greatest. It's been a while since my bar mitzvah. I find somebody in the audience who says they speak English. In my head I think, *They don't sound like they speak English*, but they say they do. So I give them a book. I explain what we're going to do and I have them choose a word. Tricks like this are impressive because the mentalist builds tension, teases it out, piques anticipation. The mentalist doesn't have the volunteer just say the word; that's not entertaining. The audience wants to watch the process unfold, they want to feel that suspense, the back-and-forth. The act of anticipation releases dopamine and the effect is greater for experiences than it is for material possessions.[3] What I'm saying is, for the audience, the slow reveal of the information and build up is the whole crux of the trick.

I have the person in front of me and I say, "Look at me. I'm going to guess the first letter." I continue, "Good, are you thinking of the first letter? Shhh, keep it inside your head." And they're supposed to agree and say something like, "Yes, I have the letter," as we continue our dance. Instead, the audience member blurts out the whole word. No suspense, no anticipation, no dopamine, no bueno. So I try harder to get them to understand how we're going to perform this trick together, where they *do not say the quiet part out loud*.

I try this three more times, and essentially beg them, "Please, just *think* of the first letter. Do you have the first letter? Keep it quiet inside your head. Don't tell me. Don't say it out loud. Do you understand?" And then they nod and then they *say* the letter, instead of silently keeping it to themself. I try explaining again, "No, you don't tell me. I have to guess it." After I say that, they again say the whole word out loud, which is precisely the exact opposite of how the trick is supposed to unfold, and of the instructions I'd repeated ad nauseum. There's no magic. There's no awe. There's just a Kurdish guy spouting random words from a book in front of me; it's a nightmare. If this wasn't so cringeworthy, it would have been absolutely hilarious; I am literally the butt of the joke.

As a quick aside that applies to all of us: Whatever it is we endeavor to do, sometimes our efforts will go off the rails. I wrote earlier about how Gaffigan had a bad show in Puerto Rico, even though he's one of the greatest comedians of all time. You're going to have a bad presentation, a failed sales call, a biffed opportunity; it happens to all of us. Everyone has an off day. Part of tapping into your inner mentalist means accepting failure and moving forward anyway, especially because it wasn't the Kurds' fault that they'd never seen stage mentalism before and didn't understand the nuances.

In the case of this show, the only way out was through, so I kept doing my tricks until the bitter end, taking comfort in knowing that at some point it would be over. I'd like for you to picture the worst bombing you could ever imagine. Now multiply that utter and complete detonation by fifty, and then throw on the fact that there's still people shaking chained doors to try to get in because they sold too many tickets, and also people clawing at the windows. This is the level of crash and burn where my inner voice appears and starts questioning if maybe I chose the wrong path in life altogether; even knowing consciously that external factors are mostly to blame, I still can't get over how much of a failure I am at every moment. The loop playing over and over in my head is *Oh God, please let it be over soon. Get. Me. Outta. HERE!*

This is easily one of the top three worst shows of my life. My performance gets to the point where it turns from tragedy to comedy because it's so terrible, it's just funny. (Usually *comedy* = *tragedy* + *time*, but this was so tragic that it was immediately and painfully hilarious.) I'm trapped in an absurd situation and there's nothing I can do as I'm surrounded by Kurds yelling words because they're so excited to have been visited by a semi-famous American magician.

Mercifully, the event finally ends. I want nothing more than to hightail it out of there, but alas I still need to get paid. I didn't suffer like that for nothing. The check will take a bit of the sting out of the situation.

Instead of presenting me with an envelope at the end, we have to go to the promoter's home to pick up my compensation. He lives in a house with all of his family, including cousins, grandparents, etc. There's easily thirty people under this one roof. The village isn't what I'd consider archaic, because they have satellite dishes, so it's not something rustic you might envision in the middle of the Sahara. Basically, they're exactly what I saw in the movie *Zero Dark Thirty* when SEAL Team Six killed bin Laden, which is really not the scene I want to have at the top of my mind while I'm here.

There are rugs covering the entire floor. I enter and take off my shoes, as custom would dictate, then sit on one of the rugs. They warm tea and coffee over an open fire and we all just sit there. I know that culturally, it is not appropriate to start our interactions by talking business. You have to park yourself with your host for an extended stay, drink coffee, eat—there's a rhythm. I could sense there was a courting process I was unaware of and, honestly, had no patience for. I mean, I'm a New Yorker. I'm like, "Lemme get the money. Lemme get out of here. I want to be gone. I'm flop-sweating. This is one of the worst experiences of my life. Just let me go." And my mom's there, getting nervous, yet still trusting that it would all work out. She's from a small town, where life has a slower pace, so she doesn't have my frenetic NYC energy. As we wait, everyone's talking but we don't know what they're saying. They're making us cool our heels and we're trying to be polite.

The whole scene drags on and on. As I sit cross-legged on the floor and pretend to sip my cup of tea, I'm realizing more and more that this guy has never done this before. He's not a promoter. He just works at my mom's company, heard that I could do mentalism, and he started getting big ideas. When I've been there for nearly an hour and exhausted all my compliments about the tea and the rugs, I can tell that this situation is getting tense, because things are starting to feel weird between my host and his pseudo partners in this endeavor—maybe they're his family members? I keep shooting looks to my mother, who got me into this mess. *When can we go? Do we just leave? Are they not going to pay us?* I don't want to be rude or aggressive because there's so many of them. But there's a distinct undercurrent that *something* is going on and I don't know how to proceed.

The powers that be in the compound end up negotiating me down to a third of what was supposed to be paid, and the night cost me hours and hours of my time and a good deal of my sanity. And while I adamantly swore to myself, "Never again," I do wonder if, should the circumstances ever arise again, I could be sucked in once more, because it's science's fault that I struggle to say no to my mother. Having built a career on pleasing people, I find it especially challenging to disappoint anyone, especially those to whom I'm closest.

Let's learn from my mistakes—by determining where we're weak before we end up falling into our own trap—so we can grow stronger.

Half the Battle

Let's first acknowledge that wanting to address our weaknesses is not our default setting. Like me with my conflict avoidance. Due to the fact that I hate drama, I will often give people a pass and forgive them when they've wronged me, even knowing that leaving things unaddressed only makes it more likely that the situation will repeat itself. This is the people pleaser in me; I'm like most performers and seek approval from my audiences. So many of us are guilty of the "If it's not broke, don't fix it" mindset. (Or, "If it's broken, any fix will do.") But that doesn't work for us, nor should it, largely because denial is unhealthy.

A funny example that I see all the time is on TikTok, people post videos how the guy next to them is hogging the armrest on an airplane, or manspreading into their limited leg room. But why is it that the person being crowded is much more likely to remain uncomfortable and post a shot of some stranger's kneecap on social media, rather than just politely saying, "Excuse me. Could you please give me some space?" and reclaiming their personal space?

Like me, maybe one of your weaknesses is not speaking up for yourself, which is a first cousin to conflict avoidance. This is common and there's a reason for it: Our avoidance stems from fear of rejection. Rejection hurts because it triggers the same neural pathways that are activated when we experience physical pain.[4] In a 2021 study conducted by Crucial Learning, a Utah-based performance and leadership training company, out of 1,300 people surveyed, 74 percent of them feared speaking out about social and political issues.[5] Whoa. So, if you struggle to make your opinion heard, you're in the majority. But when you suppress your emotions, it costs you. If your weakness is not speaking out, it can impair your incidental memory, which means what your brain picks up and stores without effort, as well as increase your cardiovascular activation, which is when your heart and blood vessels have to work harder to move blood through your body.[6]

If you want to, say, advocate for yourself, you have to acknowledge that an issue exists in the first place. And that holds true for whatever you consider to be your weakness. I'm actively working on this skill myself. Especially in business, I'm willing to allow people the benefit of the doubt. I always see the positive. I'm the first to say, "You know what, it's fine, I'll just do this guy a favor," and my manager will get mad at me and remind me, "He's treating you like crap; look at this example and that one. He hasn't earned the passes you keep giving."

A lot of us know where we can improve. So, congratulations—knowing is half the battle. In this case, even trying for slight growth or awareness is better than doing nothing. For example, I'm very controlling in certain elements of my business. Because my need to control things is a weakness—exerting control doesn't always benefit me and often works to my detriment—for years I did not take on a bigger team. I was not willing to let in people who would give me synergies and assistance, who would take a lot of meaningless busywork off my plate. I'm not even talking about big things. I mean emails, administrative stuff, back-office things. I kept that work all to myself for years. I didn't even farm out the manufacture of my props, even though I was earning enough. My old habits were so deeply engrained and I secretly enjoyed the monotony and the light suffering involved. It felt important to me to do the grunt work myself, as though it would keep me grounded. Ultimately, this was a great example of not reading my own mind.

But to level up the caliber of gigs and compensation I was working, I needed to free up time, and I had to recognize that my need for control was holding me back. I had to come to terms with the notion that spending money would make me more money, or that by taking a task off my plate, I'd get more hours in my day. Hell, I'd get more out of my life.

I had to learn to switch to quality in lieu of quantity for my gigs. My time is finite, so I must maximize it by charging accordingly. When I found that I was getting a yes for every booking, I realized that I was undercharging for my service. There's an inflection point when you finally ask for enough that they say no; it took a lot of trial and error to properly price myself. With quality over quantity, I've freed up more time to be in service of bigger things—like finding ways to get on television so tens of millions of people can see me and potentially book me.

Think about what your hours are worth. Not just in terms of dollars and cents, but bigger picture. What are the losses and costs to you—are they greater than if you actually did something about them? What can you do creatively if you're freed up? Personally, I thought, *What's it worth for me on a weekend to not look at my phone for four hours? And just play with my kids and swim in the pool and be fully checked out?* Not everything can be quantified, nor should it be. A lot of things have their own unique value that's even more important than money. You've only got one life to live.

Seek Out Discomfort

It's not enough just to be able to identify where you're not proficient. If you want to spur true growth, you must have the discipline to pursue what feels uncomfortable. I don't even mean addressing your flaws or your annoying traits, because everyone has those. I want you to look at bigger-picture things that make you uncomfortable, situations or instances that might keep you from living your "best life." Find those changes that might induce panic now, but long term will enable you to level up. The only way for me to grow in my profession was to get a better team around me, to let go of control; figuring out how to do that was profoundly uncomfortable.

The thing about discomfort is that if we can view it as part of our learning process—instead of regarding it as something to avoid—we experience more positive emotions, better motivation, and expanded growth, according to a study by researchers at Cornell and The University of Chicago.[7]

Let's fold my ultramarathons into this point about forcing discomfort. For example, I like to give myself rewards, especially when it comes to eating, because I run so much that I feel as though I am allowed to overindulge. But Mother Nature and metabolism can catch up with anyone and I'm guilty just as much as the next guy of letting loose, especially over the summer. So that means when I commit to the next race, I also commit to facing my weakness, and that's when I decide, *Hey, I'm on health lockdown for the next three months.* And so, I'll create my own zero tolerance policy on X, Y, Z.

Guess what? The first two weeks are abject misery. They're just torture, as I get used to this new routine that I hate and that I rebel against. But I keep going. I make myself sit with the discomfort. Part of overcoming means you have to make it through that beginning portion; that's the hardest part because you don't yet have momentum.

Then the amazing part is when I get used to my new rules and I begin to love the new spaces they're opening; I might love how I feel, or love my improved performance. The better habits become a lifestyle and soon the rewards start happening. I'm fitter. I'm running faster. I feel like a fine-tuned machine without the sugar and the grease clogging the works. And there's something to be said for being able to go to bed and quickly fall asleep because I haven't gorged myself. Without the crutch of bad habits, I find other ways to reach fulfillment, and the discipline of the new routine becomes its own driver, *even though it's not comfortable.*

I wouldn't know what to do if I landed in a new city for a gig and I couldn't go running once I'm there. Ironically, *that's* a weakness. I like to avoid certain busywork. I don't want to do boring stuff on the computer.

I don't want to write emails, so I will instead procrastinate by running twenty miles, which to the normal person sounds insane, but to me, it's an escape. In fact, I've done everything possible to avoid writing these very words you are reading right now! You hold in your hands certifiable proof that you can achieve your goals when you set your mind to them.

It sounds like an oxymoron, but to get comfortable being uncomfortable, you have to do it consistently. And that is often what burns out those who try to embrace a pursuit they don't enjoy. If you're just faking your way through something, it won't work long term. If you hate running, good luck running regularly. If you hate math, getting your accounting degree will be torture. So instead, you either have to love what you set your mind to or break through those inner limitations. I think you can do that with a lot of pursuits. You can find a way to love something that makes you uncomfortable if you can show yourself how the discomfort makes you better.

Be advised, your success will make other people feel insecure. I get this all the time with my running. I hear, "Oz, you're destroying your knees, you're doing this, you're doing that." When you take up self-improvement, when you decide you want more, when you really tap into the full power of your mind, you're going to have many haters and naysayers. There will be people around you who want to drag you down, who can't do what you're doing. Instead of saying to you, "This is amazing!" they'll give you all the reasons why you shouldn't be exceeding their expectations. You'll hear a lot of warnings from people, not because they're actually concerned, but because they're projecting their own issues and their own insecurities onto you. That's *their* self-defense mechanism that they employ because they can't handle their own feelings.

Use their negativity to spur yourself on.

Those haters, along with the people around you who might not nec-essarily like what you're doing, can be incredible motivation. Know that it takes a unique person to continue pushing and to change for the bet-ter, and that I believe in you. Quitting is the easiest thing in the world. Many people will casually diminish my profession saying to me, "Yeah, I had a magic set when I was a kid." And I'll think, "I did, too. So what's different between us?"

Think about this when someone challenges you on whatever your self-improvement entails as you address your weakness, whether it's training for a race, traveling across the country solo, deciding to enroll in law school at fifty, whatever. Why is it that you're somehow doing this and they're not? Why are you able to push on?

Spoiler alert: It's because you're willing to sit with discomfort.

Look at movie stars. Why are there so few of them? In part, because there's no playbook for it. Many actors carved their own path toward movie stardom, which is what I did with mentalism. If you could just go to school for four years, graduate, and say, "I have a bachelor's degree in movie star," there'd be a heck of a lot more of them. Right? So there are paths that you can carve out for yourself if you're willing to put in the work, to live with being challenged. The world has changed from pre-vious generations and there are less surefire road maps for success. Our grandparents could graduate from high school and get a manufacturing job that allowed them to buy a home, raise a family, and send the next generation to college. With our parents, the college degree was the ticket to a limitless future. But the rules are different now and there are no more guarantees, so it's more important than ever to plot your own path.

Back to the movie star example: I believe the public admires movie stars because they understand that becoming a star is not like becoming a doctor. Mind you, a doctor is a much more important role in civilization than being a movie star . . . or, let's be honest, a mentalist. But I'll never forget when a physician called me to work a party and he found out how much I charge. He said, "That's more than I make." And I said, "It's classic Economics 101 . . . look how many doctors there are in New York City. Now, look how many magicians there are. There's a thousand of you for every one of me. Supply and demand!" He laughed; he wasn't even offended. He goes, "Oh my God, you're right. I'm getting my kid to be a magician!"

Is it easy to remain uncomfortable? Of course not. Complicating matters is the fact that the neural circuits that are responsible for self-control can buckle under stress and cause our primal impulses to go unchecked. If I have a bad day or a lousy gig while I'm training for an ultramarathon, my impulses to self-soothe kick in and I'll want to inhale a pint of Häagen-Dazs. Everybody has the same stumbling blocks: No one wants to be seen as failing, no one wants to be embarrassed, and our default setting is to get rid of things that make us uncomfortable. But the more you fight that urge, the better off you'll be.

A while back, I read a study about tennis legends. Arguably the greatest tennis player of all time is Roger Federer. He's won 80 percent of his matches. What's interesting is, in looking at the points he won in each match, you might assume that he'd also won approximately 80 percent of all the points. In the lifetime of his career, however, his percentage of points won was only 54. *That means he lost 46 percent of all points.*

To me, this is a wild data point to fully absorb because it means that you don't need to be successful *every* time. Instead, it means *you'll win if you're successful most of the time.* (It is even more pronounced in baseball, if you only succeed at the plate three times in ten, you're likely headed to the Hall of Fame.) And "successful most of the time" doesn't have to be 90 percent or 80 percent. If you're willing to keep going and going and going, your persistence at putting yourself in a situation that's uncomfortable is what's going to get you to those record wins. Federer is the perfect example of someone who has mastered his mental game and leveraged the razor-thin margins that separate the GOAT from the thousands before him that never won a single tournament.

Know that you don't have to get it right every time, so that you'll be game to try again. I mean, even the best don't come out on top every time. And they are comfortable with that fact.

Life Is a Team Sport

You can feel weak in what you're trying to accomplish when you don't have a lot of mutually beneficial relationships. You have to let people in; you're not meant to do it all on your own. Remember, almost everything in life requires some degree of teamwork, whether at work or at home, so my last piece of advice is to improve your relationships if you want to work on your weaknesses.

What I mean is, find a way to help those who help you. Create your own posse if you don't have one, where everyone assists with the heavy lifting. And be actively thoughtful, whether it's giving those who've helped you little gifts, sending thoughtful thank-you cards, or making that extra effort. Always acknowledge. When you do that, people reciprocate. I love it when I go on a podcast and the host says, "Oz, you killed it for us! Thank you. Now, what can we do for you?" I always reply, "Wow. I don't know. Let me think about it. Maybe nothing. But even just saying that helped me." Try it on for size . . . make it a mission this week to ask at least one or two people that you interact with if you can do anything for them or help them. It is so rare that someone asks that question that I guarantee there will be a light look of surprise on their face.

We often default to being self-contained because it feels safer to construct a cocoon around ourselves. So when you actively show other people who you are, it sets you apart, even though it can be scary. We live in a world where so many people feel like they're disposable and unappreciated. We're in a gig economy, where you can get anything, anywhere, anytime, very quickly at your fingertips, so what others do often doesn't feel valued. You can foster strength by taking the time to improve your relationships. Maintain networks over time, check in with people in your orbit regularly. That's been a secret to my success—regular check-ins.

Everyone's got a busy life, no one's ignoring you on purpose. Let others know you exist. Do this in a way that will add value to their life, be it via a dose of joy, a hit of dopamine, or some useful info. Anytime I write a newsletter, I want it to be something that would genuinely appeal to whoever's reading it. And I don't care if that means leaning into the lowest common denominator, like memes about cute puppies. In my newsletter to friends and clients, I'm a proud dad, a proud husband. I want to include my family here, as I leave them off my social media. What's funny is that I get more responses based on my kids and my running than I do about mentalism, probably because those areas of my life are the most genuine, and by sharing I let people know I'm a "real" person. It's like, "Hey, he's not just this guy who did these tricks at our national sales conference. He's got a real life, he's a fully formed person." What I do looks seamless and effortless, so when I allow others to witness something that I'm really putting effort in on or that I'm struggling with, it's humanizing. (Like when I had four kids with norovirus at the same time. Ugh, don't ask!)

Nothing, even in the most singular solo pursuits, happens in a vacuum. Life is a team sport and how we interact with others makes a huge difference. My career took off when I allowed myself to open up to others and to create mutually beneficial relationships, because acknowledging your community is the final piece of the puzzle.

Remember, recognizing an area where you're weak is an opportunity for growth and improvement. Even though addressing this area may be difficult and will almost certainly feel uncomfortable, you have no idea the kind of doors you will open for yourself by sitting in that discomfort. If I hadn't actively pursued things outside of my comfort zone, my life would be very different right now. I might be chained to limited ideas that kept me from being home, unable to spend the kind of time I want with my wife and children.

When you put effort into maintaining relationships and enhancing your network, there's no reason your weaknesses can't ultimately become your strongest attributes. Plus, you'll likely avoid being roped into performing for an audience that will never "get" your work. That fact alone is worth whatever the cost may be.

TEN

Make Memory Your Superpower

We've all lived this dreadful moment: You just introduced yourself to someone and vice versa when—Poof!—their name disappears out of your head like a rabbit from a top hat. That little slip is not only embarrassing, but it can also cost you personally and professionally.

The good news is that your memory can be trained just like a muscle, and even a few minutes of "working out" will yield major rewards. What's funny is that most of us, when asked, will say our memories are not that good. But in reality, it's not an issue of memory but rather of poor imprinting. You never knew the information in the first place. In most instances, the problem is related more to poor listening than to poor recall. In this chapter I will walk you through some tricks of the trade on how to train your memory. I'll teach you to turn information into an anchor in your brain so that it sticks, using the techniques and exercises I teach at corporate team-building seminars.

People assume my memory is ironclad, but that is honestly not the case. Instead, I have a variety of strategies up my sleeve. Some I already revealed in an earlier section, which includes writing everything down and taking meticulous notes. I take notes on what people tell me and what I do at every show; that way, if I see those same folks in a few months, or even a few years, I'll be able to review what I wrote and get credit for having incredible recall. While being this diligent takes a little extra effort, doing so pays dividends in the long run. What's so great about not forgetting info is that the longer you hold on to information, the more valuable it becomes.

When taking notes is not an option, there are other tools and tricks I use to anchor information; I will reveal them to you, so that you, too, will get credit for having an amazing memory. It is easier than you think!

So, let's learn how to be unforgettable.

Practice Makes Perfect

Your memory is essentially a muscle, meaning it can be coached and trained to be more effective. Consider this: Unless we're injured or ill, almost all of us have the strength to do a set of bicep curls with a one-pound weight. But successfully curling a twenty-five-pound weight for multiple reps could take some training first. And that's exactly what we're going to do with your memory; we're going to give it a solid work-out, to feel the burn. Right now, your memory might not be jacked enough to remember fifty names in a room, but remembering one name, two names, or even three names is something every single one of us can do. So let's build on that by first breaking down how memory works.

Memories are not movie flashbacks. They are not perfect recordings nor are they complete records. Information can be misremembered and falsified by oneself or others. Or by oneself *and* others, when you consider the Mandela Effect, which is when a group of people collectively misremembers an event or piece of pop culture. For example, many of us recall Tom Hanks's character Forrest Gump saying, "Life is like a box of chocolates," when what he actually said is, "Life *was* like a box of chocolates." The term *Mandela Effect* was first used by Fiona Broome when speaking with others about remembering Nelson Mandela dying in prison in the 1980s, and learning that she wasn't the only one who had that memory . . . which is strange, considering that he didn't pass until 2013.[1]

This example demonstrates that memories are extremely fragile. On top of that, it takes a lot of energy to remember something, so your brain wants to forget, filtering out whatever it doesn't consider necessary to conserve energy—and that is most things.

Memories are made every time you experience a new sensory activity, because this action forges a connection between your brain's neurons. These connections are called synapses. Synapses are already present, but they're reinforced when, say, you learn a better but more confusing way to come home from the store. The more you travel that new route, the more you remember the directions and the less confusing it becomes, until you can forget even taking it because you are thinking about something else. The good news is, your capacity to remember is practically unlimited, as your brain has eighty-six billion neurons.[2]

In the 1970s, Eric Kandel, a professor of biophysics at Columbia University, established that changes in the chemical signals between neurons are the biological basis for what makes a memory.[3] Kandel, who won a Nobel Prize for this discovery, went on to explain that the strength of a memory has to do with how often it's revisited and repeated. The more you revisit a memory, the stronger it imprints.

What's interesting is that our brains give precedence to certain memories. According to Ilker Yildirim, an assistant professor of psychology at Yale, "The mind prioritizes remembering things that it is not able to explain very well. If a scene is predictable, and not surprising, it might be ignored."[4] This goes back to my point in an earlier chapter about the complexity of slipping into autopilot, which is why you're less likely to recall an uneventful drive home from work versus when you've made the same trip in a raging snowstorm. If you're in a learning environment, note that your brain also prioritizes information you study first (called the "primacy effect") as well as what's been most recently studied (called the "recency effect").[5]

If you want to maximize your potential for preventing memory loss, understand that an active mind now will help stave off memory loss later. You've got to keep your brain busy and engaged. Researchers at Harvard University found that, in a study of participants with mild cognitive impairment, those who did crossword puzzles improved their cognition by a couple of points.[6] This is because crosswords are shown to connect short-term working memory with long-term permanent memory.[7]

While gaining a couple of points can sound paltry, this is the same amount of improvement they'd have seen from an FDA-approved memory-enhancing medication. So even a small increase is quite significant.

I also recommend practicing meditation because it's linked to increasing cortical thickness in the brain, which decreases as we age. This is important because cortical thickness is linked to intelligence, meaning a thicker cortex means stronger brain function. Cortex thickness directly impacts our cognitive abilities, like problem-solving, memory, attention, and coming up with a snappy retort on the spot, instead of hours later when it doesn't count. And another benefit is that meditation can reduce ruminative thinking—meaning when your brain gets stuck on repeat, amplifying negative thoughts again and again—which can improve the way we process our emotions.[8] So, with meditation, you can structurally alter the neuroplasticity of the brain, meaning you'll create growth in the hippocampus, which basically impacts your memory capacity.[9]

We want to make your memory your superpower, and adopting healthier habits will give you that running start.

What's in a Name?

Is there anything worse than forgetting someone's name, especially mere seconds after you just met them? How mortifying is that? Say good-bye to that feeling because I have a virtually foolproof technique to prevent this from happening to you again. Here's the kicker, though, you likely aren't forgetting their name . . . you never actually *knew* it in the first place! Memory has very little to do with it, rather this is a listening issue.

Last year, I presented at a high-profile conference, speaking along-side Netflix cofounder Reed Hastings, Katie Couric, and Paris Hilton. I gave a workshop right before the main event and had twenty-three students in my breakout session. The plan was not only to amaze them with some mentalism, but also to show them the power of their own minds and how to supercharge their memories. I would tell each of them their names and what company they worked for as a fun and fast demonstration.

Again, lest you believe I have a photographic memory or supernatural powers, I can assure you that I do not. In fact, if you ask my wife how often I forget things around the house, she will have a field day on that topic!

So, as each person walked in the room, I asked them to please remove their name badges and place them into their pockets, which right away received a quizzical expression suggesting, "What in the world is this guy about to do?" Once everyone was seated, I did a quick, secret head count, because I wanted to make sure that if extra people had come in, I could account for them. I'm so glad I knew to do this, because two extra women came in who looked an awful lot like each other, and I'd have been so embarrassed if I got it wrong. I then proceeded to go around the room and rattle off each of their names. Ever the showman, it wasn't enough to simply say their names, but I also added in the various companies they each worked for and some brand-specific jokes, too. Like, I said, "Sara, she works for Campari. Doesn't matter if I have an Aperol Spritz or a Negroni later tonight; either way, you're happy, right?" and everyone laughed.

As we got down to the last guy, I feigned panic like I couldn't recall his name, and I said, "Oh no, give me a second." Then I paused before saying, "How many of you have had this exact same feeling when you're at a party, or even at a work event, and you literally just met someone three seconds ago? And you think, *Uh-oh, what is their name? What did they just say?* Now you're sweating and your heart is pounding. You can't hear anything they're saying, because all you're focused on is, *What is their name, damn it?* Not knowing is completely consuming you. It's like you're stuck in quicksand up to your knees and sinking fast. You have this awkward interaction where you're trying to find a way to find out, because you're too embarrassed to ask them their name again. Your eyes scour the room side to side hoping and praying you find someone you know to bring over and casually say, 'Oh, do you guys know each other?' and then pray to the Lord above that they spill the beans as they introduce themselves, and a flood of relief washes over you. Heaven help you if they say, 'Yes, we know each other, great to see you again.' You're too panicked to even be mad at yourself for such an unnecessary stressor. So, how would that feel?"

Consensus? Everyone agreed they'd feel pretty bad.

Then, to the guy whose name I "forgot," I said, "I bet that doesn't feel so great for you right now, Russell, does it? But I know who you are, Russell. I would never forget you. I want you on my good side, because you work for Live Nation." He sat last, and the whole thing brought down the house, and that's how I opened up the session.

Nobody wants memory tools that will take days, weeks, or years to figure out. If you hear a name, you want to know *now* how to recall it. Like with that group, I want to teach you some tips and tricks that you can master in ten minutes and still be using *ten years* from now. Because forgetting someone's name isn't just embarrassing; it's potentially damaging. In fact, researchers at Scotland's University of Aberdeen found that forgetting someone else's name can "create a downward spiral in which forgetting undermines investment in [that] relationship."[10]

The group I'd been addressing at the conference that day were all chief marketing officers, so I wanted to use an example they could relate to. I said to them, "Everyone in the world has used shampoo, and it's a marketer's dream, because the instructions are simply three words. How can anyone get confused, much less forget those three simple words: *lather, rinse, repeat.* The repeat doesn't even matter, but Pantene needs to sell some more product so best believe they want you to repeat. Say it to yourself, *lather, rinse, repeat,* and now say it again, and again. Repetition is our friend; it imprints info on our mind. We're going to repurpose that three-word catchphrase into the following—Listen, Repeat, Reply—and you'll never again forget the name of someone you just met!"

As a quick aside, not long ago, I had the opportunity to meet and perform for Barack Obama. I've never encountered somebody in my whole life who locks in better than he does. I watched him do a meet and greet for forty-five minutes, and with every single person that he

spoke to, he acted like nobody else was in the room, even though people were circling him like a frenzy of sharks. Everyone in his peripheral
vision was waiting for their chance to come over, but he did not look
around. He did not do that rushing thing—you know, where you're
talking to somebody but they're looking over their shoulder for who's
next. He didn't do that at all. If he committed thirty, forty-five, or sixty
seconds to you, you had his full attention. For him, that brief exchange
was just a Tuesday at 8:07 p.m. But for everyone in attendance—myself
included—those forty-five seconds are most likely ones that they will
remember vividly and talk about for the rest of their lives. (No, I did
not use my minute to ask if he'd gotten his paper-cutout silhouette
from Sir Richard Branson, if you're curious.)

When Obama meets you, he knows that the time he's giving you is
valuable. When he shakes your hand, he looks you right in the eye. He
focuses on you. He looks into *you*, not just into your eyes. And he's
somebody who's met countless numbers of people. What I'm describing him doing is a trick that so few people know . . . it's called "listening." Most of us don't really do it.

What I want you to do, when you listen to another person, is to turn
your mind off and truly *hear*. Easier said than done, as our mind rarely
likes to be quiet. Instead, a hundred different thoughts could race
through it, such as, *What am I about to say next? Oh my God. Who is this person? Do I know them?* But I want you to make your mind completely
blank. I'm talking complete attention. We are going to *actively listen*.

When you go up to someone, tell yourself right now to do nothing
but tune into them as they introduce themselves. I don't mean tune in
with your ears, I mean with every part of your brain; tune out your
thoughts and truly hear the words that they say. And when they say
their name, repeat it back to them immediately. Always repeat it. You
should say, "Ashley, oh, I love that. Do you spell it *A-S-H-L-E-Y*, the

traditional spelling? Yes? Great!" We'll call this technique "Listen, Repeat, Reply." Tear a page out of my playbook and pause right now: Quiet your mind and say it out loud three times: "Listen, Repeat, Reply; Listen, Repeat, Reply; LISTEN, REPEAT, REPLY." *Listen* means you make your mind a blank. Doing so will exponentially increase your chances of remembering the name, especially if you follow up your attentive moment by repeating their name.

Here's a great visual metaphor: Let's say I gave you a stick and told you to go to the beach, to the damp sand right at the shoreline. When the water recedes from a wave, quickly write your name. If you do that one time and a wave comes by, it will probably sweep away the writing and there'd be nothing left. But if you take that stick and write your name, and then go over each letter a few more times, really pressing down with all your might, it will make a far deeper impression. Now it will take many waves to wash it away completely and leave no trace.

Brain science reveals that repetition solidifies memory because it leads to more stable representations in the cortex, meaning repetition shifts information from short-term to long-term memory.[11] The more times you can carve that person's name into your mind, the less chance there is that it will get washed away by the tide. You will retain that information, I promise you. And you don't need to retain it for life, but if you can retain it for the next minute, three minutes, five minutes, then you'll avoid embarrassment, especially if you have a profession or a social life that involves meeting new people. And don't most of us experience those situations? They might not be daily occurrences, and if they're not, you've got all the more time to practice.

We've covered *listen* and *repeat*. As for *reply*, my advice falls into three different categories. The first one is spelling the name back to the person you've just met. Simply put, make sure that you are spelling it correctly. Next, comment on the spelling. "Is that *Brian* with a *y* or an *i*?"

No matter the answer, I say, "Yes, that's the best way to spell it for sure." If their name has a very obvious spelling such as *Bob* or *Bill*, then I say, "I assume *Bill* is shortened from *William*, is that right? But you go by *Bill*?" Another way to comment on someone's name is to pay them a compliment; everyone loves to be flattered. So when you reply, use their name in a compliment, and say something like, "Brian, I love those glasses. I'm just so curious, Brian, where did you get those?" You say their name again with the glasses. Now you think, *Brian with the cool glasses.* This gives you a psychological hook, an imprint that links someone's name to how they look to you. Remember, our brains retain the thing that's different. Think about if you meet somebody with one side of their head shaved and the other side is dyed blue. When they tell you their name, you're likely to remember that person far more than attendees dressed in khakis and Patagonia vests who look like your cookie-cutter hedge fund managers. Finally, make a personal connection if there is one, or you're welcome to lie and make one up as long as you won't get caught later. Choose wisely in this case! For example, after meeting Brian, you could say, "Oh how funny, my cousin is married to a Brian!" Now is my cousin really married to a man named Brian? Absolutely not, I'm a total liar, but guess what? I also won't forget that name now.

If instead of trying to just remember someone's name, you need to remember a list of things, you can build a memory palace, a technique used in literature by the character Sherlock Holmes. To create your own memory palace, you first visualize a familiar space—it can be any place you go to or have been frequently—your childhood home, your office, or your favorite coffee shop. Then determine a course of travel through that place. In the example of your childhood home, maybe you enter through the living room, then walk through the dining room, kitchen, and family room to get to the back porch.

Once you have your place and your route mapped out, determine what it is you want to remember—say, the periodic table—and place each element along the way. If you start with hydrogen, you can picture a hydrogen-powered rocket ship on the sofa next to the front door, and then for lithium, a pack of batteries on the table. These can be found next to a salt shaker for sodium and a banana for potassium. You'll have to be creative for the more difficult elements, but maybe next you can use a mnemonic device to imagine your pretty-but-not-smart cat lazing by the fireplace. You bend down to pet that cat, associating rubidium with the motion of "rubbing the belly of a dum-dum." The more you walk through and explore your memory palace, the more that info will stick.

When I preselect people in my shows who I want to use for audience participation, I have to remember them, so I look for people wearing bright colors, big jewelry, bushy beards, etc. That way, if I'm in a crowd with hundreds or even thousands of people, and I'm onstage and I run out in the audience, I can spot them from far away.

While it can be harder to do when you're with more people, these techniques still work. Let's say you go up to a group and they introduce themselves, "That's Megan, that's Susan, that's Bill, that's Nathan, and I'm Adrian." Too many people, right? I like giving compliments when it's a smaller group, but this practice doesn't scale. If you do compliment, saying, "Megan, love the earrings. Susan, where'd you get those pants? Bill, fantastic moustache. Nathan, I dig your watch. And, yo, Adrian, I loved *Rocky*," you've tipped the balance from friendly to full-blown psycho.

If you're in a larger group, take your time as you repeat their names. Make a joke out of it. Say, "Is there going to be a quiz later? You said you're Megan. Megan, so good to meet you, and Susan. Susan, so great to meet you." Say their names back three times. People appreciate this because it shows that you took the time and the effort to commit to knowing their names, which most people don't do; that extra beat sets you apart.

As for those twenty-three marketers that day, how did I do it? Here's the inside scoop: I don't have an infallible memory. While I do work at it, it's not something I need at my level. The night before my session, at the conference registration, they gave out little yearbooks with all the attendees listed and pictured. I went through and cut out their faces. I showed everyone in class these pseudo flash cards and thought there'd be a laugh or chuckle, but suffice it to say, I may have given light kidnapper vibes. I still found it funny and promise I use my powers strictly for good!

Because I always have a plan B, while I was brushing my teeth, I made piles of the faces that were easy to recall. Some people were simple to recall because they had unique names, features, or for whatever reason, their name matched their face in my mind. Sometimes a Bob just looks like a Bob. On my first round of quizzing myself, I identified eight or nine out of the twenty-three immediately.

As I practiced and made up jokes about them, more names began to gel and I added them to the "got" file. I repeated this while flossing—gotta keep that dental hygiene y'all—then while getting dressed, and packing up my things. (Put a pin in this: Your day is full of mentally empty moments that could be filled with some purpose.) I probably did four or five passes with my flash cards. By the time I was ready to go, I had twenty-one or twenty-two of the names down 100 percent. The last two or three were more of a struggle, so I said them over and over with rapid-fire delivery.

When I arrived at the class, I tested myself as they walked in, verifying via their badges that I had the details straight. That's when I said, "Take off your name tags." In my head, it was one final pop quiz. I was like, *Oh, I know her. I know him. I know her, I know him. I know him.* So I nailed it. I got everybody right and then I taught them to do the same.

Don't worry if you still forget a name after learning this technique and aren't perfect. No one is. There have been times when I've just met somebody and I forget their name, and I'm the one here telling you how not to forget. Whenever that happens, it's because I messed up step 1. Say it with me again, do it out loud for real, I don't care if you're hunkered down in a Starbucks or in seat 24F of a plane, "Listen, Repeat, Reply." Usually, what trips me up is the *listen* portion. Often, it's when I'm about to do a trick and somebody's calling out, "Hey, come over and meet this group." I'm so busy thinking about my trick that I can't make my mind blank and receptive. It's not a faulty memory if I never knew the name in the first place. It wasn't imprinted and so it was washed away. This used to happen to me frequently at sound checks before my show, as I walked backstage and suddenly was met in the dark by a group of people all at once. I'd be going over all the technical details of my upcoming performance in my head, so I would completely screw up step 1, which is to listen. I always want to make sure that the people setting up for my show feel seen and heard, as in many ways, they are the unsung heroes putting together the entire production. Also, I'm well aware that everyone talks and word spreads, and I want to ensure that I'm easy to work with and known for being kind and polite to others. Word spreads even wider if you're the opposite! Yet sometimes I'm stressed and flustered and will completely forget someone's name because I didn't listen to it in the first place. When this happens, the very best thing is to immediately say, "Could you please remind me of your name? It's Ryan? Oh, great. I thought I heard Brian and I didn't want to get it wrong. Ryan, thank you so much for your hard work." When you show them that you wanted to clarify, it affords them an extra level of respect that you cared enough to get it right.

If you're able to wash your hair, then you're able to remember our three-word trick for names. Lather, rinse, repeat becomes Listen, Repeat, Reply. The next time you're in a social or work setting with new people, challenge yourself to remember five names. Then as you're about to leave, close your eyes and picture each person's face, and see if you can remember their name. I bet you will surprise yourself, even on the first try!

Write Everything Down

Being able to recall something about someone else creates a stronger bond and builds trust, and that connection can work to your advantage. Your secret weapon here is something everyone possesses but few do— the ability to jot it down. We went over this earlier in the book, but it is so important I feel it bears repeating and I am therefore writing it down again (pun intended!)

Taking notes was, for me, born out of necessity. I started getting repeat calls for shows. I found myself struggling, wondering, *What did I do at that show?* While I have a number of tricks, I definitely don't want to repeat them for the same audience because it takes away some of the delight of the experience for them. I want to leave crowds with a sense of wonder each time; the element of surprise plays a huge role in my act.

Writing down facts about the lives of the people you meet is the fast track to building rapport, which is so important to anyone who regularly interacts with other human beings, whether it's your child's principal or a potential romantic partner or the sales lead you've been trying to close forever. Asking something like, "Hey, how did your son do at the basketball championship? Did he win again this year?" can create so much goodwill. When people feel like you've recalled something important about them, it's huge. You don't have to train to be a mentalist to harness the sorcery of giving back information that people gave you in the past, as everyone assumes you will have forgotten it.

If you're not sure how to record relevant details, here's what I do. As soon as I'm done with my show, I write everything that happened while it's fresh. If you're in sales, build time into your schedule to log these notes as soon as you get back to your car. If you're headed to the subway, leave yourself a voice message. Just don't let too much time lapse, or you may not retain everything you should.

When you pair effort with human touch, you're unstoppable. Imagine getting brownie points for simply giving people the information that they already shared with you. And it's not cheating! My job is tricking people into thinking I can read their minds, despite my going onstage and saying, "I don't read minds, I read people." The whole game is knowing how to integrate information in a way that seems truly amazing. And this is one of those life hacks that you can begin using today. I mean, just imagine how useful it would be if you're really junior at your job. If you can remember something about the big boss when you're in the elevator, you'll be noticed, and that's a pathway to success.

Any information that's given to you, anything that's been revealed, don't just let that go. Keep it and pull it out later, because that's the kind of impression that will make you stick in *their* memories.

Anchoring Information

As I transitioned from the party circuit to working primarily in the corporate sector, it struck me that pure entertainment was no longer enough; I really wanted to provide tangible value to my clients. I realized I could be most impactful by taking the information the client wanted to convey to the audience, which has a real dollars and cents value, and making it more unforgettable. I'd say to those who hired me, "Hey, what if your clients leave your event and truly remember the three key messages or data points you are targeting? What if I could do this in such a way that the information becomes 'sticky' and remains embedded in their long-term memory because it is presented under the guise of entertainment?" Think about this for a moment: Memorizing a thirty-line poem seems an overwhelming and daunting task for most of us. Yet you can easily recall the lyrics to dozens of your favorite songs. The delivery vehicle for information determines how well it will be retained.

Turns out, authentically engaging the audience and sneaking key messages and takeaways into my presentation is a very valuable addition for my corporate clients.

Standing on the dais lecturing people tends to be less effective because only so much information can be processed, and not all of the info can ever be retained. Remember, our brains give precedence to the memories that come with higher rewards, and that isn't a lecture. According to Charan Ranganath, a professor at UC Davis's Center for Neuroscience, "Rewards help you remember things, because you want future rewards. The brain prioritizes memories that are going to be useful for future decisions."[12] So with my corporate clients, I relay the information that they want their target consumer to retain. And I do that as part of an incredibly entertaining mind-reading show. This creates a greater value proposition for their company and it's been a huge ticket to my success.

When what clients want the audience to remember is included as part of a trick, they don't really see the takeaways as part of a sales pitch or lecture anymore. When presented within the form of entertainment or humor, that core message suddenly sticks a lot better because of the way everyone pays attention. We home in on entertainment. For example, if I'm working with a charity, I will reveal a series of numbers, such as someone's birthday, the jersey number of another person's favorite football player, and maybe one final person's ATM PIN. Everyone is thoroughly blown away at this point. We then multiply those numbers together and find that the total is precisely our fundraising goal for the gala and printed on the flyer everyone has in their hands. They are absolutely floored and that's when I explain what is being done with the money and how much we appreciate the generosity of all the attendees. The audience loves it because everyone's still reeling from the trick, yet the point seamlessly sticks. The charity's patrons walk away knowing where their money is going and with a great feeling in their hearts.

There's something incredibly powerful when a speaker can shift between humor and seriousness. I once saw an exceptional presenter recount his experience summiting Mount Everest—a journey during which three people tragically died. The room grew heavy with emotion. Just as the weight settled in, he slipped in a well-timed joke, breaking the tension. That sudden shift helped guide the audience through a roller coaster of feelings and drew them in even deeper, thereby helping them to remember what's being communicated. It all comes back to our brains prioritizing things that feel different.

Even the work I do with ESPN has a purpose behind it. I'm trying to get the team to walk out of practice having shared an incredible memory; that's a huge morale boost, which is in itself an anchor. Keep in mind, even though these guys are on the same team, they aren't on the *same team*. I can assure you, there's a big difference between the player who's the star quarterback and the second-string QB and whose butt is warming that bench. The second-stringers are not wishing the starter a spectacular injury-free season, because they might see that person as standing between them and a bigger paycheck, more fame, and a better career. So I try to create team unity, and I especially try to humanize the coaches and make them more accessible. The more unified a team is, the more satisfied the players are and the more effective they'll be on the field.

If I visited the team you root for and they end up winning the big game this year?

You're welcome.

Because we've been exercising your memory in this chapter, you should be feeling the burn. Now that you're better versed in anchoring information, you'll be far more adept at remembering strangers' names, and that can foster new relationships while your new techniques for remembering information they share about themselves will help strengthen existing connections.

There's no downside to having a more powerful memory, and the more actively you listen, the stronger your memory will get. You don't have to be a mind reader; you just need to put in the effort. And if you write down the information you want to keep, it can pay dividends in the long run, creating good for you and those around you, and that is unforgettable.

The Backward Alphabet Exercise

I want to leave you with the ability to use your memory to stun your friends, so I'm going to show you how to memorize the alphabet backward, saying it in reverse as easily as you can say it forward.

If I'm teaching this at a seminar, the first thing I'll do is have someone sing the alphabet song, which is very funny, because when people are watching us, it can get nerve-racking and even the smartest person falters (or at the very least sings brutally off-key).

After I do that, I'll tell them "Now say it backward." Most people hesitate, "Ummm, *Z, Y . . .*" and they start to crumble. Then in rapid fire, I'll rattle off the whole alphabet in reverse lightning fast. Then I'll drop the stunner and let them know, "In ten minutes, every one of you will be able to say it that fast backward for the rest of your life."

To teach this skill, I'll create teams who break down different letters and remember them in sections. (This is less about teams and more about recalling info in digestible chunks via association.) Again, memorizing the alphabet backward is probably not something you'll use in your day-to-day life, but this is a huge confidence builder that gives you a window into how your brain works, not to mention a fun party trick. In my workshop, everyone in the room gets a poster and a thick marker. I'll tell them that we'll start by breaking this exercise down into pieces across each team. As with any goal or problem, the best way to approach it is to chop it into bite-size chunks. To make it stick, I'll add an emotional hook, something they can quickly associate with the data.

In the first group, I'll talk about how in econ courses in college, they always call the company "XYZ Corp." I'll say, "But we're disrupting the game. We just created a company that's going to change everything. You know what we should do? Let's flip things on their head. We'll call it ZYX Corp. Who's with me?"

The first group will write *ZYX* on their posterboard and we'll all say it out loud. I find that the sillier we get, the more they'll remember this. Then I'll walk over to the next table and ask, "Where did you go to school?" As attendees tell me all the places they graduated from, I'll interject, "No, you didn't. All of you went to West Virginia University, and you bleed blue and old gold. WVU! So what's our war cry? *W, V, U!*"

I'll make everyone cheer and then we'll go back to the first table, saying, "Where do we work? ZYX! Who do we cheer for? WVU, right?" After this, I'll talk about my son who is eight. I'll say, "He loves *Guinness World Records*. He likes to quiz me with his esoteric knowledge, asking things like, 'Can you guess how much the most expensive kitchen sink in the world costs?' Well, he told us that the most expensive teaspoon in the world sold for twelve million dollars, after being handed down from generation to generation." Is this true? Absolutely not. But is it outlandish enough to stick in your brain? I sure hope so. The next group will write down *TS* for that teaspoon. I'll tell them this teaspoon is made out of platinum and I have everyone imagine holding it in their hand. Together, we'll chant, "*T, S,* teaspoon, teaspoon."

Then I'll say the person who bought the teaspoon at auction did not want his name made public, so he called himself Robert Q. Public. Initials *RQP*. I'll tell them, "Imagine those initials engraved into this teaspoon, *TS*. His name is Robert Q. Public. *R, Q, P.*" Then we'll run down the line again, starting back with *ZYX*.

To the next team, I'll start with, "You guys lucked out. It's January. It's cold. I want a day off work. And you know, the third Monday, we get to celebrate a truly legendary figure in our nation's history, Dr. Martin Luther King Jr., aka you get the day off ON MLK Jr. day. That's *O, N, M, L, K, J*. So you guys get the easiest string." I go down the line and have every team yell out their letters and let everyone know that we've already learned seventeen out of the twenty-six letters, and it has only been a few minutes, more than halfway there!

At this point, I'll make a heart with my hands. I'll say, "Do you know this gesture? It's a heart. Everyone in the room do this. I heart, *I, H*. I heart, *I, H*. Everybody make that gesture," and we all do it. And we'll keep doing that three or four times, and then we'll go down the line. We'll reinforce it over and over.

Next, I'll talk about how I have a new girlfriend. I'll say, "Okay, everyone write *G, F*, girlfriend, girlfriend." And so they write *GF*. I'll say, "You're my girlfriend. *GF*. Do you know her name? Her name is Edna, but she makes me call her Ed in public, which is very embarrassing, because that sounds weird. But she wants me to call her Ed (as in spelled E-D) not Edna. So girlfriend Edna, *G, F, E, D*." And we lather, rinse, repeat.

Finally, I'll end with a rather silly story, "The last bit is *C, B, A*, so it's very easy, because it's the opposite of *ABC*. Like my accountant told me he's got his CBA. And I thought, *Isn't that a CPA?* And he goes, 'Nope, it's a CBA,' so he kept arguing. And I think a CBA is like a fake version of a CPA." We repeat it a few times, and then we do the whole thing.

Everybody remembers the alphabet this way. If you're willing to be silly, say this to three people that you meet throughout the course of the day. Go through it three more times at different intervals, and then go home and tell your kids, your dog, or your spouse, and then tell them again tomorrow. If you do it that many times, you will retain it for the next year. It will stick, I promise you.

I've had people come up to me years after a seminar and tell me how crazy it is that they still remember it!

Keep in mind, it's not that your memory is bad; it's simply that it's out of shape, but now you have the tools to exercise it!

ELEVEN

Disarm with Charm

I can't restate this enough: I don't read minds, I read people. And at my shows, I always seek out those audience members I feel will give the biggest, most over-the-top reactions. But in life you can't always choose who you have to deal with, be it your boss or your brother-in-law. This is why learning to disarm with charm will come in exceptionally handy!

Let's start off with how I define *charm*. To me, charm is the ability to influence people, and there are a lot of different ways to go about this. Ultimately, charm involves getting people on your team; it's finding a way to persuade them to root for you. It's about using your personality and your skills to win them over, whether it's smiling your way out of a speeding ticket with a harried traffic cop or showing empathy to the poor airline employee trying to deal with two hundred angry passengers who just deboarded a canceled flight to Dallas. What's so great about charm is it doesn't feel one-sided. When you're able to charm someone, you both leave the interaction feeling more positive. (Especially when you're the only passenger that the gate agent accommodates because you were the one of two hundred who was kind.)

Charm is like a Swiss Army Knife, useful in so many different situations. Because that presence is not only about winning a person over, but also about being able to show your appreciation. That charisma is the light that shines on all of us at the same time.

Inevitably, you'll find yourself in situations where you're forced to deal with someone who's angry or upset, whether you're negotiating with difficult coworkers, unengaged committee members, a room full of NFL players who are ready to go home after a grueling day of practice, or cranky children. I'll show you ways to use your charm to shift their energy. (I know a lot about cranky children. *A lot.*) And when you use their negative energy to your advantage, it's like a mental judo move . . . and they'll never even see it coming!

Break the Ice

I absolutely adore stand-up comedy. It is my favorite form of entertainment . . . far more than mentalism if you can believe it. Comedians are masters of charm and use it from the moment their feet touch that stage. They need the audience on the same page as them or it's going to be the longest, unfunniest fifteen minutes of everyone's lives. Humor is the tool that stand-up uses to charm the audience into going along for the ride, to tip the scales their way.

If you've never been onstage trying to break the ice with an audience, you might not realize that those seated in front of you are not immediately on your side. They're not obligated to pull for your success. It makes no difference to the audience. They can be entertained by your brilliant comedy or by the flaming dumpster fire of your failure. It's not like when your parents would come to your elementary school and applaud wildly as you played Tree No. 3 in the musical, no matter how talented (or untalented) you actually were. Odds are they still took you out for ice cream afterward.

At best, an audience is neutral and it's on the comic to win them over. Every part of the performance, from how that performer grabs the mic to the clothes they wear to the way they style their hair, is part of that charm initiative. The gestures, the actions, all of it has been planned in advance and rehearsed ad nauseam. Each choice is deliberate and orchestrated for a result, even though the performance feels totally spontaneous and natural to the audience.

Now, if we're talking about the noun itself, the dictionary definition of *charm* is the power or quality of giving delight or arousing admiration. For the verb, the definition gets at attracting or delighting as if by magic. What the dictionary doesn't say is that charm—both the noun and the verb—is the linchpin to success.

But how do you become more charming in your life? We'll break it down in this chapter because charm will power your success.

I Know What You're Thinking

In order to succeed as a mentalist, I need to ensure that audience members aren't worried or apprehensive about what's going to happen when they're involved in my performance, and potentially thinking, *Yikes, he's watching everything I do. And he knows what I'm thinking right now; I don't like anything about this scenario.* That's why the first thing I do is try to put the audience at ease, telling them that I call BS on people even being able to read minds.

Without the secret ingredient of using charm to make people feel comfortable with me, an audience could turn on me pretty quickly. I call what I'm able to do the "have a drink with you after the show" test.

I strive to leave those who see me perform wanting to say hello at the bar after the performance, because that means I connected with them. My warmth won them over. Being able to guess their ATM PIN or naming the first person they ever kissed is disconcerting and can make people feel vulnerable and unprotected. But when that information is presented with some magnetism, the equation changes and suddenly everyone's lining up to have their minds read.

We are hardwired to have an expectation of what others are going to be like. We define people by the narrative we see, for better or worse. We're often judged immediately on our appearance, regardless of whether or not this is fair. In fact, according to behavioral science professor Alexander Todorov, we can make decisions about other people's trustworthiness, competence, and likability after looking at their faces for only a fraction of a second.[1] Whoa.

But what swings them back to us (and us back to them) is charm.

For example, let's say you see a big, scary biker-type in his road-worn leathers, all muscled and tatted-up. You are likely to immediately jump to conclusions about him because our minds rapidly categorize people and situations as a way to help us respond to them.[2] This happens in the region of the brain called the amygdala, which is the part that warns us about potential threats.[3] Yet the second that guy opens his mouth to say how he's been struggling to get his daughter to eat her broccoli, it changes the way we look at him. *Wait, this isn't a scary guy at all,* we think. *He's a concerned parent—just like I am—only he happens to ride a Harley.*

When I say we're trying to charm to disarm, what I mean is disrupting people's preconceived notions, clearing them off the table. Creating a shortcut past who they think we might be to how we *want* them to see us. We all have our own preconceived notions about others, based on our pasts, upbringings, and the ways we are wired. How often have you met someone and ended up saying, "Wow, you're so different from what I thought you'd be like." It's just staggering how much we hold on to our own stereotypes. What I learned over time is that when people see me, they think, *Oh, he's a magician, he's going to do a trick*, or *Ugh, he's going to challenge me intellectually*, and that raises their guard. I have to dispel those notions quickly.

Personally, when it comes to preconceived notions about what I do, I like to immediately lay everything out in the open, telling people, "If I can read your mind, that's super off-putting, right?" I even say this during my show. I make sure to verbalize their inner monologue as soon as I anticipate their thoughts—which kind of is *real* mind reading! Then I will address their reticence to take away any residual unease and instead lean into how intriguing the methods I'm using are, and if they can start to catch how I'm doing it.

What's so monumental is that charm is a skill anyone can learn to master. And even better, you'll find that the art of mastering charm—especially when you see immediate results—is fun!

Honesty Is the Best Policy

Charm is a property that people think you have naturally, like it's part of your DNA, but that's not accurate. Charm is a tool that you can absolutely learn how to use and a skill you can build. Of course, it's true that some people are imbued with natural charisma, which isn't quite the same thing as charm. As writer Jason Vu Nguyen puts it, the difference between charm and charisma is: "Charm is 'I come to you' and charisma is 'you come to me.'"[4]

In my view, charm consists of equal parts humor, vulnerability, and honesty. Honesty truly is at the core. People can sniff out someone who's fake from a mile away. There's nothing more off-putting than insincerity, because we have an evolutionary need to establish social trust. Inauthenticity sets off our internal alarm bells and spurs psychological discomfort.[5] So when you find yourself disliking someone because you perceive that they're acting fake, there's a whole lot churning under the surface of your psyche that makes you feel that way, even if you can't put your finger on the *why*, exactly.

To me? Insincerity just grates. Insincerity makes us feel like we're being played and manipulated. I've seen many videos of magicians or people that do what I do, and when I watch them perform, I instantly say, "That's not who they really are." And I don't like it. They feel to me like a caricature of the actual person.

When I'm onstage, I'm authentically myself, but maybe dialed up an extra point or two so everyone in the back row feels included. (If I were this exuberant at home, it would be insufferable.)

What draws people in is *authenticity*. In fact, authenticity is so important, Merriam-Webster made *authentic* their word of the year in 2023.[6] Being authentic is highly valued, especially as people seek out genuineness and transparency in the digital age, as the rise of AI is causing us to question all our perceptions. Importantly, authenticity cannot be faked.

I remember once seeing an interview with Oprah where she was asked what her greatest talent was. She explained that she was especially skilled at acting in front of the camera exactly the way she'd act if she were off camera. While Oprah makes it sound so simple, that's an incredible skill to have. For so many people, when the camera goes on, they change. They feel ill at ease at the realization that they're being observed, possibly judged. By the way, freezing on camera is a real phenomenon. This happens because the camera triggers our bodies' stress responses, even though we're not in any physical danger. Just the perceived threat of having eyes on us makes our stress hormones spike in a fight-or-flight response. We feel self-conscious or we're overcome by performance anxiety. Then, that spiking cortisol impacts our cognitive function, interfering with our ability to express ourselves naturally . . . so we literally freeze up and can't find our words.

Again, the camera can be metaphorical here, meaning that anytime you're in a novel situation outside of your comfort zone, the fight-or-flight response is still real. Perhaps this happens when you're in a business setting or with new people you don't know so well. Your insecurities come to the forefront and they affect the way you behave, and suddenly you're not making the impression you'd hoped.

The good news is, employing some charm will help you turn that right around.

I feel like everybody has two different selves: There's the self we are when we're with people we love or know really well. And then there's the self we take on when we're less comfortable, when we're on guard. That first self is our most effective self, but it's not what everyone sees, because we're afraid of rejection, so we sometimes keep the best of ourselves hidden and that is a shame.

How do we fight this? Well, we have to become aware of when and how we slip away from presenting our best selves.

Now let's go back to the situation where you're by yourself in a room full of new people. The urge is to just busy yourself on your phone, right? Just avoid the unknown until it's over? But what if you used charm instead? Because charm is synonymous with honesty. If you're somewhere you don't know anyone and everyone else is in the same situation, I suggest you lean into it. Almost everyone feels awkward in a setting like this; it's human nature. So name it and claim it. Walk up to someone you don't know and say with a warm smile, "I'm a fish out of water, I don't know anyone here. Definitely nervous talking to all these strangers."

When you say that to somebody, people are disarmed and grateful that you took the risk. You're saying what they're feeling, but they're too anxious to be vulnerable and open and they're not showing their best selves, either. That creates a connection. Your honesty builds a bridge. And it will be disarming because most are so afraid to let anybody see behind the curtain, to be vulnerable. It's like we hesitate to show that we're human.

So, what are the active steps you can take to up your charm? Let's get into them.

Time to Listen

Are you ready for a staggering statistic? Eighty-five percent of all that we know, we have learned by listening.[7] So, if you want to immediately up your charm level, it's a must that you listen and be present. Per a study at the University of California, Berkeley, researchers found that when participants listened to a speaker telling a personal story, the audiences' brain activity synched up with that of the speaker.[8] What a powerful takeaway.

Listening means you're actively engaging with what the other person is saying, and you're not just going, "Uh-huh, yep, uh-huh," while you wait impatiently to say your piece. As author Jim Kwik says in an article on the science of active listening, there are five steps everyone can—and should—take when trying to improve their ability to listen.

First of all, stuff your phone in your pocket and pay attention to what's said. This is universally important, whether you're sitting in front of your child's teacher or at the conference room table with a potential client or at a trendy fusion restaurant with a date you'd like to impress. People will often tell us everything we need to know, but if we're distracted by texts or a stock-ticker push notification or the hockey game on the TV above the bar, we might miss something important.

Second, a great way to intensify the impact of your listening is to express an interest in what's being said. Not only does this kind of engagement show respect and common courtesy, but there's also science that reinforces the effectiveness of this approach. Researchers in Japan have found that "neural activation in the ventral striatum was enhanced by perceiving active listening, suggesting that this was processed as rewarding. It also activated the right anterior insula, representing positive emotional reappraisal processes."[9] In plain English? When you actively listen to someone, they get a reward of that sweet brain candy I've spoken about in previous chapters.

Kwik's next suggestion is often easier said than done, but let's do it anyway. We need to make sure we're not peppering the conversation with a lot of interruptions. Respond? Yes. Leap in and take over the convo? Absolutely not. Interruptions aren't just rude; in fact, they trigger the flight-or-fight response in the amygdala. There are times when people have interrupted me that I could clearly feel my muscles tense and my heart rate increase.

When you resist the urge to interrupt and allow the person to conclude their point, you're aiding them in activating their prefrontal cortex, leading to cognitive and emotional regulation, per Kwik. But there will be times that you have to add something for a better shared understanding, so if you do need to jump in, do so in a way that won't alienate that person. ("Wait, let me stop you right there, Bob," are words that should never come out of your mouth if you're trying to charm someone.)

Kwik recommends that you engage in the conversation, asking meaningful questions to ensure mutual understanding. This works in any situation because this kind of deft, patient manner of interjecting communicates to the speaker that they're being heard. If you say a phrase like, "Wow, I've never thought of X that way before. In your experience, how would this also apply to Y and Z?" there's not a yes and no answer there; whomever you're speaking with will absolutely want to engage more. Consider this: When you meet someone, you tend to ask the same ten questions, from "What do you do?" to "Where are you from?" Everyone has their rote answers for these questions—they don't snap us out of autopilot. But what if when you met someone, you asked, "If I met a six-year-old version of you, what would they think of you as an adult?" That takes most people by surprise and is designed to bring out some introspection. The more branches you can open in a conversation, the more you indicate interest and you can use that interest to enchant and amaze people, even if you're in a professional environment. It's also for your own benefit: When you ask questions, you engage your hippocampus, and this is key because language and memory are intimately linked.[10] Also, the more you ask about someone else, the more interesting they think *you* are. It's a win-win. So right now, I want you to think of three questions you can ask someone that will really make them stop, think, and engage.

Finally, if you want to improve your listening, one of the best ways to do that is to summarize the conversation. This is crucial because not only does it reinforce the fact that you've been interested and engaged, but it pings your prefrontal cortex and will help you retain the information.

Bottom line? Active listening is flat-out charming.

If you're ready for a master class in listening, let me tell you about how I defensively listen when it comes to my business. When I say "defensively listen," I mean that you listen not only to understand, but to prepare yourself to react in a myriad of ways. It's listening to the nth degree, both actively and strategically. One of the reasons I've experienced as much growth as I have is that I collect as much information as I possibly can. Information is power. In the early days of doing gigs, I'd take my own booking phone calls. People would call me and they'd say, "I'm having a party on such and such date." I used to field those calls anywhere because I wanted to be as accessible as possible.

I was fixated on never losing a show by missing a call, my concern being that the client or event planner would immediately call another performer who would get booked instead. Yet answering every call also put me at a disadvantage, because I'd pick up not knowing who I was talking to. I realized that if I answered the phone when I was busy, I couldn't look up info about this person, so I'd ask them where they found me. I'd drill down, querying, "Oh, was it in Roslyn? Was it Jeffrey's bar mitzvah?" If I could discern that it was Jeffrey Rose's bar mitzvah, I'd know a lot of things, including how much I charged at that event or if I offered different types of packages, or if my rates had varied over time.

Honestly, it can mean a deal slipping through your fingers if you go into something blind versus if you go into something knowing that the guy's a huge baseball fan and two of his kids play college ball, because then you can make references that are topical to him. Defensive listening is about knowing your crowd, as the more familiar you are with them, the more likely you are to be able to charm them. If you start making sports references to someone who hates sports, that material will fall on deaf ears. Defensive listening is about being a chameleon, ingratiating yourself. Building rapport with somebody because connection is a cornerstone of charm.

What I started doing was answering the phone, and after the initial pleasantries, asking, "When's the date of your event?" and then, "Listen, I'm so sorry. I'm walking into a meeting right now. I'm letting you know that I am available. I would love to be there but, respectfully, need to get back to you once I'm back in the office so our call isn't rushed. When is a good time later today or tomorrow that we can talk?"

Then I'd say, "Let me quickly text you my information-gathering form so you can fill this all out and to make your life easier." What I've done is, I've answered their phone call, I've been very responsive in the moment, I've let them know that I'm available, and I've hooked them, so that hopefully they're not calling someone else immediately after me. Also, I've used benefits-oriented language to steer them toward my booking form where they provide all of their information, including where they first saw me or who referred them. From there, I can google their names, find out who they are, where they live, where they work. Those details are useful to know going into a negotiation. Information is power and the more you know, the better positioned you are in every business.

Now that I've done my homework before the call and am better informed on how this lead originated, I'm ready with relevant info for the negotiation. So, if that caller were to come back and say, "But you gave this deal to the person who referred me," I have an immediate and honest answer as to why that is. As opposed to being defensive, I can say, "I'm so glad you mentioned that. That's absolutely true. So, the deal I had with Jared is because he hired me for three upcoming events at once and therefore received a bulk booking discount; I'd be happy to extend that same deal if you're interested" I got ahead of their objection. When you defensively listen, you're not a used car salesman. Instead, you're readily prepared with the right answers.

The bottom line is the better you listen, whether it's actively or defensively, the more charming everyone will find you because, more than anything, people want to be heard.

Charm Offensive

Being charming is another way of describing being likable. A lot of what it takes to disarm with charm is the desire to genuinely connect. Obviously, listening is a key component. But there are other areas where you can improve as well.

I've talked about how special it makes people feel when you recall their little details, whether it's about how their college kid is enjoying a semester abroad or what's happening with their plans to finally buy that vacation home in Maine. It's not enough for you to know these things— instead, you have to use them to reinforce the idea that what's going on in their life is meaningful enough for you to remember.

Let's take a question and compare a charming version that uses personal details with one that doesn't.

> Question One: "How was your summer?"
>
> Question Two: "How was the new place in
> Kennebunkport this summer? Congrats on that, by the
> way. Did you love being by the ocean? How did the kids
> enjoy all that boating? Did you get your fill of lobster?
> How great was the weather?"

Question One requires nothing but a rote answer. They could say, "Fine," and that could sum up the whole summer. But the second set of questions expresses genuine interest and will lead to a more fulfilling conversation on all sides, especially if the exchange reveals more commonalities, for example, "No, I'm allergic to lobster." "No way, me too!" Ultimately, people like to be remembered, and when you can recall the details of their life, when you can ask them questions that are meaningful, it will make you both feel good, especially when your approach is positive and upbeat.

Remember that conversation is a give-and-take, not a monologue. If you want to be charming, be interested. In *How to Win Friends and Influence People*, Dale Carnegie often referred to Publilius Syrus's quote, "We are interested in others when they are interested in us."[11] Being curious is a game changer. Asking sincere questions can be your superpower. Again, let's look at how I felt when I spent half an hour with Steven Spielberg. He was so engaged with me that he left me feeling like I was the most interesting person in the world, despite my not getting one question in about *Jaws*—not one!

Another way to up your charm is to offer sincere compliments. Again, *sincerity* is the goal here. If you hand out compliments like you're passing out Halloween candy, it will feel weird and disingenuous. But something well-timed and heartfelt will almost always hit. For example, let's say you spot and admire someone's ring. You say something like, "What a gorgeous piece of jewelry. Is that an heirloom? Is there a story behind it?" Suddenly, this person who may have never thought twice about you is creating an emotional connection with you as she relays a tale about the grandmother who sewed it into the hem of her skirt so she could smuggle it out of Poland during the war. And now you're looking at them like they're the most fascinating person in the world because it's a hell of a story, and that's how they're feeling, too. Try to walk away from that conversation without a grin on your face. Remember, when you offer up sincere compliments, you open the door to a deeper sense of connection.

If you want to take your charm to the next level, mind your manners and be respectful and polite, even if it's you who happens to be in the more powerful position. If you have the opportunity to extend a little grace, do it. Be the guy who holds the elevator for the person running down the hall. Be the woman who says, "No, after you, I insist."

While confidence is always a plus, arrogance isn't, so let's keep the bragging to a minimum. It might feel good to boast, but that good feeling is definitely one-sided, as it can trigger feelings of inferiority in the other person and, now, they're not rooting for you. (Hello, social media.) Also, bragging makes you come across as less trustworthy, according to researchers at the University of Arizona.[12] So if you're bragging to someone you hope to attract as a client, you're actually *less* likely to win the account. Sure, you can talk about your wins, but couch them in humility.

Whenever you can and when appropriate, use humor in your interactions. This is across-the-board advice, but it's especially relevant if you're dating, because the use of humor shapes the perception of creativity, intelligence, and social competence, all traits everyone wants in a partner.[13] According to Michelle Shiota of Arizona State University's Department of Psychology, "In this work, we propose that people are attracted to funny romantic partners because humor acts as a cue that leads people to perceive a potential partner as possessing other desirable traits. Of the candidate traits we examined, creative ingenuity— the ability to think and act in original and inventive ways to solve problems—emerged as the trait people most reliably inferred from humor."[14] I'm not saying you have to join an improv troupe if you're hoping to find love, but it wouldn't hurt. Humor bonds us, so no matter what you're doing, offering a funny line or a wry comeback will absolutely up your charm.

If you want to be your most charming, you have to pay attention both to the verbal and the nonverbal cues the other person is giving you. The science of positive body language is something studied in "kinesics." Kinesics encompasses so much, from gestures to shrugs to the flush of our cheeks or our intake of breath. Negative body language can be the rolling of the eyes or the stiffening of the spine.

Let me ask you this—how many times have you received a text and agonized over someone's intended meaning? (Trust me, it happens to everyone.) This is because all we have are the words—there's no body language to give us contextual clues. A recent article notes that body language accounts for between 60 and 65 percent of all communication, so it's an enormous piece of the puzzle.[15] That article's figure largely aligns with what Albert Mehrabian, UCLA professor, had to say. In the late 1960s to early 1970s, he came up with the 7-38-55 model, meaning that verbal language only constitutes 7 percent of communication, nonverbal signals being the other 93 percent, specifically breaking down nonverbal communication into 55 percent body language and 38 percent voice and tone.[16] So, yes, he established that body language is a significant component of how we get our points across.

Let's say you're in a job interview for a position you really want. You're likely to be more successful in this endeavor if you're mirroring that interviewer's body language. If they rest their hand on their chin, you do the same, because that mirroring is a nonverbal way of confirming you're on the same page as your interviewer. The more you pick up on how they present themselves in gestures and speech patterns, the more you'll subliminally convince them that you're of similar mindsets. Mirroring establishes rapport.

Your body language is something you can easily control, and doing so can be as simple as keeping your palms open rather than bunching your hands into fists, pointing your feet in the same direction as someone else, making eye contact, or leaning in when you're talking to someone. Here's a weird fact—we're attracted to being able to see people's hands. There have been studies about hands, and what researchers have found is that when you can't see someone else's hands, it impacts your degree of trust in them. If a person is concealing their hands, like having them shoved in their pockets, it can even decrease how attractive we find them.[17]

As part of my act, I pay close attention to a few things, particularly eye movements, because our eye movements indicate that we're thinking. For example, if a person looks up and to the left after being asked a question, it usually means they're accessing memories. Yet if they look up to the right, it typically means they are constructing an idea. Big difference.

For my tricks to work, I have to be 100 percent sure that the participant comprehends what I'm asking of them. In my act—and in life—it's so important to make sure you're not only heard but also understood. Your spidey senses will tell you when someone's not fully engaged, like their mouth said, "Yep," but their brain said, "Nope." So double-check because ultimately the buck stops with you.

While paying attention to these quirks and bits of movement seems like such a small gesture, it packs a major punch when it comes to increasing your charm, because these little things trace back through our evolution to when being in limbic synchrony was key to the survival of your group.[18] As it may have been awhile since you had your last bio class, limbic synchrony occurs when two people's brains start coordinating, meaning you're on the same wavelength, not just emotionally but also as your heart rates, breathing, and brain wave patterns begin to synch.

Finally, here's the greatest weapon in your arsenal. And it's a biggie that accomplishes so much, from releasing dopamine and endorphins to reducing stress hormones to improving your relationships to even boosting your immune system, because it increases the production of antibodies.

What is this sorcery, you ask?

Simple. It's a smile.

At the end of the day, charm is all about drawing people in, and if you do the above, you'll be unstoppable.

Put Yourself in Their Shoes

It's an unfortunate fact that even the best of us have bad days. It's an even more unfortunate fact that sometimes people are jerks. The good news is that the human brain is coded for compassion and empathy, so here's how to deal with someone who is not yet won over by your charms.

If somebody comes at you with negative energy, your best bet is always to kill with kindness. Shift that energy. If somebody's coming at you with a vibe that's confrontational, reply with gratitude, because that disarms people. If you want to immediately de-escalate, make the person on the other end of the conversation feel heard. Repeat what they say and empathize, "I'm so sorry you had this experience. That had to be uncomfortable and that's just not right." When you give them back empathy, you smother the fire, rather than stoke the flames.

Imagine you're the gate attendant I mentioned earlier and you're dealing with all those angry passengers. If you're a weary traveler who is desperate to get on the next flight home to your family, you're going to have the best luck winning that person over if you remain calm and speak to them respectfully. Now is not the time to make threats or invoke your million-mile club membership. Use your empathy by saying something like, "I'm so sorry you have to deal with this. This probably isn't how you hoped your day was going to go when you got up, right?" The more you can make them feel heard and understood, the faster you're going to get to your bulkhead seat. More important, by employing your charm, you're going to lighten their load, too.

Now, if I were trying to de-escalate the meltdown one of my kids was having before bed, my approach would be to first validate their feelings and to make my voice quieter. The last thing I'd want to do was be louder. Kids can lose control and it's not their fault—instead, it's often a nervous system response, so I don't want to pile on any more stress.[19] I'd probably get down on their level so they could look me in the eye, to decrease their perception of any imbalance of power. I might distract them by offering them something they like, or I'd offer them other choices, like, "Do you want to wear the red pajamas or the blue ones?"

Regardless of what kind of tyrant you're dealing with, whether it's a toddler or someone acting like a toddler, you're not going to move forward if you get caught up taking their abuse personally. Treat them with respect, with kindness, while asking them questions to clarify the root cause of an issue and showing them that you're on the same team.

This is *not* the opportunity to mirror their body language, and it's especially not the time to interrupt them, as they're already in fight-or-fight mode.

When you disarm with charm, you set yourself up for success because charm impacts everyone involved. When people root for you, they win as well. Charm is how you connect, communicate, and conjure up the best of feelings.

When there are times that your natural charms aren't enough, remember to lead with empathy and do everything in your power to de-escalate tense situations with kindness, repetition, and acknowledgment. Because at the end of the day, when you can show people that they're seen and heard, they will eventually come around. And if they don't? At least you didn't make a bad situation worse.

TWELVE

Tie It All Together with a Story

In this chapter, I'll share my greatest communication tool—being a storyteller—as I recount a couple of the tales that made me who I am today. I will kick it off with the *Ocean's Eleven*–style caper I pulled off with a group of Merrill Lynch analysts as we all channeled our inner mentalists . . . along with Prince Harry. (It's a story so shocking, even Prince Harry himself can't believe it's true!)

We jump from one of the most exhilarating nights of my life to one of the worst, which held consequences so severe they nearly derailed my entire career path, coming within a hair's breadth of preventing me from working on Wall Street. Lessons I learned on that fateful night enabled me to discover the right path moving forward, and taught me how to focus less on myself and more on the people around me. The unlikely benefit of that way of thinking made all the difference in the world. From stacking the deck in my favor and figuring out how to work my charm to planning for the unexpected, I had to pull every trick out of my mentalist tool belt to save my own skin. It's been two decades since then, and I'm only now starting to laugh about it. Let me preface the story with these three pieces of advice: Day drinking is a bad idea, orange will never be the new black, and everyone should learn a card trick as your get-out-of-jail-free card . . . literally!

As we draw to a close, let me say this—your best life is waiting for you. Your hopes, your dreams, your goals are ready to come true, and the tools and tricks I've shared will allow you to define them by reading your own mind.

The fourteen-year-old version of me performing at Zia's restaurant could not fathom all that he would achieve over the next three decades. The time is now for you to define your future.

And it all ties together with the art of storytelling.

Be a Storyteller

If you want to truly tap into your inner mentalist, there's no better way to do so than by delivering your message in story form instead of as a straightforward recitation of facts and figures or a routine PowerPoint. It doesn't matter how dynamic a speaker is, how animated, how enthusiastic or knowledgeable; what they say hits differently if that information is delivered as a story. This is scientific fact. When we were little kids, we begged our parents for a story before bed, and we've haven't outgrown this desire. That's because when a message is delivered in a narrative form, information not only pings the language-processing centers of our brain, but can also engage the sensory and motor cortices . . . and that is so powerful.

Stories help connect and inspire us by adding emotions and texture to cold hard facts and data points. Storytelling is built into our DNA and traces back thousands of years—an integral part of the human experience like creating music. It greatly enhances the audience's ability to remember and recount information, as well as sneak in lessons you might otherwise have quickly forgotten (recall the backward alphabet example we talked about . . . quick, which university did we all attend?).

Storytelling is particularly effective, because as Lani Peterson, PsyD, put it in a *Harvard Business Publishing* article:

> Scientists are discovering that chemicals like cortisol, dopamine and oxytocin are released in the brain when we're told a story. Why does that matter? If we are trying to make a point stick, cortisol assists with our formulating memories. Dopamine, which helps regulate our emotional responses, keeps us engaged. When it comes to creating deeper connections with others, oxytocin is associated with empathy, an important element in building, deepening or maintaining good relationships.[1]

Paul Zak, a renowned neuroscientist, conducted a series of experiments to determine how the use of storytelling might impact the brain. Per Zak:

> As social creatures, we depend on others for our survival and happiness. A decade ago, my lab discovered that a neurochemical called oxytocin is a key 'it's safe to approach others' signal in the brain. Oxytocin is produced when we feel trusted or shown a kindness, and it motivates cooperation with others. It does this by enhancing the sense of empathy, our ability to experience others' emotions. Empathy is important for social creatures because it allows us to understand how others are likely to react to a situation, including those with whom we work.[2]

In Zak's experiment, he divided the volunteers into two groups. One watched a video about a dying boy where the information was presented in a clinical, straightforward manner. With the other, he created a narrative arc—all the same information but told in the context of a story, including the perspective of the boy's father. Afterward, he took blood samples from all the volunteers, and those who'd seen the video that used storytelling showed an increase of oxytocin in their blood.[3]

What's particularly profound about Zak's experiment is that when he ran it a second time, he gave all the subjects money, which they were allowed to spend as they wanted. He discovered that the subjects who'd been found to have the highest levels of oxytocin and cortisol were the most likely to generously donate that money.[4] This absolutely aligns with what I do for my clients that raise money for various charities—when I relay the information they want to share using a narrative arc and an emotional hook, their fundraising is far more successful.

We tell stories not only to connect and entertain, but also to assert a degree of control over the listener or reader.[5] When we're in the middle of a remarkable story, we're holding that audience rapt—they're on the edge of their seats. Humanity has been telling stories since the inception of language because stories not only allow us to share information about what could be a threat, but also how we might maneuver past that threat. Storytelling has been a necessary part of how we've survived and evolved. And really, does anything feel better than having an audience in the palm of your hand?

So pull up a chair and gather close as I share two of my best dinner party stories, and try to spot all the concepts we've discussed in this book.

His Royal Highness

For years, magic was my way of approaching a group or a stranger. It was my secret power. Magic was how I made my fear of rejection disappear.

Instead of presenting them Clark Kent, the guy who was boring and plain and vanilla, I wanted to show them Superman. That was my cheat code to walk up to anyone and not let them know who I really was as a person. Instead, they got to know the slightly exaggerated version of me, a showman who can change a one dollar bill into a hundred dollar bill faster than a speeding bullet, who can turn the mirror back on the group and make them look good. Bringing out your inner mentalist is not so much about discovering your superpower as it is figuring out what makes you unique and special. It also helped provide me with my best dinner party story ever.

This story begins with my entry-level position at Merrill Lynch after graduating from college. I worked in the financial district right near the World Financial Center. I'd interned there the summer before and apparently performed well enough for the firm to offer me a full-time position upon graduation. Back in those days, Merrill Lynch put trainees through a ten-week analyst program. I was in the global technology sector, which is the IT division of an investment bank. Forty of us were US-based and ten were from the UK. Two of the Brits in our group were exceedingly tall, and I'm only saying this because it will be important later. (I'd say those guys were nerdy, but let me be honest, we all were.) The tall dudes were named John and Mike and we called them, respectfully, Big John and Big Mike. Yes, I know . . . very creative nicknames. One was about six-eight and one was nearly six-ten, and both of them were really lanky. Think less tough guy, more Mr. Bean.

Everyone in the program hung out together during the day as we were in a glorified version of school. Merrill Lynch would have executives speak to us throughout the morning and afternoon sessions, discussing various policies and procedures, as well as their personal journeys. Then, of course, we'd go out drinking every night. Imagine, ten weeks of being paid full salaries to have fun in New York. Those were the glory days of Wall Street.

The UK contingent lived together in long-term corporate housing, a situation that was somewhere between a hotel and a condo. (To us, it was basically a fancy dorm.) They had two rooms, and it felt almost like a fraternity. Being fresh out of college from the University of Michigan, this scenario felt happily familiar. All fifty of us partied together all the time. There was a clique of twenty who were inseparable—we just had a blast.

One night we all playing poker. In our group, a guy named Bing was an excellent communicator and connector. He was profoundly skilled at turning the mirror on other people, getting them to open up and let down their guard. Bing was an expert at walking into a room and instantly warming the group with a megawatt smile, while looking deeply into your eyes when you're speaking to him in a way that makes it feel as if nothing else exists. (Bing reminded me a lot of Barack Obama in that respect.)

This was 2003, a time when I'd say people were very familiar with British royalty as a whole however less so of the youngest heir to the throne, Prince Harry. He wasn't the household name he is now and nowhere near as recognizable. He was still quite young back then, fresh out of Eton. Apparently, there was an unwritten contract between the royals and the press at the time. The paparazzi largely left Harry alone during college, so between that and the internet still in its infancy, he was still a mystery to many Americans.

At one point, I looked across the poker table, and exclaimed to my British friend Michael Coates, "You look just like Prince Harry, bro." We all laughed because he didn't resemble him that much, save for the ginger hair. Again, how would we really know what he looked like? That's when I had a light-bulb moment.

I said, "Here's what we're going to do," and I started to lay out my plan to Michael, Bing, and the rest of our crew. Bing was a get-stuff-done kind of guy. That always impressed me about him. He was dating a girl who worked at the biggest PR firm in the city representing many notable celebs. My idea was that we go "big," creating one huge, unforgettable night by making everyone believe we were out with Prince Harry. I figured we already had a redheaded Brit and that was half the battle.

I said that Bing should have his girlfriend call a high-end nightclub and tell them we were vetting various venues for a possible visit by Prince Harry. Our plan wasn't about scoring anything free; it was about creating a splash. We all thought the idea was funny, but Michael wasn't buying it. He said, "You guys are crazy. No one's ever going to believe us." I said, "They will if we go big." I genuinely believed that if we sold people on the concept, if we played roles and committed to them, they would.

I started giving everyone tasks that night. I said, "Big John, Big Mike, you're going to be security. You guys wear black suits." Bobby was part of our group. He was British but of Pakistani descent and he looked just like Jason Statham. He was a hustler, the type of guy with an edge who may have, say, scalped concert tickets in college. He was already a master in disarming with charm.

As the idea grew in my head, I went around the poker table, assigning roles. We all had a good laugh playing out the scenario but then got back to the card game and typical witty banter. My so-called brilliant idea seemed to be forgotten. This was the second week of the ten weeks into our program. Fast-forward seven weeks later, when Bing stopped me in the hallway and said, "Dude." He could convey so much with a single word. "We're doing it."

Puzzled, I replied, "Doing what?"

Remember, I spelled out my idea one night a month and a half ago. Over the course of those weeks, I spit out *a lot* of stupid ideas. (You con't want to know.) Bing said, "We're going to do the Prince Harry thing." Having noted my confusion, he explained, "I got my girl in. She's willing to make the call."

I couldn't believe it—and I couldn't pass up the opportunity. My mind began to assemble the pieces we'd need to build a believable puzzle. How would we sell everyone else on this? Immediately, I realized that we needed to scout the right location. We decided on Underbar. This place was in the W Hotel in Union Square, which was a known celebrity hot spot. The location ticked all the boxes—centrally located, fun, a see-and-be-seen spot, very dark lighting—so it seemed like the perfect venue, largely because it felt so credible. We had Bing's girl-friend call Underbar and set up a meeting with the manager, keeping it light on details and heavy on intrigue. The first rule of show biz: Sell the sizzle, not the steak.

All of us guys picked out our suits—we wanted to look the part, as that's the only way our ploy would work—and we created dossiers on our official roles. Bobby would be the prince's official consort. We weren't sure if that was the term for it, but we barreled on. We did what research we could about our official titles and decided on our roles. I was the US affiliate liaison.

The four-person "advance team" rolled up to meet the people at the club in the afternoon. Our plan was to discuss protocol, security, what areas to cordon off, how we didn't want press interference, etc. We acted very serious because that's exactly how we figured Harry's real team would have done it. We were the living embodiment of fake it till you make it.

This story was a precursor to what I do for a living now; that night was all about mentalism, pure and simple. My job now is to fool people in a certain way, to get inside their heads. Long before I was a professional mentalist, I'd learned how people think, so when we showed up that day, I made sure that everyone committed to the fake out. I was engineering the outcome in our favor starting today. If any of us hesitated, we'd have been lost.

When you're pulling the ultimate prank, it's imperative you do everything the right way. The key is that you don't break character, no matter what. We went into the meeting and were ruthless with our questions, humorless and dour, making the W staffers feel like they weren't interviewing *us*, we were interviewing *them*. We drilled them relentlessly, asking things like, "Is this the right place? Is this not? We might have to take our business elsewhere. We need to be assured there will be no leaks. We want no paparazzi."

Ours was a basic sales technique, with the threat of the take-away, like we might gift our huge prize of a royal in attendance to a different establishment if they didn't have their act together. We got *them* to sell *us* on the Underbar. We went in there planning for every eventuality and what's so funny is it never occurred to them we'd be perpetrating this level of deception.

And why would they?

We explained to the club that we did not want word of this to get out . . . which is the best way to ensure that word will spread. It's straight-up human nature. That night, we rolled up with about fifteen of us in total. The royal escort group along with a handful of women who were in our training program, all of us dressed to the nines. We bought those little earpieces that the Secret Service wear, that loop over the ear and down the back. The cords dangled beneath our starched shirts, connected to nothing as we didn't have radios. (We barely had credit ratings!) We all wore black suits, crisp white shirts, and we were just so *bloody serious*. I mean, we were selling our association with someone in the line of succession to the British monarchy.

The plan was, any time ~~Prince Harry~~ Prince Michael walked around, I'd position myself in the front, Bobby behind, and the bodyguards left and right. We were entirely convincing as we confidently approached our velvet-roped section of the club. It was all about projecting confidence and acting like we belonged there; I was reliving that first day pitching at Zia's.

Our two bodyguards—those lanky British guys—stood in front of the rope, at attention with hands neatly folded. They were unflappable, no different than the guards you might see outside of Buckingham Palace. What worked in our favor was that the Bigs were so tall it was hard to make direct eye contact with them. Word began to spread like wildfire through that place. The bar cordoned off a corner booth for us with velvet ropes and our "security guards" stood at attention.

Now, we had to have somebody put up a credit card. You can't party like a royal without the funds to back it up. We implied that a guy in our program, Adam Prichard, was Harry's royal secretary. Adam was another IT nerd who suddenly was fast-tracked to heaven. We put down Adam's credit card and all of us twenty-three-year-olds started ordering and getting into it. We were all Merrill analysts, except for one of my college friends named Jeff who worked for BlackRock. After an hour, the gawking from the crowd was too much—everyone wanted to know who we were and what we were doing. The excitement in the air made the club feel electric, like we were on the precipice of something major. We were making the best kind of scene, so we told the management, "Here's what we're willing to do."

Because we wanted to go bigger.

We had them bring us paper napkins, saying, "We're willing to give up to one hundred autographs." The crowd went crazy and everybody on the other side of the velvet rope was chomping at the bit. Please note that Underbar was a basement bar and it was exceedingly dark; that was key. It was so poorly lit that we could have said we had anyone from Brad Pitt to Michael Jackson with us. Michael started signing autographs as we shuffled people through a hasty line and they went wild.

The other factor is that this was the pre-smartphone era. Nowadays, the jig would have been up in minutes. No one could google what Harry really looked like, plus Michael was convincingly British because he *was* British. One girl in the autograph line knew my friend Jeff because they worked at BlackRock together. She normally didn't give him the time of day, but suddenly she was begging him, "Can you get me farther in line?" Worried that she might give us up once she deduced that some nerd from U of M wouldn't be pals with the real Prince Harry, we had Jeff lean into it, suave as can be, saying, "I'll see what I can do."

The reason everything worked is that we all became mentalists that night. Every single one of us kept our shit together. No one broke character. We paid attention to how the crowd was acting and we read their expressions, giving them back exactly what we could see they wanted, and we refused to be our own worst enemies.

The whole night, Prince Michael was ordering like a fiend and he was surrounded by some of the most beautiful women in New York. He kept saying, "Adam, what do the girls need?" Michael had his arms around multiple ladies. Women who'd probably cross the street normally to avoid this dork were all over him. The best part was that at one point, he had to use the lavatory. He took the bodyguards, who knocked on bathroom doors and made everybody leave. Then they stood at attention outside while Bobby, the royal consort, went inside with him.

Imagine trying to tell a New Yorker what to do—*and having them listen!*

At a certain point, we felt like we were on the cusp of overstaying cur welcome. The energy had begun to shift. The second rule of show-biz is to always leave them wanting more, so that's what we did, parting cn a high note and asking for the check. Timing, as always, is everything.

Ironically, we never discussed what we'd do if our plan worked. We were the dog who finally caught the car—What were we going to do with it? We debated getting a limo and going to another location, but we were on such a high that we didn't want to blow it. We ended up not going elsewhere because our plan had been executed so flawlessly that we didn't want to risk it crashing down.

We left the poker table while we were ahead, with a story all of us would recount for the next twenty years and counting. Again, we weren't trying to get anything over on the bar financially. We paid our tab. My share was a staggering $1,800, and that was the most expensive night of my life. I mean, this was an astronomical sum, but if we wanted to play, we had to pay, and I've never regretted a single penny.

There are certain moments in your life where you feel so alive, and I can tell you some of those moments for me are the ones you'd expect, like my wedding day, when my children were born, their birthdays, and during some big races. The moment we walked out of Underbar, it felt like *The Breakfast Club* when the Brat Pack walked out and high-fived after detention. That was a moment that tied that little group of us together for life.

All of this would have been enough, except . . . the next week, *Us Weekly* published an "About Town" blurb, saying that Prince Harry was spotted at Underbar partying for his birthday.

Even the press bought our ruse!

We did it.

We gave everyone involved, from the waitstaff to the patrons to the management to my classmates, the best night ever. And we left with a tale we're all going to tell for the rest of our lives.

So that's my favorite story. But I'll share the one that could have changed everything next.

A Weekend in Jail

During the winter of my senior year of college, I drove up to Ferris State University in Big Rapids, Michigan, to hang out with my buddies Aaron and Tubo for the weekend. That college is about three hours from Ann Arbor, smack in the middle of nowhere. Big Rapids is one of those towns where there's a college and little else. In places like that, it feels like the locals somewhat can't stand the college kids, even though it's a weird symbiotic relationship because without the university there wouldn't be much of a town. In fact, the population doubles when classes are in session. This interplay manifests in an environment where the police are always eager to catch the student body breaking the rules.

When we arrived at FSU, there was two feet of snow on the ground and almost nothing to do, save for recreational consumption. Day drinking commenced in the early afternoon at a local bar, where we waited around to see if any girls showed up and played a lot of pool and darts. Little did we realize in the moment how carefree and joyous those days were, with not a real responsibility in the world . . .

Full disclosure: I am less than pleased by the choices I made that day and am thankful to have grown up a bit since. I wasn't always one to rig the game in my own favor. So, my pals and I were fairly intoxicated by 5:00 p.m. It was pitch-dark at that point and there's nothing quite so depressing as the middle of the winter in Michigan.

We had to walk back to my friend's small house on campus, just trudging through the blackness of night and all that snow, because this was before Ubers existed and there were no taxis to be found. He lived about three quarters of a mile from the bar, and we were drunk, cold, and hungry. When we spotted a warm and bright Papa Johns looming in the distance, it was like finding a lush oasis in the middle of the scorching-hot desert.

What happened next was entirely my fault, mostly because I was an idiot that day. I can't sugarcoat it; it was all me and my bad decisions. At Papa Johns, they had a bank of about twenty phones on the counter; this was before it was common to have one phone with dozens of lines. So there were these red phones that the employees were constantly answering, thanks to their brisk delivery business.

After I paid for our late-night eats, the crew and I were sitting there waiting as the pizzas baked. I noticed that one phone was broken— cracked down the middle, nonfunctional, and not plugged in. I was wearing a poofy puffer jacket so voluminous I could hide anything under it.

And the wheels inside my head started turning. A plan was hatched with not all that much thought for the consequences, just the here and the now. I said to myself, "Well naturally, I should steal that broken phone . . . and then peer-pressure my friends to also steal something." Totally logical thought, right? My plan was to use misdirection to distract the employees and sleight of hand to hide the phone under my jacket. What could possibly go wrong?

Again, since I'm giving the unvarnished truth, this wasn't the first time I'd stolen something. I used to shoplift as a teenager because I enjoyed the rush. I'd take things I would not even use. For example, I didn't smoke cigars. But at 7-Eleven, I always made it a mission to swipe a pack of Swisher Sweets and then give them to friends.

To me, stealing cigars felt like doing a trick, given the element of excitement. I liked the fact that theft required a sleight of hand, that I needed to employ misdirection. I'd wait for the right moment and palm the package, my hand shoved up my sleeve. I'd learned to be casual years before, because I would have items, such as cards and coins, hidden in my hands throughout the day as a way to practice. I'd trained my hands to palm a coin by lightly squeezing the muscles; it doesn't change how your hand looks, yet you can hold the coin in place. In fact, I could be holding three coins and you'd never know it. So when I'd shoplift cigars, in my head it was less *crime* and more *magic*.

Listen, it made sense when I was sixteen, but as I write this, I'm cringing.

Heady with the thrill of taking what wasn't mine, I turned into the ringleader because I was my own worst enemy. I commanded my friends, "You guys steal something, too." They quickly found the bathroom, which doubled as a locker room for the employees. They ran across a laundry bin and swiped three dirty Papa Johns T-shirts, shrugging them into their own puffer coats.

Remember, we paid for the pizzas; this certainly wasn't a full-blown robbery. We went back to my friend's house, where his roommate was throwing a proper house party, the entire reason we'd come. The living room was maybe three hundred square feet and it was packed with fifty people. Amazing. The drinking continued and I ended up passing out on the futon in my buddy's bedroom, likely before the prime-time shows were even over that night. Don't forget, I'd started early.

Fun fact, I was almost legally blind without my contacts or glasses at the time. I have since had LASIK and now enjoy perfect vision. In the middle of the night, I was woken up and I didn't have my contacts in and had no idea where my glasses were. I was basically blind and completely confused. Further, I wasn't even hungover because I suspect I was still lightly drunk.

Some guy I didn't know nudged me and said, "The cops are here."
Um, *what?*

I told him, "I don't live here, bro. I don't care." But he argued with me, saying, "You have to get up, they're here for you."

Again, *what?*

When we'd arrived at the party the night before, I had vague memories of putting on our Papa Johns shirts and walking around the party with the broken phone, asking, "Who wants Papa Johns?" and taking everyone's order. Because I entered college early, I was only twenty years old, so I thought our performance the night before was the height of hilarity. That is, until a virtual SWAT team came busting into the room where I was clad in a pair of tighty-whities and a Papa Johns shirt.

I was *literally* wearing the evidence.

The officer grilled me, saying, "Do you work at Papa Johns?"

I responded, "I fell asleep in the shirt," which was technically true, but the officer saw right through my ruse. I implored him to please let me put in my contacts before we did anything else. While he allowed me that small dignity, his compassion ended there. The rest of his team perp-walked me with my hands cuffed behind my back, wearing only my skimpy underwear and the stupid T-shirt that smelled of yeast. I had to wait outside half naked in minus-ten-degree weather while they collected my felon friends.

They took us to jail and put me and Aaron in one holding cell and Tubo in a separate one by himself, which had to be so scary. This was around 3:00 a.m. The detectives interviewed each of us separately. Before the interview, they put me in a prison jumpsuit. Until then, I'd been in the holding tank in my underwear, yet my friend was fully dressed. I was like, "Dude, how are you in pants?"

When I was questioned, I mustered up all the bravado a still-drunk 20-year-old could, saying, "I need to talk to a lawyer." I'd watched enough *Law & Order* and *CSI* to at least know that. I was told we were being charged with felony larceny and that sobered me right up. I was scared out of my mind, but also confused, asking, "What do you mean, a felony?" One of the men questioning me replied, "Papa Johns said you stole three T-shirts and a phone."

Even in my state, I had the presence of mind to ask, "Isn't a felony over a certain amount of money?" My superpower of a memory was pulling all up the random police procedural episodes I'd ever seen, trying to find a kernel of info that could benefit me. The officer explained that we'd stolen things the pizza place didn't sell. Had we taken $999 worth of their not-great pizza, it would still be a misdemeanor. But because we took objects that weren't for sale, what we did was considered a felony.

Shit.

Part of me needed to believe this was all scare tactics, but Big Rapids PD *did not mess around*. The following morning, they took me from the tank and placed me in gen pop at the county jail. They treated us as though we were serial killers, and not three young idiots who were trying to make people at a party laugh.

This was dead serious. I was separated from my friends, was processed and fingerprinted, and had my mug shots taken. Aaron and Tubo were taken to a separate wing, and I was on my own, the deck decidedly not stacked in my favor.

If you've never been in gen pop at a county jail, the scene doesn't quite look like the movies. Instead of cells with bars, there are doors that close with plastic windows. When I came in, the doors were open and no one was in their cells during the day, as it was minimal security.

Everything in this open bay at the county jail is self-segregated. There's a section where Black inmates are and a section where white inmates are, with a divide between them so profound there may as well have been a wall erected between them. I'm shown to the space that's my room, and the whole time my stomach is sinking—and it's not just the hangover kicking in. Instead, I am coming face-to-face with the consequences of my actions and that is not a safe space. After I put down the pillow and blanket I was given on the hard bunk, I don't really know what to do, but again, I'd watched enough *Law & Order* to know that I was considered a "fish," which is not a great thing to be.

As I took in my surroundings, I noticed that some people were watching TV, others were seated around two long tables, and again, everyone was segregated by race. For lack of another idea, I decided to lean into the one thing I did know: I decided to make my fear of rejection magically disappear. With no hesitation, I walked over to the table of Black guys playing cards, and full of confidence *I did not feel*, I said, "Hey man, how's it going? Can I see those cards?"

It felt like in a movie where the record scratches; everyone stops talking and looks at me. The guy was so shocked that the fish had walked up to him and demanded the cards that he wasn't even mad. I pressed my good fortune at not being pounded into a damp spot on the concrete floor and said, "Let me show you something with those cards."

There I was, a punk college kid reeking of privilege, bad decisions, and Jack Daniel's, demanding they give me their cards. I guess he must have wanted to see what was going to happen next, so he handed me the deck.

I performed card tricks for probably five hours straight, and what was so wild about it was that both sides of the jail came together to watch me. Black, white, it didn't matter because they were drawn together by magic.

I had won them over, one card up my sleeve at a time.

At the end of the day when I wanted to take a shower and wash the stench of fear off me, I was promised protection from all sides. Guys from both factions kept everyone out of the open shower bay so I could bathe in privacy.

Finally, around 6:00 p.m., I was allowed to call my girlfriend. I started crying because the magnitude of this screwup was really beginning to sink in. My roommate in jail was serving a year's time for his third DUI. He was fascinated that I was from Israel. When he found out I had a passport, he said, "Dude, you've got to get out of here. You make bail, you fly to Israel." I replied, "I stole a T-shirt. I'm going back to college. I'm not fleeing; I have class on Monday."

That's when I found out there was no bail and I wasn't seeing a judge until Monday or Tuesday, so I'd be there for a while.

Again, shit.

All this goes back to my point about when you set yourself up for success, you don't know what success is going to look like in the future. Sure, success now looks like Oz the Mentalist predicting the Super Bowl winner or blowing Jim Cramer's mind on CNBC. But back then, it meant that the last seven years of my life—not only practicing card tricks but performing them on video for Penguin Magic—had given me an encyclopedic knowledge of tricks in my repertoire.

Success meant I had enough tricks to make it through a weekend almost without repeating a single one. I had Travelers, two-card monte, invisible palm aces, ambitious card, assemblies, poker deals, and the list went on and on. I had an endless array of magic to perform because I'd put in the requisite ten thousand hours it took to become an expert.

It was almost as though I were set up for this scenario: seeing a magician on the cruise ship, my mentorship with Bruce Kessler and all the hours, days, months, and years spent learning and practicing magic. I performed and then performed some more. And the guards were so blown away that I later found out they were asking my buddies in a different wing if they knew how I did it. My friends found this both hilarious and a great source of relief, knowing that I was alive, given I'd been sent off by myself while they were rooming together.

Apparently over the course of that miserable weekend, I'd become a living legend in the facility—all four wings of the jail had heard about me. And to this day, I've never had a more appreciative audience. That Monday when I was finally arraigned, guards chained my friends and I together to walk into court, attached to the person in front and behind, like an old-timey chain gang. We were led through the maze of unattached buildings that make up the Mecosta County jail, courtroom, and city hall.

Fortunately, at this point, my girlfriend had helped me find an attorney and everything that I'd messed up was set to be expunged, meaning my record would carry no whiff of this incident. The lawyer employed the Holmes Youthful Trainee Act, which states that if you've never committed a violent offense or had any criminal record, you could get your misdeeds permanently removed from your record. If you perform community service, do two years of probation, and never get in trouble again, there will be no record of the arrest. It's all erased, thank God.

I didn't even have to give a Not Guilty plea, which is very lucky because if I'd had to make a plea for a larceny, it's a financial crime and I couldn't have worked on Wall Street. When I stood in front of the courtroom, the judge started reading through my file and she said, "You're the magician, right?" I was astounded. How in the world did she know? I'd never met this person, but somehow word had gotten to her too!

My bail was set at $2,000. Fortunately, I'd also set myself up for success with the Wolverine Spartan Boat Docks company, which is the only reason I had that much money in my savings account. What's funny is when my girlfriend went to pay the bail to get me out, the bondsman and the city clerk asked, "Wait, are you the magician's girlfriend?"

I was out and I was damn fortunate. I have to believe that my ability to disarm with charm was a huge factor in my freedom.

My friends and I found out later that one of the people at the party had a roommate that worked at Papa Johns and called them to tell on us. That employee in turn sent the cops to the house party and they pressed charges. I've never met that person who told on us, but for years truly detested them from afar. I must say that now with this firmly in the rearview mirror, I would thank them for giving a much-needed wakeup call to get my life on the straight and narrow.

The lesson I learned during this experience was incredibly valuable. Importantly, I learned to never steal anything again, and to be smarter. To always have a plan, and a backup plan. That lesson would not have been learned without consequences. Maybe someone could have said it to me, but without that sting, without touching that metaphorical oven and getting burned, the lesson wouldn't have stuck. Thank God it happened in a way that didn't impact my life negatively.

All things considered, I got off very lightly and I'm truly thankful for that.

But I took all those lessons, and I've carried them with me for the rest of my life in a story that I'm only now starting to tell.

Conclusion

You've now taken a journey behind the curtain—not just into the world of mentalism but also the untapped power of your own mind. At some point, we've all wished we could read someone else's mind, myself included! Everything would be easier if we if we could figure out what other people are actually thinking. I'm not able to give you a superpower or magic bullet. The techniques I have shared aren't illusions or tricks; they're proven tools that you can use daily. Over time, they will become habits, ingrained in your muscle memory. Acting preemptively saves everyone a whole lot of time and effort and that's something you now have the ability to do.

When you're in a position of weakness, you have the formula to flip that power dynamic to your benefit. When you're feeling unsure, you can shelve that fear of rejection. You can get out of your own way, and you can lend—or take—a hand when needed. Your weaknesses are now your strengths and your memory is your superpower.

Now that you can deduce what's in another person's head, your ability to influence and win them over will grow tremendously. Anticipating the thoughts and actions of those around you makes you better at understanding human nature; it's the ultimate hack *and you have the key*. Because you can tap into your motivations and learn how to change your outcomes, you're going to push past what's kept you stuck, unable to move on and level up.

Remember that real transformation doesn't happen overnight. It happens in the small choices you make each day, the new habits you form, the beliefs you challenge, and the fears you face. By taking the time to learn how to read your own mind, and those of others around you, you are setting yourself up for success in the long term.

When you can read people—especially yourself—and when you can use all the tools I've shared—from planning for the unexpected to understanding how to captivate others with a story—the world becomes your oyster. This is an inherent trait that you only needed to recognize and hone. Like Dorothy in *The Wizard of Oz*, you always had the ability.

You have the skills, you have the instincts, and now, you have the techniques. So it's time to step up and take that metaphorical swing at the ball.

Pretend to look surprised when you knock it out of the park.

ACKNOWLEDGMENTS

I've read hundreds of these sections before and never realized how daunting the task is until writing my own. So many start with "it takes a village," which seems so cliché, but I have to tell you that it is actually true! There are countless people to thank, without whom I would never have taken on, much less completed, the Herculean task of writing my book. First and foremost, and without a single doubt, this book would not have been possible without my wife, Elisa Rosen, the love of my life and mother of our five children. You are a true force of nature and the foundation of our family. You were instrumental every step of the way, pushed me when I needed it, attempted to keep me focused (near impossible), and gave me the tough love required to put pen to paper no matter how much I complained. I love you and can't imagine my life without you. To my parents, for giving me life, picking a card (any card) at least a million times during my teenage years, and always believing in me, along with my twin sisters for your love. To my publishing and book team, thank you for your patience and guidance, your enthusiasm and energy, your humor and humanity, I fed off it throughout the entire process and it gave me confidence when I felt way in over my head: Laura Tisdel and the entire Viking team, as well as Jen Lancaster, Kevin Anderson, and Stephen Power. To my literary agent, Jim Levine, I love that every email you send tells me to please confirm receipt, that your eyes light up like a child's every time I read your mind, how genuine your reactions are, your sage advice no matter where in the world you might be, and your oh so casual yet oh so superb negotiation skills. To Pete Garceau, you knocked it out of the park with the cover design, incredible work! To Adam Grant, your generosity, willingness to answer my questions no matter how absurd, and your honesty meant more than you can imagine. To David Goggins, who I've been inspired by for many years and whose voice was in my head at times when I thought about quitting, but then instantly knew there was simply no way I could DNF or he would never let me hear the end of it. To Adam Skolnick, your *New York Times* article planted the initial seed that maybe I was worthy of writing a book and have a story to tell that might interest people, so thank you for inspiring me. To Adam Schefter, you've always believed in me and been my champion. Thank you for opening so many doors, being so selfless and being a great friend. To Jason Raff, *AGT* changed my life, and I will never forget all the crazy moments we shared behind the scenes, dumpster diving, your always calm demeanor, and what a surreal experience that show was. To Rmax Goodwin, your woodworking is superb, and I've heard that you're a decent mentalist, too. One day if you're lucky I will teach you the mouth coil trick.

There are so many more people that directly or indirectly have been a part of my life, career, and journey. To every person who has had me on their TV show or podcast, written a story about me, been in my audience and gasped or applauded or heckled me later, all my friends, extended family, my fans . . . thank you! To my brothers in the mentalism community, JFab, EBos, Nimrod, Kvine, Majornation, I appreciate your lending an ear and helping me brainstorm. To Bruce Kessler and Doug Anderson, you helped me catch the magic bug and it's hard to believe where it has taken me. And for the reader, I truly appreciate you and hope that these tools help you to achieve your goals and improve your life.

NOTES

CHAPTER ONE—CHANNEL YOUR INNER MENTALIST

1. Jennifer Guttman, "The Slippery Slope of Relying on Non-Verbal Communication," *Psychology Today*, November 17, 2017, psychologytoday.com/us/blog/sustainable-life-satisfaction/202111/the-slippery-slope-of-relying-on-non-verbal-communication.
2. Kristin Koch et al., "How *Much* the Eye Tells the Brain," *Current Biology* 16, no. 14 (July 2006): 1428–34, doi.org/10.1016/j.cub.2006.05.056.
3. Kendra Cherry, "What Is the Negativity Bias?" Verywell Mind, updated November 13, 2023, verywellmind.com/negative-bias-4589618.

CHAPTER TWO—BELIEVE IT TO ACHIEVE IT

1. Lindsey J. Byom and Bilge Mutlu, "Theory of Mind: Mechanisms, Methods, and New Directions," *Frontiers in Human Neuroscience* 7 (August 2013): 413, doi.org/10.3389/fnhum.2013.00413.
2. "How Much of Communication Is Nonverbal?" The University of Texas Permian Basin, accessed May 12, 2025, online.utpb.edu/about-us/articles/communication/how-much-of-communication-is-nonverbal.
3. Mark K. Ho, Rebecca Saxe, and Fiery Cushman, "Planning with Theory of Mind," *Trends in Cognitive Science* 26, no. 11 (November 2022): 959–71, doi.org/10.1016/j.tics.2022.08.003.
4. "Michael Phelps—The Journey—Ep 5—Visualization," interview with Michael Phelps

and Bob Bowman, posted August 20, 2018, by ProSwimwear, YouTube, 1 min., 57 sec., youtube.com/watch?v=p-mZhvxeK_k.

5. NASA, LSIC Excavation & Construction Focus Group, "Lunar Landing and Launch Pads," October 20, 2020, chrome-extension://efaidnbmnnnibpcajpcglclefindmkaj /https://ntrs.nasa.gov/api/citations/20205009125/downloads/Lunar%20Lard ing%20%20%26%20Launch%20Pads%20v1.pdf. See also NASA's mission overview page, nasa.gov/history/apollo-11-mission-overview.

6. Shaffer Grubb and Amina Khan, "The Apollo 11 Mission as Measured by Heart-beats," *Los Angeles Times*, July 17, 2019, latimes.com/projects/la-sci-apollo-11-mission -as-measured-by-heartbeats.

7. James Devitt, "What's Going On in Our Brains When We Plan?" New York University, June 7, 2024, nyu.edu/about/news-publications/news/2024/june/what-s-going -on-in-our-brains-when-we-plan-.html.

8. "Watch Mentalist Oz Pearlman Get Into TODAY Anchors' Heads," *Today* segment, posted March 10, 2016, by TODAY, YouTube, youtube.com/watch?v=K_K3f-f YKAY.

CHAPTER THREE—MAKE YOUR FEAR OF REJECTION MAGICALLY DISAPPEAR

1. Kirsten Weir, "The Pain of Social Rejection," *Monitor on Psychology* 43, no. 4 (April 2012): 50, apa.org/monitor/2012/04/rejection.

2. Mary Beckman, "Rejection Is Like Pain to the Brain," *Science*, October 9, 2003, science.org/content/article/rejection-pain-brain.

3. Elitsa Dermendzhiyska, "Rejection Kills," *Aeon*, April 30, 2019, aeon.co/essays /health-warning-social-rejection-doesnt-only-hurt-it-kills.

4. Guy Winch, "10 Surprising Facts About Rejection," *Psychology Today*, July 3, 2013, psychologytoday.com/us/blog/the-squeaky-wheel/201307/10-surprising-facts -about-rejection.

5. Ana Sandoiu, "Do You Fear Embarrassment? Here's How to Overcome It," *Medical News Today*, April 1, 2018, medicalnewstoday.com/articles/321378.

6. Yanhua Cheng and Daniel Grühn, "Age Differences in Reactions to Social Rejection: The Role of Cognitive Resources and Appraisals," *The Journals of Gerontology: Series B* 70, no. 6 (November 2015): 830–39, doi.org/10.1093/geronb/gbu054.

7. "Carrie Rescued from the Bin | Mark Lawson Talks to Stephen King," Interview, posted June 5, 2009, by BBC Studios, YouTube, youtube.com/watch?v=xgqj7dbLSa.

8. Lucas Reilly, "How Stephen King's Wife Saved 'Carrie' and Helped Launch His Career," *Mental Floss*, April 5, 2024, mentalfloss.com/article/53235/how-stephen-kings -wife-saved-carrie-and-launched-his-career.

9. "6 Famous Authors Who Once Faced Rejection," *WildMind* (blog), accessed May 12, 2025, wildmindcreative.com/bookmarketing/6-famous-authors-who-once-faced

-rejection; Sughen Yongo, "The Best Stephen King Books, Ranked and in Order," *Forbes*, June 9, 2025, forbes.com/sites/entertainment/article/stephen-king-books.

10. Scott Mautz, "11 Famous Failures That Will Inspire You to Success," *Inc.*, September 12, 2017, inc.com/scott-mautz/11-famous-failures-that-will-inspire-you-to-succes.html.

11. Liadan Gunter, "Neuroscience: What Social Media Does to Your Brain," *Nivati*, updated May 27, 2025, nivati.com/blog/neuroscience-what-social-media-does-to-your-brain.

12. Pam Belluck, "Memories Weaken Without Reinforcement, Study Finds," *New York Times*, March 16, 2015, nytimes.com/2015/03/17/science/memories-become-weaker-without-reinforcement-study-finds.html.

CHAPTER FOUR—FOCUS ON OTHERS

1. Kate Lunau, "King of Beer Sales, Amigo," *Maclean's*, August 13, 2009, macleans.ca/economy/business/king-of-beer-sales-amigo.

2. Harneet Kaur, "The Lost Art of Empathy," *Psychiatric Times*, February 17, 2022, psychiatrictimes.com/view/the-lost-art-of-empathy.

3. Alison Jane Martingano, "Social Media and Empathy Around the Globe," *Character & Context* (blog), *The Society for Personality and Social Psychology*, March 3, 2023, spsp.org/news/character-and-context-blog/martingano-social-media-use-lower-empathy.

4. "How Social Media Impedes Empathy," *Move This World*, January 15, 2019, movethisworld.com/mental-health-awareness/2019-1-15-how-social-media-impedes-empathy.

CHAPTER FIVE—FORGET TOMORROW, START TODAY

1. "Limbic System," Cleveland Clinic, accessed May 12, 2025, my.clevelandclinic.org/health/body/limbic-system.

2. Amy Spencer, "Want to Train Your Brain to Stop Procrastinating? Read These Tips from a Neuroscientist," *Real Simple*, last updated May 1, 2023, realsimple.com/work-life/life-strategies/time-management/procrastination.

3. Aniesa Hanson, "The Paralysis of Fear: How Fear of Failure Contributes to Unhappiness," Hanson Complete Wellness, accessed May 12, 2025, hansoncomplete.com/fear.

4. Magdalena Bak-Maier, "The Psychology Behind Task Completion: A Student's Guide," *Make Time Count* (blog), accessed May 12, 2025, maketimecount.com/how-completion-helps-students-build-confidence.

5. Mya Care Editorial Team, "The Zeigarnik Effect: Why Do Unfinished Tasks Haunt Us?" Mya Care, January 4, 2024, myacare.com/blog/the-zeigarnik-effect-why-do-unfinished-tasks-haunt-us.

6. Rishi Sriram, "The Neuroscience Behind Productive Struggle," *Edutopia*, April 13, 2020, edutopia.org/article/neuroscience-behind-productive-struggle.

7. Keiichiro Susuki, "Myelin: A Specialized Membrane for Cell Communication," *Nature Education* 3, no. 9 (2010): 59, nature.com/scitable/topicpage/myelin-a-specialized -membrane-for-cell-communication-14367205.

8. Matt Puderbaugh and Prabhu D. Emmady, "Neuroplasticity," StatPearls Publishing, January 2025, ncbi.nlm.nih.gov/books/NBK557811.

9. Duncan Haughey, "A Brief History of SMART Goals," ProjectSmart, December 13, 2014, projectsmart.co.uk/smart-goals/brief-history-of-smart-goals.php.

10. Stacey McLachlan, "The Science of Habit," Healthline, December 22, 2021, health line.com/health/the-science-of-habit#1.

11. James Clear, "The Cardinal Rule of Behavior Change," *James Clear*, jamesclear.com /quotes/the-cardinal-rule-of-behavior-change.

12. Katie Doll, "The Habit Loop: Charles Duhigg's Theory for Continuous Actions," Shortform, July 3, 2023, shortform.com/blog/the-habit-loop-2.

13. "Oxytocin," Cleveland Clinic, accessed May 12, 2025, my.clevelandclinic.org/health /articles/22618-oxytocin.

14. Lisa Nutter and Tim Freundlich, "A Social Movement Requires Momentum," *Stanford Social Innovation Review*, March 29, 2023, ssir.org/articles/entry/a_social_movement _requires_momentum.

CHAPTER SIX—STACK THE DECK IN YOUR FAVOR

1. Michael John O'Keeffe, "Science Is Just Starting to Understand the Benefits of Athletes Putting Their Brains in 'Auto Pilot,'" *The Conversation,* June 26, 2024, thecon versation.com/science-is-just-starting-to-understand-the-benefits-of-athletes -putting-their-brains-in-auto-pilot-232596.

2. Colleen Walsh, "Give Her Some Space: Psychologist's Perspective on Simone Biles at the Olympics Includes Message for Parents, Coaches," *The Harvard Gazette,* July 20, 2021, news.harvard.edu/gazette/story/2021/07/a-harvard-psychologists-perspective -on-biles-at-the-olympics.

3. John Kounios and David S. Rosen, "Brain Scans of Jazz Musicians Reveal How to Reach a Creative 'Flow State,'" *Scientific American* 331, no. 3 (October 2024): 66, scien tificamerican.com/article/brain-scans-of-jazz-musicians-reveal-how-to-reach-a -creative-flow-state.

4. Nathan Cross, "Neuroscience of Peak Performance: Unlocking the Secrets of Elite Athletes and Entrepreneurs," *Medium*, September 16, 2023, medium.com/@NC _16/neuroscience-of-peak-performance-unlocking-the-secrets-of-elite-athletes-and -entrepreneurs-72ce73b026.

5. Richard Lewis, "Mindful Mistakes: How Brains Learn from Errors," *Neuroscience News*, November 9, 2023, neurosciencenews.com/errorr-learning-brain-25183.

6. Krissy Brady, "This Is Why You Get More Anxious After Something Good Hap-

pens," *HuffPost*, April 9, 2019, huffpost.com/entry/anxiety-good-things_l_5ca78f c1e4b047edf959e2fe.

7. Devrupa Rakshit, "Is This Normal? 'Every Time I Start to Feel Happy, I Get Scared Bad Things Will Happen,'" *The Swaddle*, September 7, 2020, theswaddle.com/is-this -normal-every-time-i-start-to-feel-happy-i-get-scared-bad-things-will-happen.

8. Alicia Clark, *Hack Your Anxiety* (Sourcebooks: 2018).

9. "How to Regulate Your Nervous System and Restore Calm: 12 Proven Techniques," Calm.com, accessed May 12, 2025, https://calm.com/blog/how-to-regulate-nervous -system.

CHAPTER SEVEN—DON'T BE YOUR OWN WORST ENEMY

1. Caroline Bologna, "'Fake It Till You Make It' Isn't Just a Cliché. It's Backed by Science," *HuffPost*, August 3, 2022, huffpost.com/entry/behavioral-activation-fake-it -til-you-make-it_l_62d7140ae4b0aad58d139763.

2. Lisa Lavigna, "The Dangers of Negative Thinking and How to Master Positive Self-Talk," Excelsior University, September 21, 2023, excelsior.edu/article/the-dangers -of-negative-thinking-and-how-to-master-positive-self-talk.

3. Shefali Raina, "Four Brain Science Habits to Help Neutralize Negative Self-Talk," *Forbes*, May 06, 2021, forbes.com/councils/forbescoachescouncil/2021/05/06/four -brain-science-habits-to-help-neutralize-negative-self-talk.

4. "Catch It, Check It, Change It," Headroom Wellbeing Guide, BBC, accessed May 12, 2025, downloads.bbc.co.uk/headroom/cbt/catch_it.pdf.

5. "Implementing the EASE Shift Perspective Principle: CBT Techniques," Veterans Affairs, accessed May 12, 2025, mirecc.va.gov/visn5/training/docs/Handout_Shift _Persp.pdf.

6. J. M. Dutcher et al., "Self-Affirmation Activates the Ventral Striatum: A Possible Reward-Related Mechanism for Self-Affirmation," *Psychol Science* 27, no. 4 (April 2016): 455–66, doi.org/10.1177/0956797615625989.

7. Fernando Gomez-Pinilla and Charles Hillman, "The Influence of Exercise on Cognitive Abilities," *Comprehensive Physiology* 3, no. 1 (January 2013): 403–28, pmc.ncbi .nlm.nih.gov/articles/PMC3951958.

8. Grace McGregor, "How Exercise Affects the Brain," Brigham Young University, February 8, 2021, lifesciences.byu.edu/how-exercise-affects-your-brain.

CHAPTER EIGHT—ASK FOR HELP

1. Dan Schawbel, "Brene Brown: How Vulnerability Can Make Our Lives Better," *Forbes*, April 21, 2013, forbes.com/sites/danschawbel/2013/04/21/brene-brown-how -vulnerability-can-make-our-lives-better.

2. "Oxytocin: The Love Hormone," Harvard Health Publishing, June 13, 2023, health .harvard.edu/mind-and-mood/oxytocin-the-love-hormone.

3. Jennifer Caspari, "Embracing Vulnerability," *Psychology Today*, May 7, 2023, psychol ogytoday.com/us/blog/living-well-when-your-body-doesnt-cooperate/202305/em bracing-vulnerability.

4. Paul J. Zak, "The Neuroscience of Trust," *Harvard Business Review* (January/February 2017), hbr.org/2017/01/the-neuroscience-of-trust.

5. Alexander Heffner, "The Neuroscience of Friendship," *The American Prospect*, February 9, 2020, prospect.org/health/the-neuroscience-of-friendship.

6. Julianne Holt-Lunstad, Timothy B. Smith, and J. Bradley Layton, "Social Relationships and Mortality Risk: A Meta-analytic Review," *PLOS Medicine* 7, no. 7 (July 2010): e1000316, doi.org/10.1371/journal.pmed.1000316.

7. Lindsay Hindle, "What Does Neuroscience Have to Do with Mentorship?" International Association of Business Communicators British Columbia, April 8, 2014, iabc. bc.ca/blog/what-does-neuroscience-have-to-do-with-mentorship.

8. Angela Byars-Winston and Maria Lund Dahlberg, "The Science of Mentoring Relationships: What Is Mentorship?" chapter 2 in *The Science of Effective Mentorship in STEMM* (National Academies Press, 2019), ncbi.nlm.nih.gov/books/NBK552775.

9. "Using Neuroscience in Coaching and Mentoring for Improved Results," Vorecol, August 28, 2024, vorecol.com/blogs/blog-using-neuroscience-in-coaching-and-men toring-for-improved-results-9248.

10. Sarah Wilson, "The Power of Persuasion," *The Guardian*, March 7, 2009, theguardian .com/lifeandstyle/2009/mar/08/power-of-persuasion.

CHAPTER NINE—TURN YOUR WEAKNESSES INTO YOUR STRENGTHS

1. Katie A. McLaughlin, et al., "Neglect as a Violation of Species-Expectant Experience: Neurodevelopmental Consequences," *Biological Psychiatry* 82, no. 7 (October 2017): 462–71, doi.org/10.1016/j.biopsych.2017.02.1096.

2. "Who Are the Kurds?" *BBC News*, October 15, 2019, bbc.com/news/world-middle -east-29702440.

3. "Anticipation: The Psychology of Waiting in Line," Association for Psychological Science, July 15, 2014, psychologicalscience.org/news/were-only-human/anticipation -the-psychology-of-waiting-in-line.html.

4. Judith E. Glaser, "Why We Don't Speak Up," *Psychology Today*, May 22, 2018, psychol ogytoday.com/us/blog/conversational-intelligence/201805/why-we-dont -speak-up.

5. Jacob Rueda, "New Study Shows Percentage of People Fearful of Speaking Out on Their Beliefs," *ABC4 Utah News*, November 10, 2021, abc4.com/news/new-study -shows-percentage-of-people-fearful-of-speaking-out-on-their-beliefs.

6. Jane M. Richards and James J. Gross, "Composure at Any Cost? The Cognitive Consequences of Emotion Suppression," *Personality and Social Psychology Bulletin* 25, no. 8 (August 1999): 1033–44, doi.org/10.1177/01461672992511010.

7. Polly Campbell, "What We Gain by Being Uncomfortable," *Psychology Today*, June 21, 2022, psychologytoday.com/us/blog/imperfect-spirituality/202206/what-we-gain-by -being-uncomfortable.

CHAPTER TEN—MAKE MEMORY YOUR SUPERPOWER

1. Arlin Cuncic, "The Mandela Effect: How Masses of People Can Have the Same False Memory," Verywell Mind, January 3, 2024, verywellmind.com/what-is-the-mandela -effect-4589394.

2. Bradley Voytek, "Are There Really as Many Neurons in the Human Brain as Stars in the Milky Way?" *Brain Metrics* (blog), Scitable, May 20, 2013, nature.com/scitable /blog/brain-metrics/are_there_really_as_many.

3. Corinne Purtill, "The New Science of Forgetting," *Time*, April 28, 2022, time.com /6171190/new-science-of-forgetting.

4. Bill Hathaway, "What Makes a Memory? It May Be Related to How Hard Your Brain Had to Work," *YaleNews*, May 13, 2024, news.yale.edu/2024/05/13/what-makes -memory-it-may-be-related-how-hard-your-brain-had-to-work.

5. Kendra Cherry, "The Recency Effect in Psychology," Verywell Mind, January 16, 2024, verywellmind.com/the-recency-effect-4685058.

6. Andrew E. Budson, "Have You Done Your Crossword Puzzle Today?" Harvard Health Publishing, November 29, 2022, health.harvard.edu/blog/have-you-done -your-crossword-puzzle-today-202211292857.

7. "Why Crossword Puzzles Are Beneficial to Your Brain Health," Neuroelectrics, December 19, 2022, neuroelectrics.com/blog/why-crossword-puzzles-are-beneficial -to-your-brain-health.

8. Chuan-Chih Yang et al., "Alterations in Brain Structure and Amplitude of Low-Frequency After 8 Weeks of Mindfulness Meditation Training in Meditation-Naïve Subjects," *Scientific Reports* 9 (July 2019): 10977, doi.org/10.1038/s41598-019-47470-4.

9. "Unleashing the Mind: The Neuroscience of Meditation and Its Impact on Memory," *Neuroscience News*, June 7, 2023, neurosciencenews.com/memory-meditation-23414.

10. Rachelle Hampton, "New Study Shows How Even Innocently Forgetting Names and Personal Details Can Harm Relationships," *Slate*, October 16, 2018, slate.com/hu man-interest/2018/10/forgetting-names-friendship-harm-study.html.

11. Will Houston, "How Repetition Solidifies Memory," *Neuroscience News*, May 15, 2024, neurosciencenews.com/rwpwtition-memory-26114.

12. "Brain Prioritizes High-Reward Memories," UC Davis Department of Psychology, February 12, 2016, psychology.ucdavis.edu/news/brain-prioritizes-high-reward-memories.

CHAPTER ELEVEN—DISARM WITH CHARM

1. Tiffanie Wen, "The Tricks to Make Yourself Effortlessly Charming," *BBC*, June 27, 2017, bbc.com/worklife/article/20170627-the-tricks-to-make-yourself-effortlessly -charming.

2. Marianna Pogosyan, "Prejudice in the Brain," *Psychology Today,* June 23, 2020, psy chologytoday.com/us/blog/between-cultures/202006/prejudice-in-the-brain.

3. Jerry Matysik, "Implicit Bias and Law Enforcement: Reducing Blame and Under- standing the Brain," Lexipol, February 15, 2017, lexipol.com/resources/blog/im plicit-bias-law-enforcement-reducing-blame-understanding-brain.

4. Jason Vu Nguyen, "Charming vs Charismatic: Understanding the Difference and Figuring Out Which One You Are," Medium, June 16, 2022, medium.com/@jason vuvu/charming-vs-charismatic-understanding-the-difference-and-figuring-out -which-one-you-are-f64cba62125d.

5. Maya Al-Khouja et al., "Self-expression Can Be Authentic or Inauthentic, with Dif- ferential Outcomes for Well-being: Development of the Authentic and Inauthentic Expression Scale (AIES)," *Journal of Research in Personality* 97 (2022): 104191, https:// doi.org/10.1016.

6. Nancy Marshall, "Here's Why the Word of the Year Is 'Authentic,'" *Forbes,* January 31, 2024, forbes.com/councils/forbesagencycouncil/2024/01/31/heres-why-the-word-of -the-year-is-authentic.

7. Natalye Paquin, "(Really) Listening & (Really) Learning," Points of Light, March 3, 2021, pointsoflight.org/blog/really-listening-really-learning.

8. "The Science of Active Listening," JimKwik.com, March 2, 2023, jimkwik.com/the -science-of-active-listening.

9. Hiroaki Kawamichi et al., "Perceiving Active Listening Activates the Reward System and Improves the Impression of Relevant Experiences," *Social Neuroscience* 10, no. 1 (2015): 16–26, doi.org/10.1080/17470919.2014.954732.

10. Robert Sanders, "Brain's Hippocampus Helps Fill in the Blanks of Language," *UC Berkeley News,* September 19, 2016, news.berkeley.edu/2016/09/19/brains-hippocam pus-helps-fill-in-the-blanks-of-language.

11. Dale Carnegie, "Part Two: Six Ways to Make People Like You," in *How to Win Friends and Influence People* (Simon and Schuster, 1936).

12. Kyle Mittan, "Are You Good at What You Do? Bragging About It Could Make Peo- ple Trust You Less," Phys.org, July 21, 2022, phys.org/news/2022-07-good-bragging -people.html#google_vignette.

13. Brian Collisson, "Humor Is Hot: Why Being Funny Attracts Potential Partners," *Psy- chology Today,* September 26, 2024, psychologytoday.com/us/blog/dating-toxic-or -tender/202409/humor-is-hot-why-being-funny-attracts-potential-partners.

14. Dolores Tropiano, "Being Funny Has Its Benefits in the Dating World," *ASU News,*

February 13, 2024, news.asu.edu/20240213-science-and-technology-being-funny-has-its-benefits-dating-world.

15. Kendra Cherry, "Understanding Body Language and Facial Expressions," Verywell Mind, January 30, 2025, verywellmind.com/understand-body-language-and-facial-expressions-4147228.

16. Allessio Rastrelli, "Body Language," AlessioRastrelli.it, May 3, 2020, alessiorastrelli.it/en/body-language.

17. Avelo Roy, "The Science of Being Irresistibly Charming," AveloRoy.com, April 29, 2015, aveloroy.com/2015/04/29/science-irresistibly-charming-people.

18. Alannagh Kelly, "The Psychology of Mirroring," Imagine Health, October 31, 2017, imaginehealth.ie/the-psychology-of-mirroring.

19. "How Your Child's Nervous System Impacts Emotional Regulation and Meltdowns," he's-extraordinary, March 19, 2025, hes-extraordinary.com/how-your-childs-nervous-system-impacts-emotional-regulation-and-meltdowns.

CHAPTER TWELVE—TIE IT ALL TOGETHER WITH A STORY

1. Lani Peterson, "The Science Behind the Art of Storytelling," Harvard Business Publishing, November 14, 2017, lanipeterson.com/wp-content/uploads/2021/02/The-Science-Behind-teh-Art-of-Storytelling.docx.pdf.

2. Paul J. Zak, "Why Your Brain Loves Good Storytelling," *Harvard Business Review*, October 28, 2014, hbr.org/2014/10/why-your-brain-loves-good-storytelling.

3. "Storytelling and the Brain: Understanding the Neuroscience Behind Our Love for Stories," Power of Storytelling, February 7, 2023, power-of-storytelling.com/story science.

4. Giovanni René Rodriguez, "This Is Your Brain on Storytelling: The Chemistry of Modern Communication," *Forbes*, July 21, 2017, forbes.com/sites/giovannirodriguez/2017/07/21/this-is-your-brain-on-storytelling-the-chemistry-of-modern-communication.

5. Jeremy Adam Smith, "The Science of the Story," *Greater Good Magazine*, June 8, 2016, greatergood.berkeley.edu/article/item/science_of_the_story.

INDEX

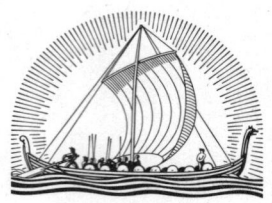

100 YEARS of PUBLISHING

Harold K. Guinzburg and George S. Oppenheimer founded Viking in 1925 with the intention of publishing books "with some claim to permanent importance rather than ephemeral popular interest." After merging with B. W. Huebsch, a small publisher with a distinguished catalog, Viking enjoyed almost fifty years of literary and commercial success before merging with Penguin Books in 1975.

Now an imprint of Penguin Random House, Viking specializes in bringing extraordinary works of fiction and nonfiction to a vast readership. In 2025, we celebrate one hundred years of excellence in publishing. Our centennial colophon features the original logo for Viking, created by the renowned American illustrator Rockwell Kent: a Viking ship that evokes enterprise, adventure, and exploration, ideas that inspired the imprint's name at its founding and continue to inspire us.

For more information on Viking's history, authors, and books, please visit penguin.com/viking.